They Can't
Kill Us All

They Can't Kill Us All

Ferguson, Baltimore, and a New Era in America's Racial Justice Movement

Wesley Lowery

Little, Brown and Company
New York Boston London

Little, Brown and Company
Hachette Book Group
1290 Avenue of the Americas, New York, NY 10104
littlebrown.com

First edition: November 2016

Little, Brown and Company is a division of Hachette Book Group, Inc. The Little, Brown name and logo are trademarks of Hachette Book Group, Inc.

The publisher is not responsible for websites (or their content) that are not owned by the publisher.

The Hachette Speakers Bureau provides a wide range of authors for speaking events. To find out more, go to hachettespeakersbureau.com or call (866) 376-6591.

Sections of this work were adapted from articles previously published in the *Washington Post*.

ISBN 978-0-316-31247-9
LCCN 2016948558

10 9 8 7 6 5 4 3 2 1

LSC-C

Printed in the United States of America

For Jance, Ty, and Feeney, from a boy
they helped grow into a man

Contents

They Can't Kill Us All

The Story

O kay, let's take him."

Within seconds two officers grabbed me, each seizing an arm, and shoved me against the soda dispenser that rested along the front wall of the McDonald's where I had been eating and working. As I released my clenched hands, my cell phone and notebook fell to the tiled floor. Then came the sharp sting of the plastic zip tie as it was sealed around my hands, pinching tight at the corners of my wrists. I'd never been arrested before, and this wasn't quite how I'd imagined it would go down.

Two days earlier I'd been sent to Ferguson, Missouri, to cover the aftermath of the police shooting of Michael Brown, an unarmed black eighteen-year-old. The fatal gunshots, fired by a white police officer, Darren Wilson, were followed by bursts of anger, in the form of both protests and riots. Hundreds, and then thousands, of local residents had flooded the streets.

They demanded answers. They demanded justice.

In the first forty-eight hours on the ground I filled a notebook: the soft words uttered through thick tears by Lezley McSpadden, Brown's mother, as she stood for the family's first press conference since "Mike Mike's" death; scenes of destruction, including the burned-down QuikTrip gas station and the rows of storefronts that now had thin wooden slabs nailed atop smashed-out windows; scribbles I'd managed while tucked in the back corner of the overflowing sanctuary of Greater St. Mark's as the Reverend Al Sharpton led an impassioned call and response: *"No justice, no peace!"*; and the green and brown stains along the corner of my notebook from the moment I was mercifully tackled to the ground, my first night in Ferguson, by a homeowner I was interviewing—a tear gas canister had landed next to us while we spoke on his lawn.

There are few things as exhilarating as parachuting into an unknown place with a bag full of pens and notebooks in pursuit of "the story." And when the phone calls, and coffee meetings, and frantic scribbling are through, piecing it all together.

But Ferguson was different because during the early days it was deeply unclear what, exactly, "the story" was. Whatever it was, I now—my arms tugged back behind my back—had become a part of it. I wasn't happy about it.

More than 150 people were taken into custody by the Ferguson and St. Louis County police departments in the week and a half that followed Mike Brown's death on August 9, 2014—the vast majority for "failure to disperse" charges that came as part of acts of peaceful protest. I was the first journalist to end up in cuffs while covering the unrest.

That claim soon became a bit of a technicality, not unlike the twin sibling who declares him- or herself "older." By the time I had been led out of the restaurant and into the bright sunlight still shining down on St. Louis early that evening, another reporter, the *Huffington Post*'s Ryan Reilly, whom I had met for the first time earlier that day, was also being led out of the restaurant, shouting that the officers had just slammed his head into the door on the way out.

For the Ferguson press corps—which would eventually swell from dozens of daily reporters for local St. Louis outlets and regional reporters for national shops into hundreds of journalists, including ones from dozens of foreign countries—the McDonald's on West Florissant Avenue became the newsroom. Not that we all had much choice in the matter; the modest-sized dining room with a single television on the wall and movie rental box in the back corner was the only spot within walking distance of the street where Mike Brown had been killed that had all three of the essentials required by a reporter on the road: bathrooms, Wi-Fi, and electrical outlets.

Because the protests were largely, in those first days, organic and not called by any specific group or set of activists, they were also unpredictable. Some of the demonstrators came to demand an immediate indictment of the officer. Others wanted officials to explain what had happened that day, to tell them who this officer was and why this young man was dead. Scores more stood on sidewalks and street corners unable to articulate their exact demands—they just knew they wanted justice. Covering Ferguson directly after the killing of Mike Brown involved hours on the streets, with clusters of reporters staked out from the early afternoon into the early hours of the morning. At any point a resident or a group of them could begin a heated argument with the police or a reporter. A demonstration that had for hours consisted of a group of local women standing and chanting on a street corner would suddenly evolve into a chain of bodies blocking traffic, or an impromptu march to the other side of town.

And as the summer sun gave way to night, the prospect of violence—both the bricks and bottles of a would-be rioter and the batons and rubber bullets of local police officers—increased exponentially. As long as the protesters and the police remained on the streets, reporters had to as well.

Not since the Boston Marathon bombings a year and a half earlier had I covered a story for which there was such intense, immediate appetite. Earlier on the day I was arrested, I tweeted digital video and photo updates from the spot where Brown had been shot and killed, from the burned-out shell of the QuikTrip gas station torched in the first night of rioting, of the peaceful crowds of church ladies who gathered that afternoon on West Florissant—a major thoroughfare not far from where the shooting occurred that played host to most of the demonstrations—as well as the heavily armored police vehicles that responded to monitor them.

For years, updates like these would have been phoned into the newsroom, with a reporter describing the unfolding situation sentence by sentence as a rewrite guy molded the news into already existing articles. Now they could be published instantaneously.

But an iPhone battery only lasts for so long, so with the deadline for the story I was writing for tomorrow's newspaper looming, I left the protest and made the three-block trek to the McDonald's, bought a Big Mac and fries, from across the room greeted Ryan, and holed up in the corner of the dining room to let my phone charge.

It wasn't long later when the riot-gear-clad officers entered, suggesting we all leave because, with protests still simmering outside, things could get dangerous once the sun went down. Then, when it became clear that we were happy to wait and see how things developed outside, they changed their tune. Now the officers were demanding we leave.

I was annoyed, but covering protests and demonstrations often means taking direction that doesn't make sense from police officers who aren't quite concerned with your convenience, much less your ability to do your job. I kept my phone, which was recording video, propped up in one hand as I shoved my notebooks into the same fading green backpack I've carried since my senior year of high school. As I packed, I attempted to ask the officer now standing in my face if I'd be able to move my rental car from the parking lot. He didn't, he said, have time for questions. Once I'd finished packing, I walked past him, making my way toward the door.

As I walked to the exit, the officers decided that all this had taken too long. It had been about one minute since they had first told me to leave when I heard one officer say, "Okay, let's take him," and then felt their arms grab me from behind. Now I stood on my tiptoes, insisting to Officer Friendly that I was, in fact, complying with his demands even though he was insisting that I wasn't.

"My hands *are* behind my back!" I shouted to the uniformed men now pressing their weight into me as they ran their gloved hands down my front and back pants pockets, which contained an abundance of pens and exactly zero weapons.

"No, you're resisting, stop resisting," an officer barked back at me, before I was led out of the building.

On August 9, 2014, the Saturday when six bullets fired by Darren Wilson entered Mike Brown's body, I was sailing in Boston Harbor with two of my former *Boston Globe* colleagues. Seated snugly in a small sailboat settled out deep in the water, we stared up at the city skyline drifting farther from us and the planes coming into Logan Airport descending low over our heads.

This was one of what had been half a dozen return trips to Boston in the seven months since I'd left a job as a metro reporter for the *Globe*, my first full-time reporting gig after college, to join the staff of the *Washington Post*. For the year or so that I had worked in Boston, I wrote breaking news for the metro desk and chipped in on the political desk, covering crime scenes and campaigns, police tape and ticker tape.

One day, I'd be in the backseat of an SUV listening to a mayoral candidate coax money out of the pockets of donors as underpaid and overcaffeinated staff members tried to run damage control. (*"Everything said in the car can be off the record, right?"*) The next day I'd get an early-morning call from Mike Bello, the *Globe*'s deputy city editor and a hard-charging, no-nonsense assignment editor who was among the favorites of my many bosses.

"*Mornin', pal,*" he'd say in low, growling yet friendly Bostonian. "*Did I wake you?*"

"Of course not. I was just getting ready to come into the office," I'd always reply.

It was one of our jokes, which we both knew was a lie. I had been passed out on my mattress, which took up more than half of the tiny room I rented not far from Boston University, until the precise moment that the buzzing vibrations of my phone, tucked beneath my drooling mouth, had jolted me awake.

"That's what I like to hear. Early mornings are good for ya!" Bello would reply before giving me the morning's task. *"We got a dead body in West Roxbury. Cops still at the scene. Go try to find some witnesses, maybe some neighbors. Send in some color. Take some iPhone video."*

The metro general assignment beat is murders, stabbings, bodies, and grieving families, with the occasional highway closure or wild turkey sighting mixed in. There was the drunk driver, so loaded one morning that she plowed into a mother walking her seven-year-old daughter, killing the child. And the elderly man, bludgeoned to death by his nephew in the living room of the apartment where he had lived for decades. Worse still was the mother in New Bedford who had a seizure while in the shower, her newborn baby nestled in her arms. They both drowned.

When two terrorists attacked the Boston Marathon, exactly one month after I began the job, I stood outside a local hospital, filing bits of information gleaned from victims and their families. The next day, I'd be on the team reporting stories of the injured. The following day, up early covering President Obama's address to the still-grieving city, and up late on the scene as local police officers engaged in a chaotic shootout with the Tsarnaev brothers.

But my goal had always been to cover politics. In 2008, I voted for the first time, and watched with envy as the campaign embeds for various outlets filed reported pieces and Twitter dispatches from Iowa rallies, and campaign buses, and election-night parties. By 2012, I was at the *Los Angeles Times*, and as part of a stint working out of the City Hall bureau I weaseled my way into a little election-night coverage—I was dispatched to an outdoor watch party for young voters who broke out in triumphant cheers when Barack Obama earned four more years in office.

In Boston, I covered the Senate race to replace John Kerry, then the mayoral race to replace Tom Menino, the city's "mayor for life." The goal was to be on the 2016 presidential trail, whether at the *Globe* or somewhere else. When, toward the end of the mayor's race, a top editor at the *Washington Post* came calling, I was hesitant—I loved Boston. But the new job was covering Congress, with a clear path toward the campaign trail. I knew I had to accept the offer.

My first year at the *Washington Post* had been both overwhelming and exhilarating. One of the last things a Boston colleague told me was that all he could think as he covered Congress was that he was working in a museum, replete with busts of the former vice-presidents lining the walkways that you dashed past as you scurried to a press conference across the Capitol.

From my perch on the *Post's* national political staff I contributed to stories far beyond the walls of Congress—a scandal in the Department of Veterans Affairs, a child migrant crisis on the country's southern border, and of course, the 2014 midterm elections.

Just a week before I arrived in Ferguson, I had been weaving through Michigan, one of a dozen or so reporters we jokingly dubbed Team America, to cover primary election night. I spent the day talking to voters at polling location after polling location— asking them general questions about their politics and motivations and picking their brains for any undercovered local political angles or leads. The last thing on my mind was policing or police shootings— it had been close to a year since I'd covered one.

I left Michigan with a notebook full of story ideas and made a pit stop in Boston for a day of relaxation with some former colleagues— and that was when I saw frantic updates from a reporter I knew in St. Louis. The police, it seemed, had shot and killed a black kid near the city. And from the looks of it, crowds were starting to gather.

Police shootings aren't uncommon, and as a reporter who is professionally acquainted with hundreds of other reporters, images of an angry vigil of grieving residents weren't particularly out of place in my social media feeds. But even in those early posts, Mike Brown's death just *felt* different. The crowds gathered near this young man's body emanated a guttural anguish. It was clear even then, for those paying attention, that this communal anger would not be easily muted or contained.

That Monday morning—after two nights on which angry daytime protests had given way to destructive waves of looting after the sun went down—the *Post*'s deputy national editor walked past my desk and overheard me discussing the ongoing situation in Ferguson. Could I get on a plane? "Sure!" I said, staring down at the still-packed bag from my trips to Michigan and Boston.

I wasn't completely excited—I'd just gotten back from the road and really wanted to spend a few days decompressing. But I knew better than to turn down an assignment. I needed to go to Ferguson, even if it was quick. I'd drop in for a day or two, gather some anecdotes for a story for one of that weekend's papers, and probably be home in time to watch Sunday football with the guys at Smoke & Barrel, our regular barbecue and whiskey spot in Adams Morgan.

An hour later, I was in a cab to the airport.

Since I'd arrived in Ferguson I had found many of the residents willing to talk, often sharing stories that seemed on their face unbelievable—officers who pulled them over repeatedly, nights spent in jail for unpaid speeding tickets, and most disturbing of all, shootings and other deaths at the hands of police officers about which they and the people of Ferguson still lacked answers.

Getting a response from the police about the death of Mike Brown had been next to impossible. Ferguson Police Chief Tom

Jackson had done a handful of press conferences, but each time he stepped to a microphone it was clear that he had been thrust forward as a sacrificial lamb. He didn't have answers—not about the death of Michael Brown, or about the ever-growing list of accusations that residents were making against his officers.

But at this particular moment, another, much more pressing reporting challenge was presenting itself: the plastic zip tie still tight around my wrists.

After marching us outside the McDonald's where we had first been detained, the officers had brought Ryan Reilly and me to the middle of the street in front of the restaurant—which had been shut down to car traffic earlier in the day due to the protests—to wait for a transport vehicle to take us to jail. We peppered the officers with questions. Cuffed or not, we were still reporters, after all. Why are we being detained? What law did we break? What are your names? Your badge numbers? Where the hell is the commanding officer? What are we being charged with?

They ignored us, for the most part. "Oh, you'll be charged with a whole lot of things," one chimed in smugly. I turned to the officer who seemed to be calling the shots and let him know that arresting credentialed journalists as they sat at their computers filing stories was a dumb move.

"This is a mistake," I said, trying to reason with him. "This is going to be on the front page of the *Washington Post* tomorrow."

"Yeah, well," he replied with a self-satisfied smirk, "you're going to be sleeping in our jail cell tonight."

He was wrong. Ryan and I would spend just about twenty minutes in the holding cells in the basement of the Ferguson Police Department, where we were driven in a police vehicle also containing one of those nice old church ladies from earlier in the day. This one was a local minister, still in her clerical collar, who sang hymns for the ten-minute drive across town while the three of us were being booked.

*Blessed assurance / Jesus is mine / oh what a foretaste / of glory
    divine*
*This is my story / this is my song / praising my savior / all the day
    long*

Other reporters had seen us being taken into custody, and much like our photos and videos from the protest earlier in the day, the story of our arrests quickly went viral. My colleagues at the *Post* knew I had been arrested before Ryan and I had even made it back to the police station.

The officers took us downstairs and placed Ryan and me in a cell that had a pay phone in the corner. We could, we were told, make as many calls as we wanted. Ryan was able to reach his dad, but the only numbers I could remember were my parents' home line and a cell phone that had, at least at one point, belonged to my high school girlfriend. After trying and failing to get ahold of my mom, I gave up—if I was going to catch up with a long-lost high school love it should probably come under different circumstances.

It wouldn't matter. About half an hour after we arrived at Ferguson police headquarters, Ryan and I were turned loose. Inundated with phone calls from other reporters and media outlets, Ferguson Police Chief Tom Jackson had ordered us released. By the time we were given back our belongings—unlaced shoes, notebooks, phones—it was clear we'd become momentary media celebrities.

My editors called and emailed. Then came the text messages, from Mom as well as nearly every friend from high school and college. Check-ins from sources and government officials. And then the overwhelming wave of radio and television producers. Within moments, we were discussing our arrest on *The Rachel Maddow Show* as we remained seated in the lobby of the Ferguson Police Department, hoping to secure paperwork that would tell us the names of the police officers who had roughed us up.

It wasn't until hours later that our arrest began to sink in. I'd arrived in Ferguson two days earlier thinking I'd be there for just a couple of days. I'd write a feature or two, and then I'd go back to DC and to writing about politics. But as I paced the carpeted floor of my hotel room in downtown St. Louis that night, it became clear that I wasn't escaping Ferguson anytime soon.

Resident after resident had told more stories of being profiled, of feeling harassed. These protests, they insisted, were not just about Mike Brown. What was clear, from the first day, was that residents of Ferguson, and all who had traveled there to join them, had no trust in, and virtually no relationship with, the police. The police, in turn, seemed to exhibit next to no humanity toward the pained residents they were charged with protecting.

Ferguson would birth a movement and set the nation on a course for a still-ongoing public hearing on race that stretched far past the killing of unarmed residents—from daily policing to Confederate imagery to respectability politics to cultural appropriation. The social justice movement spawned from Mike Brown's blood would force city after city to grapple with its own fraught histories of race and policing. As protests propelled by tweets and hashtags spread under the banner of Black Lives Matter and with cell phone and body camera video shining new light on the way police interact with minority communities, America was forced to consider that not everyone marching in the streets could be wrong. Even if you believe Mike Brown's own questionable choices sealed his fate, did Eric Garner, John Crawford, Tamir Rice, Walter Scott, Freddie Gray, and Sandra Bland all deserve to die?

It's worth remembering now, as the Obama presidency has come to its close, what it was like to live inside the moment when his ascendancy was a still-unfolding fact. After a seemingly never-ending sea of firsts—first black mayors, first black governors, and first black senators—to have reached that ultimate electoral mountaintop, the presidency, seemed then to have validated decades of struggle. But the nation's grappling with race and the legacy of its original sin — ongoing since the first slaves arrived in Jamestown in 1619 — was and is far from over. Any façade of a postracial reality was soon melted away amid the all-consuming eight-year flame of racial reckoning that Obama's election sparked.

Ferguson would mark the arrival on the national stage of a new generation of black political activists — young leaders whose parents and grandparents had been born as recently as the 1970s and 1980s, an era many considered to be post–civil rights. Their parents' parents had been largely focused on winning the opportunity to participate in the political process and gaining access to the protections promised them as citizens. Their parents focused on using the newfound opportunities and safeties provided by the Civil Rights and Voting Rights Acts to claim seats at the table, with political and activist strategies often focused on registering as many black voters and electing as many black leaders to public office as possible. For at least two decades, the days of taking the struggle to the streets had seemed, to many politically active black Americans, far in the rearview mirror.

For many of the post–Joshua Generation — the young men and women who, like me, first cast their ballots in 2008, who had grown up in integrated schools and neighborhoods in a world where black entertainers like Michaels Jackson and Jordan were widely recognized as the world's greatest — the seemingly unrelenting wave of black death required an accounting. Despite the talks so many of us of this generation received from parents, teachers, and coaches — *Don't run from the cops. Keep your hands out of your pockets. Be conscious of where you're wandering...* — the young black bodies we kept seeing in our Facebook newsfeeds could have been our own. How could we explain this to ourselves or each other?

Now we were able to share what we saw and how we felt about it instantaneously with thousands of others who were going through similar awakenings. Conversations once had at Bible studies and on barroom stools were happening on our phones and on Facebook, allowing both instant access to information and a means of instant feedback. Social media made it possible for young black people to document interactions they believed to be injustices, and exposed their white friends and family members to their experiences.

As President Obama's second term toiled on, it became increasingly clear that talk of a postracial America was no more than cheap political punditry. A new generation of black Americans were, if anything, as emboldened by our black president as they were unsurprised by the failure of his election to usher in a fantasy period of racial healing. From the death of Oscar Grant on New Year's Eve in 2009 after he was shot by a transit officer in Oakland, California, to the death of Trayvon Martin in February 2012 by the gun of neighborhood watchman George Zimmerman in Sanford, Florida, the headlines of the Obama years often seemed a yearbook of black death, raising a morbid and depressing quandary for black men and women: Why had the promise and potential of such a transformative presidency not yet reached down to the lives of those who elected him? Even the historic Obama presidency could not suspend the injunction that playing by the rules wasn't enough to keep you safe. What protection was offered by a black presidency when, as James Baldwin once wrote, the world is white, and we are black?

By the time a grand jury concluded in November 2014 that there was not enough evidence to charge Ferguson police officer Darren Wilson with a crime in the killing of Mike Brown, I'd been in that city for the better part of three months. I didn't know then that I'd spend the next eight months crisscrossing the country, visiting city after city to report on and understand the social movement that vowed to awaken a sleeping nation and insisted it begin to truly value black life. Each day, it seemed, there was another shooting.

In city after city, I found police departments whose largely white ranks looked little like the communities of color they were charged with protecting, officers whose actions were at worst criminal and at best lacked racial sensitivity, and black and brown bodies disproportionately gunned down by those sworn to serve and protect.

How many? At the time Mike Brown was killed, it wasn't completely clear. There had been several efforts by citizen journalists to count the number of people killed by the police each year, but full, comprehensive data on police violence wasn't available at the national level, certainly not in real time. The lack of information made it impossible to have an educated conversation about race and policing during those early days—police unions and law enforcement sympathizers would claim that Mike Brown's death was a one-off, while civil rights groups and emerging young activists would claim that Brown was a stand-in for countless others. Those deaths were black communities' reality, though they were left with no way to quantify that truth to a skeptical majority-white media, or by extension the nation. In interviews over the months I spent in Ferguson, residents described Mike Brown as a symbol of their own oppression. In a city where, federal investigators would later conclude, traffic tickets and arrest warrants were used systematically to target impoverished black residents, Brown's death afforded an opportunity through protest for otherwise ignored voices to be heard. On many nights protesters would refuse to provide their names to reporters who approached them for interviews. "My name is Mike Brown," they would reply.

In the year following Ferguson, my colleagues and I at the *Post* compiled the number of police killings as a way of establishing an accurate count. The picture we painted would reveal how common it had become for unarmed black men to be killed by police officers— one unarmed black person shot and killed by police every ten days. The stories of these men, and a few women, stared out at me from the sea of white men and women who were also left dead at the hands of police officers. Almost all of these shootings—990 of them in total in 2015 alone—would be ruled legally justified. And in a plurality if not a majority of the cases, officers, it seemed, had little option but to fire their weapons. But in hundreds of the cases, the circumstances were much muddier.

What does justice look like for those who are killed by officers who, according to the way our laws are written, have committed no crime but who through tactic or restraint could have avoided taking a life? What should be said to those grieving families, what recourse awaits them once the grand jury returns no bill? Justice is a hard concept to wrestle with when your eyes are filled with scenes of death.

On that first night in Ferguson, I was sucked into the story I wanted to cover and understand, even if I would struggle for the next year to reconcile my own role in the chaos. When I'd been a reporter for all of three years, my beat became the nation's biggest domestic story line. The young leaders behind many of the protests often trusted me because we could have been classmates or childhood playmates — in some cases, we had been. The streets of Ferguson, and later Baltimore, were flooded with newly declared citizen journalists as well as writers and reporters with well-stated partisan or ideological loyalties. They, along with scores of live streamers — who used phone apps to broadcast live images and audio from the often chaotic demonstrations and nights of rioting — played a crucial role in the creation of the movement. But my role, I knew, was different. My fundamental professional obligation was to fairness and truth.

Among those truths, however, were these: I'm a black man in America who is often tasked with telling the story of black men and women killed on American streets by those who are sworn to protect them but who historically have seen and treated those men, women, and even their children as anything but American. That story didn't start or end on the streets of Ferguson.

I wrote this book from the messy notes I compiled as I reported, by looking back at what I wrote in the *Washington Post,* and from hundreds of interviews with young protest leaders, elected officials, police officers and chiefs, and the families and friends of those who in death became national symbols. The messages of the Ferguson protester, of the Cleveland protester, of the Charleston protester, the

Baltimore protester, the Missouri protester, and the Baton Rouge protester were in many ways different—nuanced demands specific to each locale. But there was an underlying message, a defiant declaration, bursting from the protest chants in each of these cities, perhaps best captured by a sign left by a demonstrator near the site of the shooting of Antonio Brown, who was the last in the string of black men killed by St. Louis police in 2014: YOU CAN'T KILL US ALL.

The story of Ferguson, Cleveland, and Baltimore is that of the fractured and neglected relationship that exists between those who walk the streets without a badge and those who wear one. This gulf of trust only widens and becomes harder still to fill with each shooting. And the conversation about accountability and reform stalls each time, as we saw earlier this year in Dallas and Baton Rouge, when an officer's life is deliberately targeted in the name of vigilante justice.

Two years after America's great awakening to the reality of police violence in the streets of Ferguson, the same distrust, pain, and suspicion that drove thousands into the streets flow through the veins of millions of black and brown Americans.

The story of Ferguson remains the story of America.

CHAPTER ONE

Ferguson: A City Holds Its Breath

The first time I saw the name Michael Brown was on Instagram. I typically checked Instagram once or twice a week to see old college friends partying, or journalism colleagues posting from airports en route to an assignment. As I scrolled through my feed on the afternoon of August 9, my finger stopped when I reached a series of videos uploaded by Brittany Noble, a local news reporter in St. Louis whom I consider an older sister. The clip showed a disheveled woman screaming, crying. The police, she said, had killed her first-born son. Over her shoulder a crowd had gathered.

I first met Brit-*tan*-ney, as she always teasingly insisted we pronounce it, at one of the annual gatherings of the National Association of Black Journalists. We were then both job-hungry college students and quickly hit it off while discussing the feedback we'd received on our résumés from recruiters and comparing invites to the conference's nightly receptions. Five years later, we remained part of a core group of friends from those conferences who stayed in semifrequent touch as we tried to navigate entry-level journalism jobs.

Brittany had graduated a few years earlier than me, and after bouncing around several smaller-market television stations, she'd settled into a gig with KMOV, the CBS affiliate in St. Louis, which was both her hometown and that of her fiancé, Mike. As they prepared for the wedding, they decided to live in a racially diverse town not far from the city: Ferguson.

Two years after taking the gig in Missouri, Brittany was working weekends, giving her Friday nights to the job and then, after a few hours of sleep, heading back out into the field for early-Saturday- and Sunday-morning live shots. It's the type of thankless work done by many young reporters, but she was glad to be back home.

The only thing bigger than Brittany's smile is her drive, and that ambition meant she was often looking for a way to stand out on the job, constantly searching for a small scoop or a neighborhood feature that her competition might have overlooked. It didn't hurt that she had connections. Her mother, before she retired, had been one of the highest-ranking black women in the history of the St. Louis Police Department. Her soon-to-be father-in-law ran a prominent black church in the city. On many days, Brittany's email and voice mail were full of story tips and ideas. Not all of the leads panned out, but it wasn't rare for her to come up with a unique angle or tidbit.

Much like my own experience at the *Globe,* working general assignment can be a mixed bag: one day you're covering a high school graduation, the next you're camped out beside crime scene tape.

And then, of course, there are the officer-involved shootings. Brittany's first came on July 1, 2012, at her first job at a station in Saginaw, Michigan. A homeless black man, Milton Hall, had been shot and killed by the police in the parking lot of a shopping plaza.

The officers responded to a 911 call about a man who had stolen a cup of coffee from a convenience store. When they arrived, they encountered Hall, who was carrying a knife, and they began to argue with him. The forty-nine-year-old had a history of mental illness and had been living on the street.

Eight officers reported to the scene, and they told investigators that when they arrived Hall threatened a female officer with the knife and closed within a few feet of her. After a standoff of several minutes, the officers—who had formed a semicircle around Hall as he staggered forward—opened fire.

With traffic driving past and several bystanders in the parking lot, the officers shot forty-seven bullets in total, with eleven of them riddling Hall's body. The shooting was caught on cell phone video and soon was playing on loop on CNN. "The community was outraged, they said they were going to protest and demonstrate and blow the whole place up if these officers didn't get indicted," Brittany recalled to me years later. "And then the officers didn't get indicted, and nothing happened."

Before Ferguson, this story line was as common as it was hidden. A community flies into rage after a questionable police shooting, leaders hold vigils and marches, figureheads call for accountability, and then, almost as quickly as the tragedy began, it ends. Everyone but the grieving family moves on with their lives until the next time a radio dispatcher puts out the call:

Need backup. Shots fired. Officer involved.

When that call came on August 9, 2014, Brittany was in St. Louis. Having worked the early-morning Saturday shift, she was across town preparing for her engagement photo shoot.

"Hey, Brittany, you see that the police shot somebody in Ferguson?" her fiancé called out before handing her the phone so she could see for herself. Perhaps he was already tiring of the engagement photos, because he knew full and well what would happen next.

In an industry dominated by white reporters and editors, young black journalists are told early and often that they've got to go above and beyond—showing up unasked for a weekend shift, coming in early and staying late on the weekdays, and always being ready, at a moment's notice, to drop everything and run toward the story. For two years that was what Brittany, one of the only black reporters at her station and one of just a few dozen in St. Louis—a major media market— had been doing. She often felt overlooked or underappreciated, but if she kept doing her job, if she kept chasing and getting "the story," she knew they couldn't ignore her and her work forever.

Brittany fired off an email to her bosses, asking if they had anyone headed to the scene. When they didn't respond, she called a producer directly.

"You need me to come in?" she asked.

Minutes later she landed the first major scoop of Ferguson: the emotional reaction of Michael Brown's mother as she arrived at the scene.

As Brittany raced across town, residents of the Canfield Green apartment complex began flooding the streets. The shooting had happened on a quiet side street, in a spot surrounded by four-level apartment buildings. As the crowds gathered, others took to windows and porches, looking down at the chaos developing below. Within minutes after the shooting, word spread through the surrounding apartments, and beyond, that Brown's hands were up in the air when the fatal shots were fired by Officer Darren Wilson, who had encountered Brown and his friend Dorian Johnson while responding to a call about two young men, matching their description, who had just been involved in the robbery of a nearby liquor store.

As police officers scrambled to secure the scene, an enraged, agitated crowd was quickly gathering. Why is Brown's body still out there? Why was he shot and killed in the first place? And why do we keep hearing that he had his hands up?

"Get us several more units over here," one of the responding officers demanded over the police radio. "There's gonna be a problem."

Johnson and Brown had entered Ferguson Market & Liquor at 11:53 that morning—with Brown, the younger of the two men, grabbing a thirty-four-dollar box of Swisher Sweets and attempting to walk out. The employee working behind the counter that day told Brown that he had to pay for the smokes, and in response the teen grabbed the man by the collar and shoved him. One of the store's security cameras captured the violent exchange, an eleven-second video clip that would be the last living image of Brown.

But in the hours and days after Brown was shot and killed by Officer Darren Wilson, none of the residents of Ferguson knew about the liquor store robbery. That information wouldn't come out for days, when still-frame images from surveillance cameras were released by Ferguson PD. In fact, in those early days, police refused to release any information or answer any question of substance.

Why had Brown been shot and killed? Who was the officer involved? What was the potential threat to the officer that prompted his use of deadly force? But a vacuum of information always finds a way to be filled, especially in a crowded apartment complex full of dozens of people who claimed to have seen the struggle and the shooting.

The Canfield Green apartments are a cluster of half a dozen cream-colored buildings with green and brown trim. The thirty-seven-acre complex contains more than 414 apartments, one- and two-bedroom units, for which Canfield's almost exclusively black residents fork over about five hundred dollars a month. It's a relatively low-income sliver of Ferguson, a city that is socioeconomically diverse. Residents complain of gang activity, of break-ins, and of their ears too frequently seizing at the sharp cackle of gunshots.

During my first days on the ground in Ferguson, many Canfield residents believed that Brown—after being confronted by Wilson for jaywalking—had been shot in the back as he ran away. Dorian Johnson, Brown's friend who was with him when he was killed, claimed that after an initial struggle and gunfire, Brown ran away from Wilson, turned around, put his hands up, and shouted out, "Don't shoot!" Johnson ran away after Brown and Wilson began struggling, ducking behind a nearby vehicle as the fatal shots were fired. An even more inflammatory rumor, later proven untrue, was soon circulating throughout Ferguson: that Officer Wilson had stood over Brown's dying body and fired an execution shot into the dying teen's chest.

For many of those first nights after Brown's death, people

believed that there was video of the shooting, with rumors flying that officers had seized residents' cell phones to keep the videos from spreading. And there was anger about the number of bullets fired by Wilson.

Why would Wilson need to shoot Mike Brown six times? Why didn't he have a Taser? Why did it take so long for Brown's body to be moved from the ground?

"I could see how [the officer] could be intimidated, but that ain't a reason to be gunned down, not nine times, not with your hands up," said Duane Finnie, thirty-six, a childhood friend of Brown's father and friend of the family, who was one of the first people I interviewed after arriving in Ferguson. "I just put myself in Mike's shoes, and like, your last seconds of life you're getting executed by somebody who is supposed to protect and serve you.

"People are tired of being misused and mistreated, and this is an outlet for them to express their outrage and anger; everyone is looking for an outlet to express their emotions," he told me on August 11, two days after the shooting. "This is a reason...all the looting and what's going on, but people want to be heard, and they don't know how to do it. So that's why they lash out."

"They're not trying to let this one get swept under the table," a friend of Finnie's, who had been standing alongside him while we spoke, chimed in.

Investigators would later conclude that Brown's hands were most likely not up and that the altercation began when the eighteen-year-old punched Darren Wilson after the officer, responding to the robbery call, attempted to stop him on the street.

Whether Brown was attempting to surrender or attempting to attack Officer Wilson when the fatal shots were fired remains murky. The evidence shows that "Hands up, don't shoot"—a national rallying cry, the chief chorus of the dead boy's defenders—was based on a falsehood. But as anger boiled into rage, no one in Ferguson could have known that yet.

They did know that the police in Ferguson looked nothing like them: an almost-all-white force charged with serving and protecting a majority black city. They knew all too well about the near-constant traffic tickets they were being given, and how often those tickets turned into warrants.

And they knew that Mike Mike, the quiet kid who got his hair cut up the street on West Florissant and who was often seen walking around in this neighborhood, was dead.

"That could be any of us. That could have been me dead on the street!" screamed Carl Union, twenty-seven, a local DJ who refused to leave one of the early protests despite multiple rounds of heavy tear gas. Union said that when he saw the images of Brown's body in the street he thought of his young daughter. When he heard that Brown had been shot by the police, he became angry and decided to join the protest. "It's like we're not even human to them," Union said through tears.

Mike Brown's body remained on the hot August ground for four and a half hours—a gruesome, dehumanizing spectacle that further traumatized the residents of Canfield Drive and would later be cited by local police officials as among their major mistakes.

For some, first in Ferguson and later around the nation, the spectacle of Brown's body cooling on the asphalt conjured images of the historic horrors of lynchings—the black body of a man robbed of his right to due process and placed on display as a warning to other black residents.

If the police were willing not only to kill Mike Brown, residents of Canfield Drive would ask me as I interviewed them, but also to let his body sit out that way, what would they be willing to do to the rest of us?

Within an hour of the shooting, word had traveled to Michael Brown's family—his mother, stepfather, and father—who each individually made their way to Canfield Drive. Police had sealed off the block, causing a bottleneck of dozens and eventually hundreds of people who began to gather at the corner at West Florissant Avenue. That was where Brittany and the videographer she had with her parked their news van, and where she first approached Lezley McSpadden, the slain boy's mother.

Another reporter at Brittany's station was supposed to interview the family, so initially Brittany focused on getting reaction quotes from enraged local residents. But Brown's mother was standing just a few feet away, and it didn't look like any of the reporters were talking to her. Finally, Brittany asked one of the residents she had interviewed—a cousin of Brown's—if he would make an introduction. Initially she didn't even bring her cameraman with her, assuming that her colleague had already interviewed the dead teen's mother. Instead, Brittany thought, she'd upload the video to Instagram—since that was where she had first heard the story.

"You didn't have to shoot him eight times!" McSpadden exclaimed to Brittany. "You just shot all through my baby's body."

Brittany ended up working late into the night, transmitting live shots for every newscast, ending with the 11:30 p.m., and watching as the crowds that gathered became more and more frustrated and angry.

The Ferguson and St. Louis County police had sent scores of officers, some in full riot gear and tactical vehicles, to deal with the growing crowds and to hold them back as they attempted to investigate for themselves the scene of the shooting. All of this is pretty standard for the scene of a police shooting—police, protesters, angered residents and families—but the scale of the immediate response from both the community and law enforcement signaled that perhaps Ferguson would be different.

"This was a scene that I had never seen before, a heartbreak that I had never felt before from the people I was interviewing," Brittany later told me. "I just felt different. Something wasn't right. This wasn't the typical police shooting scene."

And then, after four hours, as midday turned to late afternoon, officers finally removed Brown's body from the asphalt. They did not address the crowds who were hungry for answers after spending most of their Saturday hearing inflammatory rumors. "People were like: after all of that, they're just going to leave?" Brittany said. "They're not going to say anything? These people were hurt." As the police began to leave, church groups started walking down Canfield Drive, following the still-hysterical Lezley McSpadden to the spot where crimson blood still stained the ground.

When they arrived, the groups circled around McSpadden and her husband and began to pray, sing, and hug. Some were older folks from the church up the road, others were younger residents who poured out of the Canfield apartments. What had been a rambunctious crowd had composed itself to create a vigil for a violent death.

But the tranquility didn't last. As the prayer group began to break up, the residents of Canfield began to yell. Prayer wasn't going to fix this. Neither was singing. The police had to answer for this. Why was Mike Brown dead? Why had his body been left out for so long? And when would we get answers?

Amid the shouting, someone lit a Dumpster on fire. While moments earlier desperate prayers were being sent above, now it was the flash of flames floating into the night air.

Ferguson survived that first night. The Dumpster fire and the sound of distant gunshots spooked police, but they were nothing compared with what was to come.

The following day, the Ferguson Police Department still hadn't explained what had happened or apologized for keeping Brown's body out on the ground for so long. And church groups were calling for a march in the slain teen's honor.

That Sunday afternoon, after services concluded, local pastors and their flocks met at the spot where Brown was killed. Hundreds showed up, surrounding newly erected memorials made of candles, stuffed animals, and liquor bottles that together overflowed the grass shoulders on either side of the two-lane road.

The crowd started marching and chanting, for the first time, what they believed to be Michael Brown's own words in his final moments.

"Hands up, don't shoot!"

The cries rang into the air as the crowd, including many students set to begin school the following week, as well as middle-aged residents of the apartment complex, moved forward. As they hit West Florissant and turned left, they were met by a wall of police officers. Soon what had begun as a peaceful march had morphed into a heated standoff, blocking traffic in both directions.

The scene played out right in front of Brittany, who after spending Saturday night on the job woke up for her 5 a.m. live shot, worked a full day shift, and was again at the corner of Canfield Drive and West Florissant watching her community clash with police.

Night was close. The crowd continued shouting at the officers, who were shouting back. And as the church groups began to leave, young men emerged who seemed angrier and more determined to extract revenge for Mike Brown's death.

Brittany made her way toward the front of the demonstration, to the spot where the crowd was standing toe-to-toe with the police. A young girl, perhaps in her early teens, ran up and grabbed Brittany's arm, a look of terror in her eyes. "They knocked out the windows of your truck!" the girl screamed. "And now they're burning the QuikTrip."

Brittany turned to see the shattered glass of the news station van scattered across the ground, and as she moved toward it, she could see men running in and out of the QuikTrip gas station at the corner of West Florissant Avenue and Northwinds Estates Drive.

It's unclear how it started, but in the swirl of misinformation and confusion, some in the neighborhood started spreading word that the 911 call to report a robbery by Michael Brown was made by the employees of this gas station. They most likely had confused the gas station with the liquor store up the street.

That night, armed vandals took advantage of raging protests and demonstrations to break into the QuikTrip gas station that sat just a block away from the spot on Canfield Drive where Brown was killed, grabbing handfuls of chips and sodas, cigarettes and lighters as others ripped the ATM machine from the wall. Before long, the store was ablaze.

While the photos and videos from the day of Brown's death had certainly gone viral—viewed and shared thousands of times—it was the destruction of the QuikTrip, not the police shooting of Mike Brown, that brought the microscope of the national media to Ferguson. The unrest in Ferguson had now become a riot. Yet another police shooting in a working-class black neighborhood, even the breaking of a young black body left on public display, didn't catch the gaze of the national media. It was the community's enraged response—broken windows and shattered storefronts—that drew the eyes of the nation.

Most of the so-called race riots of the 1800s and early 1900s consisted of armed clashes between white and black residents—very often precipitated by a black man or woman being somewhere that black folks "didn't belong."

That began to change in the 1930s. The large-scale racial conflicts that began in 1935 consisted primarily not of white Klansmen and residents ransacking black homes and businesses but of black men and women lashing out with violence against symbols of the white establishment: businesses, storefronts, and government buildings.

And of the more than 100 such race riots since 1935, almost all have been sparked by some type of police incident.

Between the two world wars, Harlem was believed to be the shining gold standard of what a postracial, renaissance city could look like: the nation's capital of black culture and society, full of neighborhoods with relatively peaceful integration of blacks, whites, and immigrants. But so much like almost a century later, in the Obama years, to think that Harlem was then some sort of postracial mecca required a willed ignorance of the deep racial inequalities baked into the American experience.

"The end of the Harlem Renaissance had a postracial zeitgeist never seen before, which caused its own set of anxieties for both black and white residents," Dr. Khalil Gibran Muhammad, the then director of the New York Public Library's Schomburg Center for Research in Black Culture, who has written at length about race riots, told me long after Ferguson. "The truth is, it was in commercial establishments, like the neighborhood dime store, where there was a level of integration and race mixing, a decade after the Great Migration, that had never been seen before. Which meant there was a lot of racial tension."

On the afternoon of March 19, 1935, Lino Rivera, a sixteen-year-old black Puerto Rican boy, was caught stealing a penknife from S. H. Kress, a dime store across the street from the storied Apollo Theater. In the time it took for the police to arrive, a crowd gathered outside the storefront.

The store owner asked police to let Rivera go, but no one told the crowds that officers had quietly slipped the teen out the store's side door. In a vacuum of information, a story spread that a young black boy had been killed for stealing a piece of candy and that the police were hiding his body. A hearse just happened to pull up and park nearby. The crowd assumed the worst.

More than ten thousand black residents took to the Harlem streets, with some smashing storefront windows and later getting in fights with the white New York Police Department officers who arrived to break up the violent assembly.

"Police, despite their numbers, were handicapped in dealing with the rioters by the necessity of guarding the windowless stores," a reporter for the *New York Daily News* wrote the next day. "Looting of stores was the objective of hundreds of hoodlums who swarmed into the district from Manhattan and the Bronx after news of the riot spread. Burglar alarms and false alarms were ringing constantly in the district, and fires were set in several looted stores."

By the time the rioting had concluded a day later, 125 people had been arrested, 3 people were dead, and more than two million dollars of damage had been done to local businesses.

As is almost always the case after the type of unrest commonly called a race riot, local officials quickly appointed commissions and review boards to tease out what had caused the chaos. Multiple such commissions were created to examine the 1935 unrest in Harlem.

They all concluded more or less the same thing: that the unrest was as much about systemic discrimination and inequity as it was the specific case of Lino Rivera. The "bi-racial Commission of Investigation" appointed by New York's mayor, Fiorello La Guardia, called for increased access to health care, better schools and vocational training, access to better housing, and improved relationships between police officers and black residents of Harlem as its prescription for preventing another riot.

"This relatively unimportant case of juvenile pilfering would never have taken on the significance which it later took on, had not a fortuitous combination of subsequent events made it the spark which set aflame the smouldering resentments of the city of Harlem against racial discrimination and poverty in the midst of plenty," the commission wrote in its review. "The insecurity of the individual in Harlem against police aggression is one of the most potent causes for the existing hostility to authority."

Another report, titled "The Negro in Harlem: A Report on Social and Economic Conditions Responsible for the Outbreak of March 19, 1935," concluded that the unrest came as the result of the accumulating effect of "injustices of discrimination in employment, the aggressions of the police, and the racial segregation."

Those who have studied the 1935 Harlem riot say that while the underlying issues in the neighborhood spoke to deep systemic inequality, it was the perceived disregard and devaluation of the black body, and of black life, that called forth the rage that enveloped the black men and women of Harlem on that day.

The same can be said for the violence in Ferguson. Those who set fire to the QuikTrip, and who smashed the windows of Sam's Meat Market and Red's BBQ, did so, at least in part, out of communal rage over the death of Mike Brown. Yet were it not for the deep, abiding inequality through which the black residents of Ferguson lived their lives, it is unclear if those blocks of Ferguson would ever have burst into flames.

"The Harlem riot of 1935, now the subject of a comprehensive report, demonstrated that 'the Negro is not merely the man who shouldn't be forgotten; he is the man who cannot safely be ignored,'" the writer and philosopher Alain Locke, the first black Rhodes Scholar, wrote in 1936. "Eleven brief years ago Harlem was full of the thrill and ferment of sudden progress and prosperity....Today, with that same Harlem prostrate in the grip of the depression and throes of social unrest, we confront the sobering facts of a serious relapse and premature setback; indeed, find it hard to believe that the rosy enthusiasms and hopes of 1925 were more than bright illusions or a cruelly deceptive mirage. Yet after all there was a renaissance, with its poetic spurt of cultural and spiritual advance, vital with significant but uneven accomplishments; what we face in Harlem today is the first scene of the next act—the prosy ordeal of the reformation with its stubborn tasks of economic reconstruction and social and civic reform."

Decades after the 1935 Harlem riot and yet decades before Ferguson, James Baldwin, who grew up on these same Harlem streets, warned that there would be more of this brand of unrest, invoking Biblical imagery to remind a nation then grappling with the civil rights movement that a just God had promised that his next judgment on an unjust world would come by flames, not water. Baldwin wrote in 1963, "If we—and now I mean the relatively conscious blacks, who must, like lovers, insist on, or create, the consciousness of the other—do not falter in our duty now, we may be able, handful that we are, to end the racial nightmare, and achieve our country, and change the world.

"If we do not now dare everything, the fulfillment of that prophecy, re-created from the Bible in song by a slave, is upon us: *God gave Noah the rainbow sign, No more water, the fire next time.*"

By the time the sun rose over Ferguson on August 11, two days after Mike Brown's death, the QuikTrip gas station would be nothing but charred remains—the large metal post that once displayed the red and white QT logo now declaring THE QT PEOPLE'S PARK. LIBERATED 8/10/14 in black spray paint.

More than two dozen friends and family members attended an afternoon press conference at the Jennings Mason Temple church in St. Louis, where the forceful words of civil rights attorney Ben Crump echoed off the wooden fixtures and at times rattled the stained-glass windows.

This was my first stop after arriving in St. Louis, on the afternoon of August 11, two days after Mike Brown had been killed.

The press conference was just beginning as I found my way up the stairs to the second-floor sanctuary, sliding into a pew behind the local news cameramen and grabbing a seat between two correspondents for MSNBC. It was a scene we had all, unfortunately, grown familiar with. A grieving family, with T-shirts reading REST IN PEACE, would step to the microphone to demand justice, knowing how unlikely it would be that they would get it.

I'd been in this room before. Midway through an internship at the *Boston Globe*, I'd been dispatched to the scene of a police shooting of a young black man. Officers said he had fled on foot after a traffic stop, then pulled a gun on them. The investigation into the killing took well over a year, and the slain man's mother had taken to community meetings to confront police officials, sobbing and pleading with them to give her the name of the officer who had killed her son. I'd sit with my head angled down as I listened to her desperate cries.

Knowing that a police officer is responsible causes a special, deep pain for the families of those killed, because the person who gunned down their loved one was not a mythical "bad guy," not a gang-banger or a thug or a random criminal. For the families of those killed by the police, it is often most shattering that their loved one was killed by the very people sworn to protect them. A family and a community's fundamental understanding of safety and security in our society is threatened when those pledged to protect kill.

Similar cries, the frantic gasps of a mother now without her child, were coming from the back of the sanctuary as Mike Brown's family made their way to the microphone.

Immediately, I found myself with a small but consequential logis-tical decision to make. I was armed with a notebook, a phone, and my two hands. In most cases, I would opt to record audio with my phone while taking notes by hand. But that would mean not sending real-time updates on a story where a national audience was hungry for new information. So I opted against recording. This was a story that had played out on social media; I reasoned that that was where my reporting efforts should continue to focus for now. I'd use my phone to send tweets and take notes by hand—even if it meant I'd end up with a more disjointed and incomplete set of direct quotations.

"He was executed, in broad daylight, when it was clear he had no weapon," declared Crump, a Florida-based attorney who was first thrust into the national spotlight when he represented the family of Trayvon Martin. "Their baby was executed in broad daylight!" he yelled. Crump said that Martin's father had called the Brown family before listing name after name of young black men gunned down in controversial shootings in recent years—Trayvon Martin, Jordan Davis, Jonathan Ferrell.

Those names represented the first wave of black death to come during the Obama administration, a series of shootings—joined by that of Oscar Grant, subject of a police shooting that occurred in 2009 but drew sustained national attention in 2013 after being depicted in the film *Fruitvale Station*—that brought new urgency to the peril of black life.

"To some it has become a cliché, to us these are our children," Crump declared, voice booming. "Our children, don't they deserve the dignity and respect of law enforcement?"

Brown's mother stepped to the microphone, overcome with emotion as members of her family wailed in the sanctuary's front row. Along the sides of the room sat friends of the family, their shirts declaring NO JUSTICE NO PEACE. Unable to deliver her prepared remarks, Lezley McSpadden said she would have been overjoyed to drop her son off at college. Mike Brown, having finally completed the summer course he needed to get his high school diploma, was supposed to be starting his classes at a vocational school that very day. Instead, McSpadden said, she was planning his burial. "That was my firstborn son. . . . Ask anyone and they'd tell you how much I loved my son. . . . I just wish I could have been there to help him, my son . . . ," she muttered before breaking down in tears. Lifting her head as tears dropped onto the podium, she added: "No violence, just justice."

At the end of the service, I slipped out in front of the family, hoping to catch one or two of them as they made their way to their cars. But they were overcome, the pain of the death still fresh. As they neared the exit, Brown's grandmother, with whom for a time he had lived, fell to the ground as she wailed. "Oh, God, they took my baby!" Tears were bursting from her eyes as she was carried toward a car.

Moments later I found Charles Ewing, one of Brown's uncles and a local pastor, who insisted to me that there was no way his nephew would have attacked a police officer. "We called him the gentle giant, he was a gentle giant," Ewing told me, calling Brown—whose attack on the liquor store worker was not yet known—a nonviolent kid to his core. "He was like a big teddy bear," Ewing said. "We tried to get him to play football but he was too timid."

I wanted my readers to feel like they knew Michael Brown, and I wanted to know him myself. Who was this young man, what were his hopes and his dreams, his strengths and his faults? Why did he end up in that liquor store that day, with his hand gripping the collar of that cashier?

A journalist's portrait of the deceased is often used by the casual reader to decide if the tragic outcome that befell him or her could have happened to us, or, as is often implied to be the case in those killed by police officers, if this tragic fate was reserved for someone innately criminal who behaved in a way we never would.

We focus on personal details of the dead not only because readers want to know, but because we in the media do, too. We believe that if we can somehow figure out the character and life of the person at the center of the story, we can somehow understand what happened that day. We fall into the fallacy of believing we can litigate the complicated story before us into a black-and-white binary of good guys and bad guys. There are no isolated incidents, yet the media's focus on the victim and the officer inadvertently erases the context of the nation's history as it relates to race, policing, and training for law enforcement. And by focusing on the character of the victim, we inadvertently take the focus off the powerful and instead train our eyes and judgment on the powerless.

In reality, knowing whether Michael Brown liked football, was truly a "gentle giant," or was an honors student or a dropout provides little insight into what happened on Canfield Green that day. Even less relevant were the tidbits meant to "prove" Brown was somehow deserving of his fate—that he smoked weed with his friends or rapped sexual lyrics in the makeshift studio he had constructed in his grandmother's basement.

In those early days, the national media litigated Mike Brown, rather than litigating the shooting. We placed the burden of proof on the dead teenager, not the officer who had shot and killed him.

To many white Americans, Mike Brown was a young man who lived a very different life, in a very different country. He robbed a liquor store and then got in a scuffle with a police officer. The specifics of the shooting appeared to absolve the conscience of anyone who might have felt responsible for weighing whether Michael Brown's death, legally justified or not, fit a broader pattern and whether that pattern was one rooted in systemic injustice.

A shortsighted framing, divorced from historical context, led us to litigate and relitigate each specific detail of the shooting without fully grasping the groundswell of pain and frustration fuming from the pores of the people of Ferguson—which also left us blindsided by what was to come.

We had met less than a minute earlier, on the steps outside one of Greater St. Louis's largest black churches, but Netta's brow was already furrowed and a string of teasing taunts had begun its seamless flow from her lips.

"I mean, I know you said you were light-skinned, but you didn't say you were *this* light-skinned!" she said matter-of-factly, standing outside a hastily called meeting of the NAACP in response to the protests and the riots. After the family press conference, this was my second stop in Ferguson.

Netta's frank declaration and piercing facial expressions as she stared at the overdressed reporter standing in front of her were disarming.

"Okay. Well, we already have a white friend named white Wes," she said, reaching over to point to a labor organizer standing with their group. "So we can call you point-five Wes." Unyieldingly blunt, with a face that betrays both passion and skepticism, this was Johnetta Elzie.

It was August 11, and I had been in St. Louis for roughly three hours. But Netta was one of the only people I knew I needed to talk to. For days I had watched her fire off tweet after tweet from the ground, often providing vivid emotional detail along with photos and videos of the protests and the police response. She seemed to be always on the scene and always in the know about the planned demonstrations.

Netta was a "day one" protester, one of the people who flooded the streets in the hours after the shooting and who saw with their own eyes the chaos of August 9, 2014—the police dogs, the devastation of Michael Brown's parents, and the dead teen's body baking on the asphalt.

As I boarded a plane to St. Louis, I'd sent her a private message on Twitter explaining that I was on my way to Ferguson and wanted to touch base and get any context I would need to make sure I told the story accurately. She replied with her cell phone number and told me to hit her up when I landed. Before I could reply, she had sent out this tweet to her growing list of followers.

"Reporters from the Washington Post are on their way to #STL #ferguson to cover the #MikeBrown story the correct way. THIS IS LOVE."

The news of Big Mike's death wasn't broken by a local reporter, although many of them were on the scene not long after the shooting. The first dispatches came from Emanuel Freeman, a twenty-seven-year-old local rapper who goes by the stage name Thee Pharoah and who lived in the Canfield Green apartment complex. He heard the first gunshot and raced to the window, phone in hand, sending emotional updates. "I JUST SAW SOMEONE DIE OMFG," Freeman tweeted at 10:03 a.m. on August 9, 2014. "the police just shot someone dead in front of my crib yo," he sent in response to someone who inquired for more information. "no reason! He was running!" Then another update, this one containing a blurry image of Officer Darren Wilson standing over Mike Brown's body.

Johnetta Elzie quickly became the most prominent of the citizen journalists telling the story of Ferguson. To her followers, she seemed omnipresent—at the police department, at the spot where Mike Brown had been killed, outside the gas station, shocked and scared as it began to burn. And all of it was documented, line by line and exclamation by exclamation. Her unchecked emotion was captivating. If someone online attacked her, she attacked back, and hit harder— with none of the faux humility or fake good faith that colors the way most of the prominent chattering class interacts and debates on social media. Her criticism of the police and of the media was searing. For a journalist used to reading the often carefully-calculated social media dispatches of fellow political reporters and elected officials, her honesty was a refreshing burst of real, an injection of vivid life into a story about a gruesome death.

Netta had spent nearly all of her twenty-five years in St. Louis, raised by her mother, Relonda, who for years owned and operated a beauty salon she had named Ree's Hair Explosion. Netta grew up listening to the older black clientele argue about men, and fashion, and politics, picking up their mannerisms and at times hyperbolic attitudes. Things weren't always great between Netta and her mother, with frequent clashes between the strong-willed single mother and her even stronger-willed daughter.

But Netta always knew her mother was proud of the grades she brought home from Our Lady of Good Counsel, a private school paid for with money earned at the salon. For Netta, often the only black child in her classes, it was a special pride to outwork her white classmates. She longed to see the look on their faces each time a quiz or assignment was handed back and she could proudly declare that she—the girl from the rough side of town—had bested them.

As Netta entered her early teens, Relonda decided she wanted to start a nonprofit to mentor young girls—especially those like her, who found themselves young mothers. It wasn't long before she was pestering her daughter for help with paperwork, and for recommendations for speakers even if the idea never got fully off the ground.

Relonda had been sick for a long time, in and out of the hospital with a variety of ailments. Not long before Netta was set to graduate from high school and head to college came Relonda's diagnosis of lupus.

By the time Netta moved back to St. Louis after her freshman year at Southeast Missouri State, things had gotten much worse, and she was getting 2 a.m. calls from her mother for help getting to and from emergency trips to the hospital.

"A week before she died, I sat down and she looked at me and she read my whole life," Netta told me later. "'I know exactly what's going on with you,' she told me, and then she listed every worry that I had—I really wanted to be independent, I wanted to pay all of my bills on my own, I wanted to stop having to answer to or fight through my freedom with my family. She sat there and she told me that she was going to fix it all.

"And I remember looking at her and saying: 'What are you going to do, you're a sick woman.'

"Toward the end, she would tell me that she loved me, and I would tell her that I loved her back. For the first time I'd let her hug me and kiss me. I let her be my mother."

Just after 2014 began, Relonda Elzie died.

For years, Netta had turned to social media the way most men and women of her generation do—as a hybrid newsfeed, broadcasting platform, and ongoing group therapy space. Her wide eyes would oscillate between her television and Twitter feeds as she watched *Love & Hip Hop* or political news shows, her computer and smartphone serving as her second screens. She posted Facebook statuses about Trayvon Martin and Jordan Davis.

Netta tweeted her way through her freshman year as she navigated the parties and classrooms, before ultimately—after several incidents in which men on campus attempted to sexually assault her—giving up on college altogether and moving home. She tweeted about her mother's death, leaning heavily on the support provided by the small section of the Internet she had carved out for herself as she worked up the courage to explain to her younger sister that their mother was gone.

These years of posts prepared Netta for her role as one of the protest movement's chief on-the-ground correspondents in Ferguson. In fact, it was a friend she had made online who first saw news of the officer-involved shooting in St. Louis on August 9, 2014 and flagged the tweets for Netta, who at the time was home at her aunt's house, where she had been living since her mother's death.

Netta spent two or three hours glued to her Twitter timeline—searching for updates from eyewitnesses and tweeting in outrage at news outlets that seemed already, before much if any information had been released, to have decided that Mike Brown had deserved his fate. Then, around 9:30 p.m., Netta and a friend decided to make the drive to Ferguson and see the scene for themselves.

They approached Canfield Drive with apprehension. Netta had seen photos on Twitter of police trying to wash the blood from the street. Soapsuds, now illuminated by a streetlight, did little to make the pooled blood vanish. "It was devastating," Netta recalled. "It made me feel like his body might as well have still been out there."

As she paced the streets, taking video clips that she uploaded to Instagram and photos that she sent out on Twitter, Netta heard the words of several young children, residents of the Canfield Green apartment complex, repeating over and over in her mind. "I kept hearing them say that they saw Mike Mike get killed."

With that morbid chorus on loop in her brain, Netta approached another local woman, who said she was a nurse and that when she had raced into the street to render care to Michael Brown's body, one of the responding officers had raised his weapon in her face and told her to "get the fuck back!"

But Netta wasn't surprised by the police response, or by the perceived hostility. It was only a matter of time, she figured, before the local media began attacking the character of the man whose blood was still seeping into the ground in front of her.

She'd been born and raised in St. Louis. She knew how this works.

For decades, some in St. Louis had boasted proudly about their city's relative racial harmony. It was one of the only Midwestern metropolises, they were quick to note, not to have seen violent riots break out during the 1960s.

But it didn't take much research, or many conversations with black residents, to see that there was little racial harmony here. One day, months into covering Ferguson, I realized that, if anything, this city felt like a place that was constantly overcompensating, trying to convince you that everything was going to be just fine: move along, there's no race or racial tension to be seen here! But the robust memorial of Mike Brown, the protests that still raged more than a hundred days after his death, and the shells of burned-out storefronts told a much different story.

When I arrived, it had been almost two decades since Neal Peirce had first come to St. Louis. A journalist by trade, Peirce spent much of the 1980s and 1990s writing comprehensive investigative reports on the status of America's cities. Along with his coauthor, Curtis Johnson, Peirce would parachute into a major city to take the locale's temperature economically, socially, and racially by interviewing the movers and shakers — zooming out to ten thousand feet in cities that often were used to little more than granular coverage. These "Peirce Reports" would often later be published in their entirety by the local newspaper in whichever town was profiled, serving at the time and now, decades later, as some of the most comprehensive and revealing assessments of many of America's big cities pre-Internet, when it took much more than a few clicks and Google searches to collate deep social science and research with reporting. With an agreement struck to have the final product considered for publication in the *St. Louis Post-Dispatch*, Peirce and Johnson began their work.

"I recall two poignant moments," said Curtis Johnson, who co-wrote the 1997 reports about St. Louis with Peirce, when I asked him two decades later about their research. "First, when one leader, when we asked what he would regard as evidence that St. Louis was making progress on race relations, his response revealed the quiet seething among blacks. He said something like, 'When white leaders quit picking our leaders for us.' That really said it all. He had no particular animus and went out of his way to show respect for St. Louis leaders. But it was the patronizing that mostly got to him. Obviously, many less privileged blacks would have been more than quietly seething."

As they finished their interviews, Johnson and Peirce increasingly found leaders—both black and white—voicing concern that if St. Louis didn't initiate honest and robust efforts to address structural and systemic inequities, a day of reckoning would, sooner or later, arrive. "I hope the report generates fire in the belly and stimulates fear," Thomas Purcell, who ran Laclede's Landing Redevelopment Corporation, which aimed to bring new business to a historic district downtown, told Peirce when they sat for an interview. "St. Louis, if you don't fear and do something about it, there are consequences."

After conducting dozens of interviews, Peirce and Johnson issued an urgent prognosis, which was published by the *St. Louis Post-Dispatch* on March 11, 1997:

> Race pervades every St. Louis regional issue. It feeds the sprawl and all the costs of sprawl as people run from inner-city minorities. It explains the disparities in school funding and the extraordinary

percentages of private and parochial school enrollments. It limits the geographic appeal of the new rail system because far-out suburbs don't want too easy a connection to the core.

No one even bothers to deny that race relations in the St. Louis region are a tough, seemingly intractable problem. Some African-Americans say it's a "volcano destined to erupt," that the apparently calm racial atmosphere masks a seething cauldron of resentment that will inevitably explode when today's black leaders, nurtured in the hopefulness of the civil rights revolution, yield to a next, less patient generation.

It took longer than they may have imagined, but by 2014 the magma beneath the volcano that was Greater St. Louis's intractable problem had begun to stir.

For decades, many of the black residents of St. Louis County had complaints not just about policing, but also about why they had so little access to quality housing, why the region's leaders couldn't provide the number of jobs they so desperately sought, and why the trains and buses to get them to those jobs were inconveniently routed around the black parts of town.

Ferguson is in all ways suburban. One of a series of small municipalities that make up "North County," the city's residential streets cut long, weaving paths lined with duplexes. As they have for years, basketball hoops and discarded footballs rest in many front yards. Most of the suburbs were, for most of modern history, majority white. For generations, locals recall, they were "sundown towns" where blacks could work as domestics or handymen but dared not attempt to live.

But in recent decades a massive migration of black residents, both from surrounding suburbs and from parts of East St. Louis, transformed these small cities. According to US Census numbers, Ferguson was 99 percent white in 1970. A decade later, blacks made up 14 percent of the population, and by 1990 they were 25 percent of the city's population.

By the turn of the century, Ferguson had become a majority—
52 percent—black suburb. Its elected and appointed city leadership
struggled to keep up. The council remained almost all white (white
councilors recruited the only two black candidates to ever run), and
soon the city was dealing with the distrust and suspicion that come
when an almost-all-white police force is charged with monitoring a
majority-minority city.

"The American dream is if I work hard, bust my rear end, no
matter where I start I can put myself in a better place," said Jason
Johnson, a political scientist at Hiram College, who grew up in
Greater St. Louis and traveled to Ferguson to witness the protests.
"These aren't just protests of hopeless downtrodden black folk…
these are protests born of expectation. Of people who say: 'I moved
up here to get away from this crap.' It's the notion that no matter
what you do, many African-Americans still feel like they're denied
the American dream."

In hundreds of interviews, residents of the North County suburbs told me heartbreaking stories of arbitrary traffic stops and
aggressive street stops and patdowns, emergency calls ignored by
police, and the enduring perception that the deaths of black and
brown men are neither fully investigated nor solved—especially
deaths at the hands of police officers.

"There is this overwhelming feeling that they can shoot us, they
can beat us—we can even have this stuff on video and the police
officer still gets off," said Patricia Bynes, a member of the local Democratic committee who was a regular at the protests. "There is the
idea that police officers are untouchables."

This is why a local minister like Derrick Robinson left his family
night after night, grabbed a cardboard sign, and ventured into the
thick summer heat or biting winter to cry *"Justice for Mike Brown!"*
into the stone-cold faces of armed police officers. It's why he stood
on the same street corner night after night, waiting for something to
go sideways—maybe tonight it's tear gas and rubber bullets, or

maybe tonight it will be gunshots bursting from an illicit weapon fired toward the crowds from the window of a high-rise apartment.

In Ferguson, protest was a means for the many to assert, with unified voice, their humanity. Disruptive protest brought with it the promise of finally making the system listen.

"Indict, convict, send that killa cop to jail, the whole damn system is guilty as hell!"

Just a few days into covering the Ferguson protests, a question constantly leveled by editors back in Washington, as well as skeptics of the protests, was: What, exactly, do these protesters want? A grand jury was considering whether to charge the officers, after all.

Before Ferguson, most of the nation—and many of us in the media—knew very little about the process for charging a police officer with a crime. If a shooting was unjustified, most of us assumed, the officer would be charged.

Months after the Ferguson grand jury concluded its work, two of my colleagues teamed with Phil Stinson, a professor at Bowling Green State University, to conduct the most thorough review to date of how often, if ever, police officers are charged.

Out of what was likely more than ten thousand fatal police shootings by on-duty police officers between 2004 and 2014, just fifty-four officers had been charged with a crime—and in just a handful of those cases were the officers convicted.

The people of Ferguson didn't need that analysis. They already knew.

Among the first things that typically happen after a police shooting is a round of calls for a special prosecutor. Local prosecutors rely on police officers every day for both evidence and testimony, so the logic goes that a local prosecutor may be inclined against aggressively pursuing charges against police officers whom he likely knows and on whose work he relies.

St. Louis County's elected prosecutor is Bob McCulloch, a

well-known power player in Missouri's Democratic circles who has close ties to Governor Jay Nixon and Senator Claire McCaskill— who at the time of Michael Brown's shooting were the two most powerful Democrats in a once-red state that over time had begun to purple.

McCulloch came from a cop family—his father was a St. Louis policeman. When Bob was just twelve years old, his father was killed in the line of duty, during a shooting involving a black suspect. McCulloch's brother and a nephew are both St. Louis police officers, and his mother spent twenty years as the department's clerk.

The death of his father, in part, inspired McCulloch to pursue a career as a police officer, but he lost a leg after a bout with cancer during his high school years and settled instead for a long career as the county prosecutor.

McCulloch argued that he was elected to be the county's prosecutor, and that was not a responsibility he was going to relinquish willingly. And soon, Missouri's Democratic power brokers publicly stood by their prosecutor.

"I believe that Bob McCulloch will be fair," McCaskill declared in an interview with MSNBC, one of just a handful of on-the-record statements she provided during the August round of unrest in Ferguson. "You have to understand the only allegation against this prosecutor is he can't be fair. Well, what does that say about the people of this country where people are elected? You don't come along and just remove someone from that job unless it is under the powers of an emergency."

As his allies began to take to the media to defend him, I approached McCulloch's office and asked how many times they had previously considered charges against a police officer and how many times, if any, they had secured the indictment of an officer.

It took them a while—the prosecutor's office didn't keep records in a way that was searchable, and like many government agencies, the St. Louis County prosecutor's office had seen significant employee turnover in the years since McCulloch first took the job in 1991. Eventually, they produced a roster of thirty-three cases, put together by their office staff's collective memory, in which McCulloch had pursued the indictment of a police officer. But of that list, just a handful of cases had resulted in charges against an officer for exhibiting force while on the job. None of the indictments were for an on-duty shooting.

Among those cases was the 2000 Jack in the Box shooting. Two unarmed black men, Earl Murray and Ronald Beasley, were shot and killed in St. Louis County, sparking the largest police protests that St. Louis had seen until Ferguson came along a decade and a half later. Agents had been zeroing in on Murray, a small-time drug dealer, who earlier in the day had asked his friend Beasley, who worked as an auto mechanic, if he could help him fix his car, which had been acting up. McCulloch to date has refused to release video evidence in the shooting, and said at the time of the investigation that he agreed with the decision of the grand jury not to charge the two officers involved.

Then, in a series of interviews, McCulloch called the two slain men "bums" who had "spread destruction in the community." I went back and forth half a dozen times with McCulloch's spokesman, who had been inundated with media requests. In one of our last correspondences, the spokesman conceded that, with the perspective of a decade, perhaps there was little honor in calling the dead names.

"In retrospect, Mr. McCulloch believes Murray and Beasley should have been described as 'convicted felons' rather than 'bums,' as that would have been a more accurate description," the spokesman told me in an email.

At the time, local leaders and Al Sharpton had led demonstrations and blocked freeways as they called for an indictment. But, as was almost always true in the case of police violence between the early-1990s beating of Rodney King and the 2014 shooting of Mike Brown, soon enough, the commotion died down.

But the black residents of St. Louis County hadn't forgotten the Jack in the Box shooting, or the way the slain men — especially Beasley, who hadn't even been a target of the drug sting — had been described by the county prosecutor. They remembered vividly.

One afternoon, as I worked my way up and down the street protests, a middle-aged woman walked right up to me, asked if I was the reporter she had heard about on TV — the sole advantage of our arrests was that Ryan Reilly and I had become recognizable pseudo-celebrities among the protest crowd — and then urged me to focus my next story on McCulloch.

"That's the real story, that's the real scandal!" this woman insisted, before she went on to compare the mild-mannered St. Louis County prosecutor to the notorious public safety commissioner who faced off with Martin Luther King, Jr., in Birmingham in 1963. "He's our Bull Connor!"

But despite calls for him to step aside that were sustained from the day Mike Brown was killed until the day a grand jury declined to indict Darren Wilson, McCulloch was consistent in his refusal. "I have absolutely no intention of walking away from the duties and responsibilities entrusted in me by the people in this community," he told a local radio station in August 2014. "I have done it for twenty-four years, and I've done, if I do say so myself, a very good job."

There would be no special prosecutor. And there would be no indictment.

What makes a young man stand before a police line and throw a water bottle toward their armor? It's certainly part ego. And it's part the foolishness of youth.

But in Ferguson, it was also at least part helplessness.

These residents, time and time again, offered a discouraging assessment of the plight that was their reality: If, no matter what a police officer does to you, he or she will not be charged with a crime, why does it matter if you disperse at those officers' commands? If it doesn't matter how the police — the system — treats you, does it matter how you treat them?

Much of my job as a reporter consists of desperate and, more often than not, failed attempts to convince people with no reason to trust me that this is exactly what they should do.

A fellow reporter once remarked to me that a reporter deals in the extremes — showing up on what is either the best or the worst day of your life, stepping up to your doorstep to find either elation or pain. We ring your phone the morning after you've claimed the winning Powerball ticket. And we show up, notebook tucked in our back pocket, the day after your mother or brother has been killed. Maybe it was a car accident, or a murder, or a police shooting. How did you find out? And will you tell us more about them? We're so sorry for your loss. Oh, and by the way, you don't happen to have a color photo, do you?

It's not an exact science. Sometimes those closest to a news story are eager to talk to you and every other reporter, and other times just to one or two lucky souls who happen to show up with their notebook at the exact right moment. Other times, no matter the technique, no number of attempts or approaches will convince someone to submit to an interview. But every reporter works their own advantages, developed by trial and error. I knew immediately which tack I'd take with Netta Elzie, whose trust later became one of my advantages when seeking interviews with other residents and activists.

Netta was deeply suspicious of the media, not unlike many of the families and friends of police shooting victims I had encountered before. So often, distrust of police was matched, if not exceeded, by deep suspicion of the media — and very often that suspicion was born from a moment in their past. And in my experience, a man or woman who has been burned or betrayed by the media wants one thing. Not a correction, or a rehabilitative article: they want to be heard, to be able to explain the injustice they believed was dealt to them so that their pain is validated.

Netta's personal distrust of the media began earlier that year, just two weeks after her mother's death. Sitting on her aunt's couch that afternoon, surfing social media, she saw a Facebook post she didn't think could be true:

"RIP Stephon."

She got the phone call from another mutual friend. It was true. Stephon Averyhart was dead. Just weeks after losing her mother, she had lost a close friend. Netta was shattered.

They had met almost five years earlier, when one of her closest friends began dating one of his. As the friend groups began to merge, the two found that they just clicked. First they'd text each other when their friends were meeting up, to make sure the other would be attending. Then they'd make sure they linked up anytime Netta was back in town from school over a holiday.

Eventually, Stephon began inviting Netta with him to the highlight of his week: Sunday-night drag racing in downtown St. Louis. Netta remembers Stephon as a showman, a clown, who would go out of his way to make everyone laugh as they sat around someone's living room or basement, or when they'd head out to a bar or club or restaurant.

He was the friend group's Mr. Fix-It, getting much of his money from working odd jobs on cars and buying old beater vehicles, fixing them up, and reselling them. When you talk to his friends now, one of the first things they all recall is that Stephon had a hustle about him.

While everyone else had upgraded to smartphones, Stephon was still carrying around an old black flip phone.

"As long as it rings and I can keep getting my money, it works!"

Stephon would shout as his friends would burst into laughter each time his dated ringtone would interrupt a hangout.

The police said Averyhart had fled from a traffic stop—prompting a police chase that included a spike strip and a helicopter. When Averyhart crashed his car, he allegedly jumped from it and ran with a gun in his hand. Then, having trapped him in an alleyway, the officers said they saw him raise the gun in their direction.

Pieces by local television stations often mistakenly described Averyhart as a felon, but his only major crime had been fleeing the police during what ended up being his fatal encounter. Otherwise, Averyhart had no criminal record other than a few unpaid traffic tickets and a misdemeanor marijuana charge. Articles published on the websites of several St. Louis television stations repeated the erroneous charge, and a sea of online commenters called him a thug, a lowlife, someone who deserved to be killed, and whom the world was better without. "The comment section was so horrible," Netta recalled as we discussed Stephon's death more than a year later. "That was my first time really realizing that these racist people from the Internet are real-life people. This person saying these horrible things about my dead friend could be my neighbor."

But Stephon Averyhart had the misfortune of being a black man shot and killed by the police *before* Ferguson. His killing drew almost no media scrutiny, besides the occasional article in the *Riverfront Times,* a scrappy weekly newspaper in St. Louis, which continued to follow the case.

Averyhart's mother, Stacey Hill, was sitting at home when she got the phone call telling her that the St. Louis police had shot her only son. The fifty-four-year-old mother had spent her entire life in St. Louis, where she still works at a local grocery store decorating cakes for birthdays and graduations. And funerals.

Stephon had been on the way to an auto parts store to pick up supplies for one of his mechanic jobs. His mother still says he should have been a race car driver, so much did he love driving fast from the first time he ever sat behind a wheel. And he was driving fast on that day when the flashing lights pulled up behind him. He had no criminal record and, his family insists, was carrying his gun legally. But he did commit a crime—he ran from the officers who tried to pull him over.

Hill wishes her son hadn't run. But she understands why he did.

Black residents in St. Louis all fear the traffic stop. Departments in Greater St. Louis are known for using them to milk revenue for their city's bottom line, often stacking multiple violations into a single citation. When tickets go unpaid, a warrant is issued. On the day Mike Brown was killed, Ferguson had almost as many active warrants as it did residents.

Stephon Averyhart had an outstanding traffic warrant.

After the first call, Stacey Hill raced to the scene of the shooting. Unable to get answers, she tried the hospital—where workers and security guards wouldn't tell her if Stephon was dead or alive. After several hours, she went home and waited. Finally, she got a call summoning her to the medical examiner's office

Hill was heartbroken. And then she became angry. She read all the headlines calling her only son an ex-con and a felon. Those same articles declared that Stephon had pointed a gun at the officers chasing him, but she just didn't believe it. The investigation would clear her son, she knew it.

But few things move as slowly, under such a unique cloak of darkness, as an investigation into an officer-involved shooting.

It was months before she got a call from a St. Louis police sergeant, in September 2014. The shooting of Michael Brown had thrust all local police departments under public scrutiny. They wanted to give her an update. Hill says she was told that the initial police story was wrong. Her son had never actually pointed the gun; rather, he was reaching down to pick it up off the ground when he was shot.

"My son deserved to go to jail that day," Hill still says. "He did not deserve to die."

Hill begged the sergeant to have the department issue a new press release to correct the record. She asked for the officers' names and was told that those, too, were unavailable to her—the investigation was ongoing. To date, it still is.

She went home and waited. Almost two years after that meeting, she is still waiting.

For Netta, the pain that pushed her to protest began privately with the deaths of Trayvon Martin and Jordan Davis, as well as the execution of Troy Davis—a Georgia inmate whose appeals of his death sentence became a rallying cry around the same time that the story of Trayvon Martin reached its apex. This private feeling of sorrow was compounded by the two police shootings that would define the next years of Netta's life—one of a man, Stephon Averyhart, whom she knew and loved, and the other of a man, Mike Brown, whom she had never known.

In February 2016, two years after Stephon was killed and eighteen months after the unrest in Ferguson, I called the St. Louis Metropolitan Police Department and asked about the status of the investigation into Stephon's shooting. The department continued to refuse to release the names of the officers involved. They also wouldn't give me any other information about why Stephon had been pulled over or why he had been shot. All they would release in terms of documents was a two-page preliminary police report, for which they charged me six dollars. The investigation into the shooting—which occurred six months before that of Michael Brown—remains active.

I called Stacey Hill back and asked her if she had heard anything else. Sometime in 2015 the captain had called her into the police station and told her he had something to give her. During this meeting, he handed over a more-than-forty-page case file, which included the same two useless pages that I had been given as well as a full readout of the incident report.

The report, which Stacey Hill sent to me via FedEx next-day delivery, stated that a St. Louis Metropolitan Police helicopter began following Averyhart after he fled the traffic stop, around 11:50 a.m. on February 12, 2014. After officers deployed spike strips, the report says Averyhart ditched his car in an alley and began running, with a gun in his hand. Not far behind were two officers, now pursuing him on foot.

As Stephon ran down another alley, he attempted to throw the gun over a tall wooden fence, but he miscalculated the height. The pistol, according to the account of the shooting given by a police officer who was watching from a helicopter, hit the top of the fence and landed back in the alley at Averyhart's feet. Initially, Averyhart kept running. Then he paused, turned around, and bent over to pick the weapon back up. At that moment, according to the officer with the bird's-eye view, the two officers who had been running after Averyhart rounded the corner, pulled their guns, and opened fire.

"We could see the detectives draw their firearms and then the suspect fall to the ground," John Furrer, the officer in the helicopter, said in his statement to investigators. "Detectives advised over the radio that shots had been fired. The suspect laid in the alley motionless."

So what actually happened in that alley? Did Averyhart really threateningly "raise" the gun at officers, or was he in the act of picking it up when officers ran up on him, got spooked, and opened fire? Will the officers involved be charged? Probably not. And when will Stacey Hill get some of the answers she still so desperately desires? It's unclear if she ever will.

Much as they did on the last two days, crowds had gathered near the street where Michael Brown had been killed and were rallying at the charred remains of the QuikTrip gas station on the evening of August 11, 2014. Night began to fall, and the crowds grew increasingly angry as heavily armored police officers began threatening to deploy tear gas if they did not disperse.

After leaving the Brown family's press conference, I had driven across town to meet up with Netta and a handful of other young residents and soon-to-be activists outside the NAACP meeting and then asked them to direct me back into Ferguson.

"Slow down," Netta urged as I whipped my rental car around a suburban side street. "The cops around here don't play when it comes to speeding tickets." I probably should have known as much, but it was still just my first day in Ferguson.

After I parked my car just up the street, at the home of one of Netta's friends, we made our way toward the intersection of Nesbit and West Florissant, where it appeared about three dozen people were squaring off against police officers.

"I'm under siege," said Donald Harry, the owner of a single-story house that sat at the corner of Nesbit Street and West Florissant Avenue. Across the street stood dozens of residents shouting at the cops. A block in the other direction, behind Harry's home, stood armored police vehicles and an advancing line of officers. Harry was trapped in the middle of the chaos.

The previous night, rioters had shot out the back window of the black SUV that sat in Harry's driveway. When he heard yelling and commotion outside, and threatening declarations from the police officers, he got worried and left his house.

"I've got my family in here," Harry told me, pointing back at his home. I was jotting down the rest of his sentence when Harry grabbed me, shoving me sideways onto the ground and toward his shrubbery. The police had begun firing tear gas, and while my head was buried in a notebook, I hadn't noticed the canister that had landed inches from our feet.

Soon the corner on which we were standing was engulfed in a cloud of tear gas. Covering my face with the collar of my sweater, I glanced behind me in time to see Netta clutch the top of her chest.

"Are they shooting us? Did I just get hit with something?" she screamed. The rubber bullet that had struck her chest was now lying at her feet.

We both started running back toward the car.

"I was just trying to get to my sister's house!" cried one twenty-three-year-old, who lay sobbing on a lawn.

He said he was walking home when officers approached him, sprayed tear gas in his face, and peppered him with rubber bullets. His friends pleaded with an ambulance to hurry, and a neighbor offered to drive him to the hospital.

"I don't need a hospital!" the man yelled. "This is my home."

The police aggression only further incited the crowd, with some lying in the street with hands in the air: "Don't shoot!" they chanted. Others added: "Go home, killers!" Others fled, crying out for water as stinging tear gas bit at their eyes.

While many residents of Ferguson had been deeply outraged by the violence and looting of the previous night, what upset them even more was the nightly militarized response of law enforcement. These suburban families weren't used to seeing officers in riot gear, which further ingrained the image of a hostile occupying force in the minds of residents whose support would have been vital for the police to maintain order.

As the night wore on, residents who remained outside began to regroup. Many refused to leave the streets. Others were physically incapable. As police moved up West Florissant, many residents said they were trapped. The neighborhood consists of a series of cul-de-sacs with one main road stretching between them, and each one was now blocked by police.

After running to the car for a bottle of water, I decided—despite Netta's warnings—to move back up toward the tear gas to see what was going on. As I made my way up the street, I ran into twenty-five-year-old Edward Crawford.

"This is beyond Mike Brown, this is about all of us," Crawford told me, insisting that the reason he had come out into the streets was because he had previously been subject to traffic stops and searches and had felt he was harassed by Ferguson police because of the color of his skin. A young father who worked as a waiter, Crawford had joined the protests not long before the tear gas and rubber bullets were deployed. "The looting was wrong, but so is this. This is excessive force," he said as a tear gas canister landed just behind his feet.

As I made my way back to my car for the final time, I ran into Crawford again.

Two nights later, he and I would both be thrust into the national narrative—as I would sit in a jail cell in the basement of the Ferguson Police Department, Crawford would again join the protests. This time, wearing an American flag tank top and eating a bag of chips, he would race to a canister of tear gas fired on the protesters and, in an act captured by the camera of *Post-Dispatch* photographer Robert Cohen, toss it through the air back toward the police officers. The image went viral, becoming perhaps the single most recognizable symbol from the Ferguson unrest. But tonight, Crawford was no symbol, and he was no hero. He was just a scared resident who was convinced that this aggression from the police might never stop.

"You're gonna write your story, and you're gonna leave town, and nothing is going to change," Crawford told me as the late hours of Monday turned into the early hours of Tuesday. "One day, one month, one year from now, after you leave, it's still going to be fucked up in Ferguson."

Based on the early media coverage, there appeared to be little if any effort to distinguish between organic expressions of outrage and pain that manifested in peaceful protests—both those unplanned and those days later, which were more deliberately organized—and those that boiled over into violence. This was, at least in part, due to our addiction to the exciting, to "breaking" coverage, which emphasizes emotional urgency and sacrifices accuracy and nuance on the altar of immediacy. "Buildings are burning!" an anchor would declare, with little discussion of how circumstances had changed since the last dispatch from what an hour earlier had been a peaceful demonstration. Any person standing on a street was now a "protester," whether they were part of an organized demonstration or just standing on their own front stoop. You could see how it would be easy to assume that these same "protesters" waving signs and organizing groups and demonstrations were the very same "protesters" throwing rocks and starting fires. But most often, they weren't.

As the unrest stretched from days into weeks, it began to gain levels of organization. Several new activists' groups—led by time-tested local organizers like Montague Simmons, who worked with the decades-old St. Louis activism group Organization for Black Struggle, and Derek Laney of Missourians Organizing for Reform and Empowerment (MORE), as well as by young people who were relatively new to activism, like local rapper Tef Poe and Taureen "Tory" Russell, who cofounded the group Hands Up United; and Ashley Yates, Larry Fellows, Alexis Templeton, and Brittany Ferrell, who were among those who launched Millennial Activists United—began coordinating acts of civil disobedience, marches, and rallies. The bitter taste of injustice is intoxicating on the tongue of a traumatized people.

Organized protests—unlike the half dozen or so nights of rioting—almost never resulted in violence, except for tear gas from responding officers. The momentum seemed to keep growing in the streets, spurred on, in part, by the simple truth that police kept killing people.

On Tuesday, August 19, twenty-five-year-old Kajieme Powell

robbed a corner store about four miles from the site where Brown had been killed. According to the police account, the young man brandished a knife and stole two energy drinks and some donuts. Responding officers demanded he take his hands out of his pockets. Powell yelled, "Shoot me!" They obliged. Police said the boy, who had a history of mental illness, had come within three feet of the officers. Cell phone video later recorded by a witness showed that it was more like fifteen feet. Several dozen shots were fired after Powell had already been hit and was lying on the ground.

"They could have shot him in the ass, they could have shot him in the legs. They didn't have to slaughter him," said Floyd Blackwell, the former mayor of nearby Cool Valley, a two-thousand-person city that is nearly 85 percent black, and whose kids attended the same schools as Michael Brown.

In late September, a Ferguson police officer chasing a young man behind the community center was shot in the arm. But rumors quickly spread through the streets that it was the young black man, not the officer, who had been shot. Officers had to act quickly to calm an emotional crowd outside the police station, insisting that the only gunshot victim that night had been the officer.

But protesters insisted it was just a matter of time before the police killed again.

On October 8, eighteen-year-old Vonderrit D. Myers was shot multiple times by an off-duty officer in the Shaw neighborhood of St. Louis—a racially diverse, middle-class section of the city. Police said Myers, who fired three shots at an officer, was armed with a stolen gun that they recovered at the scene. Family members insisted at the time that he was armed only with a deli sandwich.

"Racial profiling will not stand in our community any longer," declared Pastor Doug Hollis, a cousin of Myers, as he presided over a candlelight memorial at the spot where the man, known in the community by the nickname Drup, was killed. More than a hundred clutched rosaries and candles and chanted, "Whose street? Drup's street," as they released red and silver balloons into the air. "We pray for every young man in this community, dear God," another local minister proclaimed during a prayer a few moments later. "That he might be safe wherever he walks."

The shooting came as hundreds were flocking to Ferguson for Ferguson October, a planned weekend of activism that had been coordinated both locally and nationally. The brunt of the work fell to the Organization for Black Struggle and MORE, as well as the new groups, such as Hands Up United and Millennial Activists United. Ferguson October was designed to show local officials that activists had not forgotten about their pursuit of justice for Michael Brown. Given the intense national coverage of the case, I was shocked that the investigation had been allowed to linger this long. Late summer was now fall, with winter fast approaching.

The weekend included carefully coordinated acts of civil disobedience, but no rioting or violence. Hundreds marched on and occupied Saint Louis University, ministers Jim Wallis and Cornel West led dozens of clergy onto the property of the Ferguson Police Department and were arrested; and young activists like DeRay Mckesson, an educator who had joined the protests from Minneapolis, and Charles Wade, a former fashion designer from Austin, helped plan roadblocks of downtown intersections that they called They Think It's a Game—during which the activists played children's games such as hopscotch and jump rope as they blocked traffic.

I'd initially been skeptical of Ferguson October. The initial protests had gone on for weeks, and it was hard to believe that these activists, many of whom had never organized demonstrations or direct action protests before, would be able to replicate the organic emotion that radiated from the crowded streets during August. But the Myers shooting had sparked a new sense of urgency. Myers's name was now being chanted along with those of Michael Brown and Kajieme Powell. While it would take months to sort out a full official version of what had happened, much of St. Louis's black community already knew everything they needed to know: another black young man had been killed by another white police officer.

A dreadful anticipation had for months hung thick in the air. The grand jury waiting game had stretched for months, and even those of us among the press who had stayed in Ferguson for weeks eventually departed. By early November, with rumors of an impending decision, the media, myself included, had started showing up again. Each day was another countdown toward the inevitable: Darren Wilson was not going to be charged with a crime for the shooting, the city would likely break out into another round of chaos, and it all would be covered wall to wall on cable television.

Netta Elzie, and many other activists who had been anointed leaders of the protests by the national media, had grown noticeably weary of all of the anticipatory coverage. Almost every night there was some sort of demonstration, often either outside the Ferguson Police Department or in the Shaw neighborhood of St. Louis where Meyers had been killed, and it wasn't uncommon to find the most recognizable and best known of the local organizers screaming at the horde of media cameras to move back so actual protesters could take spots closest to the police line. At one point, Netta and several other prominent protesters decided to sit out the ongoing preannouncement protests, arguing that it wasn't worth it to spend their nights outside in the cold on evenings when cameras outnumbered protest signs. Meanwhile, they kept getting calls from reporters like me, who to their frustration continued to ask the same slew of questions: *"What's going to happen if there is no indictment? Are you worried about violence?"* "We just had coffee with like thirty-four reporters," Netta told me one afternoon in November, about a week and a half before the grand jury decision would be announced, as the full force of the national media began rearriving on the ground. "There are a few reporters who I'll read their stories and just...," she said, trailing off. "All it takes is one bad reporter or one reporter who just constantly works to make the police look better to make me leery of talking to all of the reporters from that same newspaper or station."

And, as is often the case with competitive stories, media saturation bred frustration and at times unhealthy competition between reporters on the ground. Both local and national media had taken turns getting things wrong, parroting police and protester narratives that were later disproven and drawing the ire of readers, and each other. The national media, many local scribes quibbled, was out of touch with local context and just wanted to make itself the story. And the local media, some of the national reporters contended, was often too cozy with the police and prosecutor and was complicit in most of the deep systemic problems now exposed in the wake of the shooting.

Everyone was right, to an extent. But in reality, reporters were only lashing out at each other because we were all exhausted. It had been three months of unanswered questions, tense overnight reporting assignments, editors demanding answers that we could not provide, and, at all times, the anxiety of knowing that no matter how late into the night the protests went on we would all have to wake up the next day and do it all over again.

That anger toward the national media, particularly cable news networks, peaked in mid-November following a string of erroneous reports declaring that an announcement of the grand jury decision was imminent, only to be walked back hours or days later.

"Reporters from the large cities, the economic and the political centers, they tend to believe that they are the biggest dogs of all the big dogs, and they tend to be slow to admit that local media has better official sources," Chris King, the managing editor of the *St. Louis American*, the local black weekly newspaper, told me one day in November. King spent the months between Mike Brown's death and the grand jury announcement serving as a source and fixer for national media reporters parachuting into town. His information wasn't always right, but he was regularly in contact with police and city officials who were often reluctant to talk with the national press, certainly not on the record. A text message introduction from King could instantly set an out-of-town reporter up with an excellent source.

"It's the 'broadcast media that cried wolf' crisis," King told me, exasperated by yet another erroneous cable news report that had declared a grand jury decision had been reached. "If cable news said tomorrow morning that the sun is risen, people would walk outside to see if the sun is outside."

On one afternoon I showed up on West Florissant Avenue for an interview with Mike Brown's barber and found more television cameras than shoppers at a strip mall up the street from the shooting site. An Internet rumor had declared that this was the day of the announcement, causing the number of out-of-town reporters to spike.

"Can one of you-all call and find out about the power?" shouted Lawanda Felder, a twenty-year-old college student, who lives in a nearby apartment building, to the reporters. The power had gone out on one side of West Florissant, affecting hundreds of low-income housing units, so Felder came outside to ask the long line of reporters conducting interviews if they knew what was up. No one did, although I don't know that any of us had really inquired.

"They're just out here to see if there will be riots," Felder told me, encapsulating the chief complaint of many Ferguson residents about the ongoing anticipatory coverage. "But they don't care about the struggles we're facing in our daily lives. None of them are going to call and see why my power is out."

When the news finally broke, we were crowded in the hotel suite that the half dozen or so *Washington Post* staffers on the ground in Ferguson were using as a makeshift newsroom. It was a one-line alert from *Bloomberg News* that came just after 11:30 a.m. on a weekday just before Thanksgiving.

"BREAKING: The Ferguson grand jury considering charges against Darren Wilson has concluded its work."

The alert was a relief, because I was ready for it all to be over: the false reports that the decision was imminent, the rumors peddled by conservative news outlets that black separatist groups were going to show up with assault rifles, the declarations of liberal blogs that the KKK was going to be in Ferguson protecting businesses and targeting protesters. Each new report would prompt a wave of emails from my bosses back in DC — *Do we have this confirmed? Can we get this interview, too? How can we push this forward?* Even mainstream outlets like the *Post* and CNN got into the game of fruitless predictions triggered by sourcing veiled in anonymity. In October, several colleagues and I reported that Ferguson Police Chief Tom Jackson's resignation was imminent. We were wrong.

The consensus among the hundreds if not thousands of reporters on the ground was that, most likely, the decision not to indict would thrust the city back into chaos. There was intense pressure to pinpoint when exactly the news might be coming. Misinformed sourcing was abundant. Local attorneys who claimed to be close to prosecutor Bob McCulloch, federal law enforcement officials who claimed to have a real-time handle on the developments in Missouri despite being seated comfortably at their desks in Washington, DC, and local Congressional offices were all leaking tidbits of information to reporters at local and national outlets — more often spreading information that would prove untrue. But *Bloomberg*, a financial news outlet, had yet to be wrong. Frankly, the fact that they were the outlet breaking the news that the grand jury had concluded its work led me to believe their sourcing was solid. I texted a source of mine I had been cultivating for weeks to see if I could confirm it.

Ferguson police and city government were hopeless in terms of issuing accurate information. Other than the occasional interview or puff profile, almost no one working for Ferguson PD actually knew anything about the daily developments in the Mike Brown case, and those who did weren't talking. My best bet, I'd figured pretty early on in my reporting, was tracking down someone in the county government. The county's elected officials and police would certainly be involved in conversations about how to roll out the announcement, meaning their staffs would all be briefed. And I figured I could charm at least one of those staffers into sharing some of that information with me. So I sent a text message: Is the grand jury concluded? Is an announcement coming today?

"The gj was [sic] finished its work and discussion of how and when announcement will be made," the source replied.

And then my phone started ringing. The source was calling. The principals—prosecutor McCulloch, county police chief Jon Belmar, the county executive, and their aides—were stepping into a meeting to decide what to do. They had given consideration to a plan that would have them announce only that the grand jury had finished its process and announce a later date when the decision itself would be released. But the police unions hated that plan. Their officers were working twelve-hour shifts, and Thanksgiving was fast approaching. If the city was going to burn, they argued, they might as well get it over with before the holiday.

When news is breaking, the uncertainty and urgency spark the drive to make the calls and pester the sources needed to confirm details, but also sprout a mentally overwhelming anxiety—a pressure to get it right, and to get it first. Mostly, I hope, to get it right.

I frantically paced our hotel suite, sitting down and then abruptly shooting back up to my feet perhaps a hundred times that afternoon as we worked to confirm that the grand jury decision was coming. At 1:49 p.m., almost two hours after the grand jury had ended its session, my source texted me again. The meeting had just concluded, and a final decision had been made.

"McCulloch set to announce the GJ decision at 7pm. That could change," the source said. "Gov has a press event at 5:30 ahead of the announcement."

It all made sense. Governor Nixon would take to the microphones before the announcement to preemptively urge peace. Then, that evening, with schoolchildren safely home, parents home from work, and their teens hopefully home and under their watchful eyes, the prosecutor would break the news.

I shot a text message to a second, well-connected local source. This one wasn't quite as well placed as my first contact, but over the course of the months since Ferguson had become a national story, this person had yet to steer me wrong. A response came quickly: the decision was made, and it was coming tonight.

Meanwhile, my colleague Kimberly Kindy, whose diligence and deep sourcing had helped our Ferguson coverage avoid disaster more than once, had her own source confirming what I was hearing. We had three people—the magic number—all telling us the decision had been made and was coming that night (one of mine even went so far as to say that the grand jury had decided against an indictment). But we chose to hold back. As cable networks spent hours declaring that an announcement of the decision "could come at any moment," we wrote that the decision was expected that evening. We decided early on that we wouldn't attempt to scoop the decision itself. We would wait for the words to come out of Bob McCulloch's mouth.

The rest of the day was a blur. We knew we'd have tight newspaper deadlines, made tighter by the decision to announce whether Wilson would be charged that night. And we knew that—one way or another—the streets would erupt.

My plan had been to spend the night at the Canfield Green apartment complex, to wait and see if the neighborhood where Mike Brown lived would descend into violence. But as I sat in the car charging my phone, I got a text message from DeRay Mckesson. He wanted to know where I'd be watching the decision and invited me to a friend's apartment about ten miles away in downtown St. Louis to watch the announcement with him, Netta, and a handful of other activists.

The group I found in the living room of a third-floor downtown apartment building was calm, like a suburban family gathered around the television for the evening news. Netta and DeRay had been at the forefront of the protests, and they were joined by a few others who had also been there from the very beginning. In total there were eight of us gathered around the small television set. Initially we had settled on watching Headline News, but after a while they tired of the tone of the questions being asked by Nancy Grace. Eventually, they switched the channel to CNN. The announcement wouldn't come for more than an hour. But they already knew. As prosecutor Bob McCulloch began speaking, Mckesson let out a loud sigh.

"Here we go," said Brittany Packnett, then executive director of Teach for America—St. Louis, who had been actively involved in the protests and had quickly become close with Netta and DeRay. "Here we go."

Sent each day by either Netta, DeRay, Brittany, or Justin Hansford, a law professor at St. Louis University, the *Ferguson Protester Newsletter* had swelled to a readership of more than twenty-one thousand people. And the newsletter's writers had become masters of the text message alert system they'd crafted during Ferguson October. The news had yet to break, but they were ready. In anticipation of Wilson's not being charged, they had prepared an open letter, written primarily by Packnett, that they planned to blast out to their subscribers the moment McCulloch made his announcement.

"In Ferguson, a wound bleeds," the letter said. "The results are in. And we still don't have justice."

Wilson had not been indicted. They hit "Send" on the letter; I fired off several tweets and then asked each of the activists in the room for their reaction to the news. When I was done typing up a feed for my editors back in Washington, everyone in the room sprinted toward the apartment door to make the drive back to Ferguson.

Several miles away, hundreds gathered outside the Ferguson Police Department, some carrying the protest signs that had been held there every day since the one when Mike Brown was killed.

"Everybody want me to be calm, do you know how those bullets hit my son? What they did to his body as they entered his body?!" Lezley McSpadden screamed as the news was relayed, her husband and other loved ones wrapping her in a tight hug. "Burn this motherfucker down!" her husband, Louis Head, began screaming. "Burn this bitch down."

There were fires in the streets before DeRay, Netta, and Brittany even made it to Ferguson. By morning, dozens of businesses had been torched, Ferguson police cruisers pummeled, and above it all were the festive streetlights city officials had hung, spelling out SEASON'S GREETINGS.

CHAPTER TWO

Cleveland: Coming Home

It wasn't long after the grand jury decision in Ferguson that most of the media that had flocked to Greater St. Louis boarded planes back home. As the rest of my colleagues headed home to their families for the Thanksgiving holiday, I stayed in my hotel room to cover what remained after the riots, namely the cleanup. Dozens of properties—a Chinese food place that had been gutted, a small cupcake bakery whose equipment had been torched, a used-car lot in which every vehicle had been ignited and left to smolder—had been burned on the night of the grand jury decision.

On West Florissant, the building that had housed Heal STL, a nonprofit started by St. Louis alderman Antonio French during the months between the shooting and the nonindictment, had been burned to the ground, leaving behind a pile of ash and brick. Across town, far from the protest sites, the church where Michael Brown's father had been baptized had also been set ablaze.

I interviewed store owners and residents who had been left behind, who still had as many questions as answers, and who were only further embittered by the second round of violence after the nonindictment was announced. And then I decided I couldn't stay another day. I closed my eyes as the low, deep hum of the airplane began its rumble, lulling me to sleep for what felt like the first time since I'd arrived in Ferguson.

During the previous month, as we played the excruciating waiting game, attacks against journalists covering the story on the ground had spiked to levels that surpassed even the vitriol that Ryan Reilly and I had faced after our arrests. As they awaited word that Darren Wilson would not be charged, critics of the now-vibrant protests attempted to hack away at the sanity and credibility of the reporters telling the story.

The protests had created a countermovement of skepticism, anger, and hate, driven by some who genuinely believed that the coverage of Ferguson was overblown and amplified by others with more sinister motivations. These legions of skeptics insisted that the entire story was a fraud, that Mike Brown had deserved his fate, and that tensions in Ferguson were completely stoked by the media— based not on historical injustice, but on real-time race-baiting. The photos and videos that we had posted from the protests had unnecessarily fanned the flames, these critics insisted. And by demanding answers of the Ferguson Police Department, by wanting to know why this young man had died, the critics declared, we were now responsible for the social unrest in the streets.

A St. Louis blogger took a picture of me interviewing some demonstrators at a massive downtown rally and published it in a piece that suggested I was "marching with protesters." Meanwhile, back in DC, conservative political sites had made me a routine target— suggesting that I wasn't really black and, in what was perhaps the most infuriating moment of my experience covering Ferguson, publishing my parents' home address and details about several of my immediate family members drawn from information found on my mother's Facebook page. I spent Thanksgiving as what felt like the only national reporter still stuck in Ferguson; my mother spent the day being taught by horrified family members how to change her social media privacy settings.

The young protest leaders had it, by far, the worst, finding themselves besieged by online harassment and physical threats. Local organizers like Ashley Yates and Tef Poe, young voices among the most prominent at the demonstrations and rallies during the early days in Ferguson, were followed to and from protests by police cruisers. Others, like Charles Wade, a fashion stylist and philanthropist who had helped raise money for the budding Ferguson protest groups, found their email accounts being hacked or their credit card information posted publicly by Internet trolls who wished them harm.

"People were calling my mom's business, flooding their voice mail with hate," Wade told me. "There are times when it feels like too much, when you just want to escape back to being a random person on Twitter, and not a target."

When he told me that, I immediately understood. Feeling besieged with hostile messages, I'd withdrawn during my final stint in Ferguson. Other than a handful of other reporters, I was talking to almost no one, spending my days pacing my hotel room, working the phones as I tried to suss out new details of when the grand jury investigation would conclude. Days before the decision, I received a text message from Colin, one of my closest friends from high school, who was still living back home in Cleveland. The police had shot and killed a twelve-year-old who had been playing in a park. I don't think I ever responded; I was too caught up with Ferguson to process a shooting in Cleveland.

As my plane landed at Reagan National Airport, my phone began buzzing.

The grand jury in New York City had made its decision: the officer who months earlier had employed the choke hold that killed Eric Garner would not be charged with a crime. Hundreds had already taken to the streets in just the hour and a half that I had been in the air.

I began calling the young organizers I knew in New York, many of whom had traveled to St. Louis during the previous months, and reached out to the organizers still in Ferguson who had already begun planning demonstrations for the night. Rather than ask to be delivered home, I directed my taxi driver to head to the corner of Fifteenth and M, to what was then the location of the *Washington Post*'s offices.

When I arrived, the bosses called me into an office. I could take a day or two off, they said, but then they wanted me to get back on a plane. Not to New York, but to Cleveland.

I was running late, but I made it just in time to see the last of about two hundred protesters storm into Cleveland City Hall, their signs and T-shirts declaring BLACK LIVES MATTER and JUSTICE FOR TAMIR as they marched up to the council chambers for the body's final meeting of the year.

That night there was a stinging winter breeze blowing off Lake Erie and drifting through a largely empty downtown Cleveland. Typically, this section of the city would be quiet at this time of night, just after dinner on a weekday, with city employees gone from the public buildings—courthouse, administrative offices, City Hall— that line these blocks. But on this night, there was a strong, steady sound of dissent.

"This is a movement, not a moment," declared Lorenzo Norris, a local pastor, as he led the racially diverse if largely young group of protesters into the council chambers. The Cleveland protesters were incensed by a recent federal review that had concluded that their police officers routinely exerted excessive force during routine interactions and pulled their guns (and their triggers) inappropriately. That probe had been sparked by another shooting, the "137 bullets" shooting in November 2012, during which Cleveland police officers opened fire on a car that had led them on a chase, only to later discover that both of those killed had been unarmed. Like their protest brethren in Ferguson, the Clevelanders contended that local elected officials hadn't done enough. "We want change," Norris told me as I caught up with the group. "We must have change."

The City Hall demonstrations came a few weeks after the police shooting of twelve-year-old Tamir Rice, which my friend Colin had texted me about back in Ferguson.

Tamir Rice was shot and killed on the afternoon of November 22, 2014, after Cleveland Division of Police Officer Timothy Loehmann and his partner, Officer Frank Garmback, responded to a call about a man with a gun outside a recreation center. The man who called the police told the dispatcher that the person was possibly a child playing with a toy, information that was never given to Loehmann and Garmback.

The officers believed they were responding to an "active shooter." Loehmann and Garmback approached the boy in their cruiser, pulling directly up to a park gazebo where for the last hour Tamir had been throwing snowballs and pretending to fire the toy weapon. Their cruiser slid on the snow-covered grass as Loehmann leaped out from the passenger-side door. "I kept my eyes on the suspect the entire time," Loehmann said. "I was fixed on his waistband and hand area. I was trained to keep my eyes on his hands because 'hands may kill.'"

Loehmann claimed he yelled for the boy to show his hands, but that instead of complying, the boy lifted his shirt and reached into his waistband. Loehmann said that when he saw Tamir's elbow moving upward and the weapon coming up out of his pants, he fired two shots.

Video of the shooting, captured by a security camera installed in the parking lot just a few feet away, showed that it took less than two seconds after the officers arrived for Tamir to be shot dead. It's unclear if Tamir even knew who had pulled up on him before he was on the ground, a bullet lodged in his chest.

"At its core, Tamir's death is a tale of stunning systemic police incompetence and indifference," wrote Phillip Morris, the sole black metro columnist at the Cleveland *Plain Dealer,* in a column penned after it was revealed that Cleveland Police had hired Tim Loeh-mann, the officer who shot Rice, without checking his references or running a serious background check.

Had the city done that, they would have uncovered job reviews from the suburban department where Loehmann once worked that describe him as "weepy" and "distracted." A former supervisor, in a November 2012 note, made it clear he would not recommend that Loehmann, the son of a police officer, be given a badge and a gun, going on to say that the officer could not be trusted to follow simple instructions from commanding officers.

Months after that note was written, Loehmann entered the Cleveland police academy and in March 2014 was sworn in as a city police officer. Less than eight months later, a bullet from his department-issued weapon pierced the chest of a sixth-grade boy playing in a park.

"The city of Cleveland killed Tamir Rice when it issued Tim Loehmann a gun," Morris wrote.

"The boy's blood now flows over all of our hands."

Later that night, once the City Hall protest was wrapped up, I drove over to see Colin.

Colin and I had been like brothers since meeting early in high school. In many ways we couldn't be more different. He is confident and outgoing, well dressed and poised. When we met I was still quite dorky, a teen with wire-rim glasses who was too socially nervous to score any invites to house parties on the weekends. A basketball standout with cunning charisma, Colin was the alpha male in the group of popular young black men a year behind me. The son of one of Cleveland's most successful businessmen, he carried with him a sense of swagger and style—which, in early high school, simply meant that his clothing fit properly.

Some of my awkwardness could probably be attributed to the aura of racial ambiguity and confusion I carried with me to Cleveland when I moved there in eighth grade, well after most childhood cliques had been formed. My family moved to Shaker Heights, an East Side suburb that for decades was heralded as having one of the best and most diverse public school districts in the nation. My father is an oft-underemployed writer and editor, and my mother is a dental hygienist. Each expense I proposed growing up—from a twenty-dollar field trip to forty dollars for a new pair of khakis for homecoming—was a battle with my deeply frugal mother. More often than not, she'd say yes, but as I got older I tried to ask less and less, hoping that any extra cash would flow down to my younger brothers. I relied more on the money I banked from odd jobs and lawn mowing and, later, my gig as a busboy at a country club.

But in many ways Colin and I couldn't have been more similar—we both came from deeply loving families who cared more than anything else that we achieved. Ours were the kind of family that chose where to live based on the best-available public school education, where we'd be surrounded by a diverse set of peers, and where we could otherwise thrive.

Colin and I found each other while working for the middle school newspaper. I had joined as a last-ditch effort to find friends during the second half of my eighth-grade year. Colin was a seventh grader, thin and energetic, who wasn't quite sure if writing would be his thing, but who was happy to make a few friends a year older. And, as it often works in middle school, that set of insignificant circumstances sparked one of the most meaningful relationships in my life.

"So did you see the video?" Colin asked me as we dapped and hugged, making our way into his living room, plopping down on the same couch where we'd watched Cavs playoff games during LeBron's first stint in Cleveland. We weren't exactly surprised by Tamir Rice's death. We knew the Cleveland police weren't known for their rigor or calculated decision-making—in fact, in the last decade, the

Department of Justice had issued not just one but two sets of findings that concluded the department routinely violated the civil rights of the city's residents. As young black men from the suburbs riding through the city in cars a little too nice to have either of us behind the wheel, we'd had our fair share of colorful interactions with Cleveland's finest.

But before I could even answer Colin, a familiar voice burst from the stairwell.

"Is that Wesley I hear?" Colin's mother exclaimed as she made her way into the room, and I jumped up from the couch, took off my hat, and wrapped her in a hug. As we pulled back, she paused, her hands still on my shoulders and a huge smile creeping across her face. She'd watched me grow up, quite literally, in this living room, from that scrawny kid with the glasses who was the editor of the high school newspaper into a national correspondent for the *Washington Post* whose voice she'd occasionally hear bursting from a television at the beauty salon.

"Now, let me guess, you're writing about that Tamir Rice shooting, right?" she said. "Isn't that just so awful?"

For the next few minutes the three of us ran through the conversation that had taken place in countless other living rooms. Colin was immediately skeptical of the account of the shooting given by the officers and believed that the since-released video of the shooting raised even more questions. And besides, it was just a kid with a toy playing in a park, he reasoned. He shouldn't have ended up dead.

But why would that child be allowed out in the park alone, with a toy gun? Colin's mother demanded. Being out in that neighborhood, pointing a realistic-looking weapon at people, seemed like a death wish. Where were his parents, or his siblings?

"Yeah, but parents can't be everywhere," I offered up in response, then added with a chuckle, "Lord knows, you and my mom raised Colin and me right, but we still found our fair share of trouble when you weren't looking."

"I guess you're right," Colin's mother said with a sigh as she made her way out of the room. "You boys be safe tonight. No trouble. Well, not too much trouble."

At some point in high school, my best friends and I all had a running joke about "the talk," which most of them had been given by a father or mother or some other relative. The underlying theme of this set of warnings passed down from black parents to their children is one of self-awareness: the people you encounter, especially the police, are likely willing to break your body, if only because they subconsciously view you not only as less than, but also as a threat.

Find almost any high school–age black male and ask him about "the talk." Neither of my parents ever really gave it to me, but I heard "the talk" secondhand from the mothers of a few friends. Besides, when you grow up in a mixed-race home—my mother is white, my father black—no one has to tell you that one half of your family looks different than the other and that you need to pay attention. Close attention.

Say *"yes sir"* or *"yes ma'am"* to any officer you encounter. If you get pulled over, keep your hands on the wheel. As we rode around in Colin's car listening to Cleveland rap—Bone Thugs-N-Harmony, Chip Tha Ripper, and a young guy from our high school who would eventually adopt the name Kid Cudi—we'd keep our wallets in the center console. That way, we wouldn't have to reach into our pockets. Above all, we knew to never, ever run in the presence of a police officer. That's just asking for trouble.

Growing up, we didn't speak directly about race often in our house, but my parents made certain that my two younger brothers and I knew who we were, and where we came from. Each of us carry a Swahili middle name. It's hard to doubt your blackness with a middle name like Jabari, which means "the bravest." Tucked next to the Bible study course books on our living room bookshelf sat a library that could have belonged to any African-American history professor—*The Autobiography of Malcolm X, Roots, The Wretched of* the Earth, *Their Eyes Were Watching God,* and *Go Tell It on the Mountain.* The characters in my childhood bedtime books were black. And one year, maybe third or fourth grade, I remember my dad loading my brothers and me into the family station wagon to head to a library a town or two over to attend a nighttime program that explained the significance of each day of Kwanzaa. An ornament from that program still hangs on our family Christmas tree each year.

"I never had to tell you or your brothers that you are black," my father said to me in December 2015, in the matter-of-fact cadence that we both often transition into when speaking. "The world was going to do a pretty good job of telling you all that. My kids didn't need to be told they were black; they're smart. I just had to make sure you were surrounded by the right examples and the tools to succeed." Instead of rules, we had expectations. We were their ambassadors, representing their parenting and the last name Lowery everywhere we went. A bad grade, or a call home from a teacher because we'd acted up—which, in my case, happened not infrequently—was a grave embarrassment. We were too smart and had been given too many opportunities to squander them.

As I sat in my childhood living room listening to my father, I considered for the first time in my life that every decision my parents had made during the bulk of their adulthood had been about calibrating the best outcomes for their kids. The most important calculation had been where we went to church—the cornerstone of our family. Both of my grandfathers worked in the ministry, my father's father a Baptist pastor and my mother's father an engineer who to this day devotes his free time to mission work, helping to start several seminaries and serving as one of their lead grant writers.

Before Cleveland, our family lived in Teaneck, New Jersey, where we were regulars at First Baptist Church in Hackensack, a welcoming if at times struggling congregation that was as diverse as it was loving. Upstairs, in one of the conference rooms, a Spanish-language congregation met at the same time we were downstairs in the sanctuary. One day, I told myself then, I'd learn Spanish so I could go be a missionary to Guatemala or Ecuador or one of the other far-off places where my friends from church and their families had come from. When we moved to Cleveland in the early 2000s, we quickly joined Cedar Hill Baptist Church, once a pseudo-megachurch that had shrunk to a few hundred members. Like our church in New Jersey, Cedar Hill was diverse and had an international feel. The membership included blacks and whites and Asians and a good number of African immigrants. While we met in the sanctuary, a Chinese congregation met down the hall, in one of our conference rooms.

The next consideration was the diversity of where we lived—our parents had kept us in public schools, almost exclusively in suburbs with as many black residents as there were white ones. We were raised surrounded by success, both black and white.

As my father kept talking—about our churches, schools, and neighborhoods—I stopped him with a question. When did he, a generation earlier, and with two black parents, become aware of the reality of race in his own life?

He thought for a moment and began to tell the story of a road trip he, his three siblings, and his parents took sometime in the late 1960s or 1970s when he was not yet a teen. My father's is an expansive black family, from a deeply religious section of North Carolina near Charlotte where pretty much any black person you encounter can be safely assumed to be some sort of cousin. And depending on how much free time you have, you can probably list the names of uncles and aunts until you can confirm that yes, this person standing in front of you is a relative. My grandmother had always been strict in general, but especially about making sure that my dad and his siblings had gone to the bathroom before getting on the road. Being a child, this time my dad had the audacity to ask "Why?" The trip was only an hour, and he didn't have to go. Why did it matter so much if he went to the bathroom before they got in the car?

"Mark," my grandmother said to him. "Have you ever been in the car, and you just had to go to the bathroom so bad that you would have the driver pull the car over onto the side of the road, right then? You just have to go right now!"

Of course he had, and he said so.

"Now imagine that's you, you've got to go so badly, and finally, after miles and miles, you spot a rest stop, you pull over and run out of the car, but inside, the white man at the counter stops you before you can make it to the bathroom door . . .

"'There's no bathrooms for you in here,' he says sternly. 'Maybe a few miles down the road. Now get going.'"

My dad, he recalled to me with a laugh, wouldn't ever complain again when his mother, who had lived most of her life in a country in which people who looked like her weren't legally allowed to vote, harangued him to use the restroom before they set out on the road. He'd been awakened to the reality of his parents' and grandparents' lives and of his own. There is the pivotal moment in a black man or woman's life from which we can never return: when you realize the threat posed to you by the color of your own skin, the humiliation and danger that could befall you or your family as the result of the most human necessity, using a restroom.

It wouldn't be until years later—during my senior year of college—that I would have my own awakening to the reality that even with a black president in office, my shade of pigment remained a hazard. I was twenty-one and living in Athens, Ohio, as I finished my time at Ohio University, when an unarmed seventeen-year-old named Trayvon Martin was shot and killed by a neighborhood watchman in Sanford, Florida. Within days, the initial details of the shooting, and Trayvon's face, filled my Facebook and Twitter feeds as friends from high school and college debated the case and expressed their outrage. Trayvon had been visiting his father, who lived in Sanford, to watch the NBA All-Star Game, when he ventured out to a nearby gas station to buy iced tea and

Skittles. As he walked home, talking on the phone with a friend, with a sweatshirt hood over his head to shield him from the falling rain, he caught the eye of George Zimmerman.

Zimmerman, a self-appointed neighborhood watchman, was so concerned with a rash of break-ins that he had begun patrolling the subdivision, carrying a gun.

"Hey, we've had some break-ins in my neighborhood and there's a real suspicious guy...," Zimmerman told the 911 operator. "This guy looks like he's up to no good, or he's on drugs or something. It's raining and he's just walking around, looking about."

Zimmerman and the operator talked for a few more minutes, as a police officer began to make his way to the scene.

"These assholes, they always get away," Zimmerman said.

"Are you following him?" the operator asked.

"Yeah," Zimmerman responded.

"Okay, we don't need you to do that," the operator said.

Moments later, after hanging up with the 911 operator, Zimmerman physically confronted Trayvon Martin. According to his account, Trayvon attacked him, punching him so hard that he fell to the ground. Scared for his life, Zimmerman said he reached for the gun he was carrying and shot Trayvon in the chest. The fatal bullet left Zimmerman's gun at 7:16 p.m. By 7:30 p.m., Trayvon was pronounced dead.

There hadn't been any direct witnesses to the confrontation, but a handful of people who saw parts of it said they believed they saw Trayvon on top of Zimmerman, punching him. Citing the lack of evidence refuting Zimmerman's story that he had acted in self-defense, the local police let him go home.

Trayvon, a teen who looked not unlike one of my younger brothers, was vilified in the media, the same way Michael Brown and Tamir Rice and Eric Garner would be years later. Pictures of him smoking marijuana were published; media outlets dug through his tweets for profanities—seizing on rap lyrics they suggested somehow proved the teen's propensity for violence. He shouldn't have been wearing a hoodie, some said. He shouldn't have been out at night, others added.

How many nights during high school had I spent wandering an unfamiliar neighborhood in one of the suburbs that surrounded my own? Probably wearing a hoodie—which I wore pretty much everywhere when I was seventeen—or maybe even those jeans that didn't quite fit right and if I forgot to wear a belt slid down as I walked. How many times was I one overzealous neighborhood watchman away from death?

There was no news story in 2012 and 2013 that I followed as closely as the George Zimmerman trial. During the early days of the case, after Trayvon was killed and Zimmerman remained at large, I was blogging for a now-defunct website, Loop21, which focused on black issues and politics. The initial outrage that Zimmerman was not arrested and that no charges were filed stood in contrast to the picture of Zimmerman slowly losing his cool under the national scrutiny.

At one point, he went off the grid but made a concession to visibility by launching a low-budget fundraising website so that his growing legion of supporters could contribute to his legal defense. The story of the site was broken by one of my friends and mentors, Mara Schiavocampo, then a correspondent for NBC News. Since I owned a website myself—essentially a blog where I hosted my résumé as I searched for summer internships—I knew I'd be able to find the email address for whoever had registered the site. Sitting in the office I shared with three other editors at my college newspaper, I fired off an email at 5:35 p.m., describing myself as a freelance reporter who was trying to confirm the site's authenticity. I never expected a response; in fact, I assumed hundreds of other reporters would have done the same thing and that maybe my name would show up someday during the trial if all the emails were released. That would be cool, I thought.

Eleven minutes later, I got a reply, from george@therealgeorge
zimmerman.com.

Mr. Lowery, You are correct. www.therealgeorgezimmerman
.com is run by me, George Zimmerman.
Thanks,
George

I was floored. The man who was all over cable news, at the center
of one of the most racially charged stories of my lifetime, was emailing with me, a twenty-one-year-old sitting in his college newsroom.
I quickly responded, asking him if there was any way he could prove
that it really was him.

"Certainly," George Zimmerman replied. "You can contact Sean
Hannity. I spoke with him today and he confirmed my identity. Sin-
cerely, George Zimmerman."

I couldn't believe what was happening. And then it got even
stranger.

"Come in here, Wesley!" my friend John Nero, a fellow editor at
the paper, shouted, beckoning me into our newspaper lobby, where
the television was almost always tuned to CNN.

George Zimmerman's attorneys had called a press conference to
beg him to call them. He had started a fundraising website, and
apparently, they now revealed, he'd had a phone conversation with
Sean Hannity of Fox News earlier that day. I had been emailing
with the actual George Zimmerman.

In the coming days and weeks, thousands of people in Florida
and elsewhere took to the streets and signed online petitions demanding that Zimmerman be arrested. Eventually, he was, and was
charged with second-degree murder.

The year 2012 was a major awakening point not just for me but
also for other young black men and women across the country. We
watched the Trayvon Martin shooting play out in real time on our

Facebook pages and television screens. At the same time, the stories of Jordan Davis and Oscar Grant (a 2009 police shooting that was depicted in the film *Fruitvale Station*) solidified the undeniable feeling in our hearts that their deaths and those of other young black men were not isolated.

While "the movement" was born in Ferguson, it was conceived in the hearts and minds of young black Americans at different points in the preceding years. One of these moments came with the Florida jury's decision to find George Zimmerman, the neighborhood watchman who shot and killed Trayvon Martin, "not guilty."

On the night of that decision I was still living in Boston. The news broke on Twitter that the jury was done deliberating and that the announcement was forthcoming. Then we all saw the words: "not guilty." I sprang into reporter mode—one that was still new to me—because I didn't know what else to do. I had to do something even if I wasn't an activist, or even a normal citizen. I was a reporter. I got in my Pontiac Grand Prix and drove to a nearby church that had announced it was having a vigil. If I couldn't participate, I could at least do a few interviews and email them in to the *Globe*'s weekend editors. But by the time I had found a place to park, the vigil had concluded. I went back to my car and sat in silence as raindrops splattered on my windshield.

For months, some right-wing and white supremacist groups had warned of the impending "Trayvon Martin riots." They encouraged white Americans to brace for what they predicted would surely be a round of racial unrest once Zimmerman, at this point almost a folk hero, was acquitted.

In a column titled "What If Zimmerman Walks Free?" Pat Buchanan, once an adviser to Ronald Reagan, laid the blame for racial tension at the feet of alleged race-baiters. It was the fault of Jesse Jackson, and Maxine Waters, and the New Black Panthers—an essentially nonexistent group of about half a dozen would-be radicals—and President Obama, for having the audacity to sympathize with the family of a dead teenager who had been followed and killed by Zimmerman.

"The public mind has been so poisoned that an acquittal of George Zimmerman could ignite a reaction similar to that, twenty years ago, when the Simi Valley jury acquitted the LAPD cops in the Rodney King beating case," Buchanan declared. "Should that happen, those who fanned the flames, and those who did nothing to douse them, should themselves go on trial in the public arena." Just moments after Zimmerman was found not guilty, former speaker of the House of Representatives Newt Gingrich further fanned the hysteria.

"I watch these protesters," Gingrich said live on CNN. "None of whom read the transcript, none of whom sat through five weeks of the trial. All of whom were prepared, basically, to be a lynch mob."

History, stubborn in its nuance, proved Buchanan, Gingrich, and the rest of their lot wrong. There were no large-scale Trayvon Martin riots. In their place were vigils held throughout the country — like the one I had barely missed in Boston. Peaceful black America was awakened by the Zimmerman verdict, which reminded them anew that their lives and their bodies could be abused and destroyed without consequence. Trayvon's death epitomized the truth that the system black Americans had been told to trust was never structured to deliver justice to them.

The "not guilty" verdict prompted the creation of a round of boisterous and determined protest groups, most prominently the Dream Defenders and Million Hoodies Movement for Justice, both initially Florida-based, although the latter would eventually expand nationally.

Across the country, at a time when Twitter had yet to become the primary platform for news consumption, a then-thirty-one-year-old activist in Oakland named Alicia Garza penned a Facebook status that soon went viral.

She called the status "a love note to black people."

"the sad part is, there's a section of America who is cheering and celebrating right now. and that makes me sick to my stomach. we GOTTA get it together y'all," she wrote. "stop saying we are not surprised. that's a damn shame in itself. I continue to be surprised at how little Black lives matter. And I will continue that. stop giving up on black life."

"black people. I love you. I love us. Our lives matter," she concluded.

Her friend and fellow activist Patrisse Cullors found poetry in the post, extracting the phrase "black lives matter" and reposting the status. Soon the two women reached out to a third activist, Opal Tometi, who set up Tumblr and Twitter accounts under the slogan.

"Black Lives Matter is an ideological and political intervention in a world where Black lives are systematically and intentionally targeted for demise," Garza wrote in the group's official written history of its founding. "It is an affirmation of Black folks' contributions to this society, our humanity, and our resilience in the face of deadly oppression."

While the phrase is now the name of an organization and is often used to describe the broader protest and social justice movement, Black Lives Matter is best thought of as an ideology. Its tenets have matured and expanded over time, and not all of its adherents subscribe to them in exactly the same manner—much the way an Episcopalian and a Baptist, or a religious conservative and a deficit hawk, could both be described as a Christian or a conservative, yet still hold disagreements over policy, tactics, and lifestyle.

For the young black men and women entering the adult world during the Obama presidency, the ideology of Black Lives Matter, not yet an organization nor a movement, carried substance, even heft. It was a message that resonated with the young black men and women who had been so outraged and pained by the Zimmerman verdict. And the decision by Tometi to focus on Twitter and Tumblr, then second-tier social media outlets, instead of Facebook, proved a stroke of strategic genius. Both networks allow for more organic, democratic growth. Unlike Facebook, in which virality is determined by algorithms, visibility on

Twitter and Tumblr is determined directly by how compelling a given message, post, or dispatch is. A phrase like #blacklivesmatter, or #ferguson, or, later on, #BaltimoreUprising, can in a matter of moments transform from a singular sentence typed on an individual user's iPhone into an internationally trending topic. #blacklivesmatter didn't catch on immediately, but its time would soon come.

As writer and historian Jelani Cobb wrote in the *New Yorker,* in what remains one of the definitive profiles of the creation of the organization now known nationally as #blacklivesmatter:

> Black Lives Matter didn't reach a wider public until the following summer, when a police officer named Darren Wilson shot and killed eighteen-year-old Michael Brown in Ferguson. Darnell Moore, a writer and an activist based in Brooklyn, who knew Cullors, coordinated "freedom rides" to Missouri from New York, Chicago, Portland, Los Angeles, Philadelphia, and Boston. Within a few weeks of Brown's death, hundreds of people who had never participated in organized protests took to the streets, and that campaign eventually exposed Ferguson as a case study of structural racism in America and a metaphor for all that had gone wrong since the end of the civil-rights movement.

Many of the local organizers were excited to have reinforcements. They had been out in the streets for days, launching organizations such as Hands Up United and Millennial Activists United. The Black Lives Matter rides had brought fresh bodies for the protest lines and fresh voices for the megaphones. But they had also brought with them crowds of outsiders, who hadn't been in these streets, whose eyes and tongues had yet to feel the bitter sting of tear gas.

That tension between veterans and newcomers would eventually play out not only in cities like St. Louis and Cleveland, but also on a national stage, as the media began attempting to define the contours of the protest movement and appoint leaders. Even before the out-of-town buses had arrived, the Ferguson protesters had begun using the chant "Black Lives Matter," and were punctuating the hundreds of tweets that some of them were sending each day with #blacklivesmatter.

That hashtag, linked in the minds of its creators to their group and their network, inevitably took on a life of its own—and became a mantle under which thousands of demonstrators, activists, and groups began protesting both online and in the streets. Whether they wanted or intended it, the protest movement was being identified as the "Black Lives Matter movement" by the media, myself included, before most of us appreciated the difference between the rallying cry and the organization that preceded it. This conflation became even more complicated once the #blacklivesmatter group founded by Garza, Cullors, and Tometi began spawning chapters and organizing a more formal network of allies. Black Lives Matter was now a widely adopted slogan, a "movement," and its own organization—but that nuance and complication were lacking from nearly all media coverage, due in part to laziness but in fact more likely because at that point in the quickly moving story of the unrest in Ferguson, few reporters—myself included—could accurately grasp what exactly was happening.

This reductive media coverage became a major fault line among the activists—who began to bicker about when, exactly, this "movement" had begun, and who deserved credit for its inception: the three "founders" or the organic protesters in places like New York and Ferguson.

"This conflation was cause for concern because the project was near and dear to our hearts," Cullors wrote in an essay on the protest movement in February 2016. "As queer Black women, we are often misremembered as contributors and creators of our work, a consequence of deep-seated patriarchy, sexism, and homophobia. But more importantly, this was cause for concern because movements don't belong to any one person and we knew that this movement wasn't started by us. Its roots lie in the Black organizers of centuries ago, our ancestors who, in the face of violence like chattel slavery, lynching, whipping, rape, theft and separation of our families, fought for freedom from the state. But despite intervention after intervention with the media, they continued to conflate the two, causing a fissure among some."

While organizers and activists began attempting to sort this out among themselves, with tiffs at times spilling out onto social media, their supporters in the rest of the nation continued to carry their banner and express solidarity with a movement still working to find its footing and at some moments of infighting one misstep away from implosion. As of March 2016, the tenth anniversary of Twitter, the hashtag #blacklivesmatter had been used more than twelve million times—the third most of any hashtag related to a social cause. Atop the list, however, sits #ferguson, the most-used hashtag promoting a social cause in the history of Twitter, tweeted more than twenty-seven million times.

"#blacklivesmatter would not be recognized worldwide if it weren't for the folks in St. Louis and Ferguson who put their bodies on the line day in and day out and who continue to show up for Black lives," Cullors wrote. "And yet, we knew there was something specific about Ferguson and the efforts of the brave organizers in Ferguson that made this moment different: more radically intersectional, more attuned to the technology of our times, more in your face. Ferguson organizers shifted the energy in this country in the direction of Black liberation in the same, and different, ways as the case of Amadou Diallo, Rodney King, Jena Six, Troy Davis and Trayvon Martin."

The small entrance and modest selection on the ground floor of Guide to Kulchur are a clever mask for the West Side Cleveland bookstore's expansive basement meeting room, which, by December

2014, had for months played host to an activist collective determined to achieve police reform in this city.

After curving down the stairs, you're confronted by a lounge of sorts—a series of couches covered by a canopy of cloth. Around the corner, a large meeting table that seats well more than a dozen is surrounded by thick stacks of paperbacks. This is where the local protest movement in Cleveland incubated. Activists from the East Side and West Side, young and old, gathered—at times daily—to strategize and get to know each other.

"We all knew we needed to do something, we had to this time," said RA Washington, a musician and poet who owns the bookstore and serves as a sort of community elder in the surrounding blocks, the first time I showed up for one of the meetings.

At this point, there was no formal #blacklivesmatter chapter in Cleveland. Organizers of the ongoing demonstrations hailed from a mishmash of other activist groups and labor organizations. Unlike the leadership tug-of-war that took place in Ferguson, there was no concern in Cleveland about external interlopers—almost all of the young activists were local.

On this day, a cold afternoon about three days into my trip home, a hodgepodge of activists and organizers peppered several members of the City Council with questions. They had specific demands and insisted that each local official they meet complete a "report card"—committing to either yes or no on statements such as "the officer who killed Rice should be immediately indicted."

"We need to show that we as young black people in Cleveland are no longer going to allow these things to happen," said Joe Worthy, a key organizer with the New Abolitionist Association, one of the groups of younger protesters and activists that have driven the demonstrations here. Worthy was one of the first activists I met when I arrived home. He spoke in a sharp, polished cadence, with little patience for niceties. If a council member started to wander into talking points, it was Joe who would shout him or her down and demand that he or she address the question asked. "We wanted a public commitment to our demands at least from some council members; we also wanted a public commitment to negotiate publicly to bring change," Worthy declared during the meeting, earning a round of snaps of approval. "These things can't be negotiated by backroom deals."

Cleveland is built from a proud activist and civil rights tradition, with locals quick to note that it was here—partially in response to the civil rights movement—that the first black mayor of a major American city was elected. That legacy left a mosaic of community organizing groups—from those focused on black-on-black crime, to those left over from Occupy Wall Street, to those who have for years worked on police brutality issues. But a summit like this, featuring primarily young but also some older activists, many noted, seemed unprecedented, at least in recent local history.

When Tamir Rice was killed, it seemed, activist Cleveland jolted into action.

Determined to learn lessons from St. Louis and New York, top city officials in Cleveland took extremely deliberate steps in response to the renewed protests. The fact that half a dozen council members were gathered here in this bookstore basement to be peppered with questions was evidence of that.

Police Chief Calvin Williams, who is black, voluntarily shut down parts of the highway so that protesters could march. Police officers working nights during many of the early demonstrations talked openly and at times joked around with demonstrators.

"There are things that are wrong within the Cleveland Division of Police, and we will correct them. That is my pledge to everybody," Williams vowed during a forum titled "Is Cleveland the Next Ferguson?" that city leaders held in early December at the Word Church, the city's most influential black congregation.

While, like St. Louis, Cleveland is a heavily segregated Midwestern metropolis still battling its way out of tough economic times that have left significant portions of its black population in poverty, in many ways Cleveland had seen a much less violent and boisterous response to the Tamir Rice shooting than Greater St. Louis did in the days after Michael Brown was killed. There had been some protests, and city leaders were feeling pressure.

"Tamir Rice should not have been shot," Williams said, prompting applause from the crowd. "It is not Tamir Rice's fault, but it is also not the fault of that officer," Williams added, which earned him as many jeers as his previous remark had brought claps.

By all accounts, the Cleveland police could not have handled the protests more differently than their colleagues in St. Louis, who suited up in riot gear and deployed tear gas and fired rubber bullets not only at violent looters, but also at peaceful protesters, local elected officials, and residents who had left their suburban homes to observe the ruckus happening outside.

But not in Cleveland. In fact, after some morning commuters and media figures griped about the highway protests impeding traffic and causing "inconvenience," Mayor Jackson responded by declaring: "That's the inconvenience of freedom."

"People are rightfully angry," Cleveland City Council president Kevin Kelley told me one afternoon as we sat in his City Hall office. "In some parts of the city, the Cleveland Division of Police and the community need to have a relationship that is stronger."

Behind him, on proud display, was the yellow flag of Old Brooklyn, a West Side Cleveland neighborhood perhaps best known for its high number of law enforcement and public safety families, which lies in Kelley's district. And in police districts like those, where on some blocks it seems there's a PROUD SUPPORTER OF THE FOP affixed to at least one car in every other driveway, Kelley and others told me, there are stronger relationships between officers and the community.

"[In my district] most residents are on a cell phone basis with the district commander. We know the person who we're going to call," said Kelley. "I think that if in every edge of the city we did as good a job as that, we'd be able to use those relationships as a vehicle to push for progress."

I knew he was right, in large part because I knew people who had spent their entire lives in his district. My college roommate at Ohio University hailed from a police family in Old Brooklyn. His aunts and uncles were cops, and his cousins—who would crash on our futon on their nearly monthly visits to campus—all seemed to want to grow up to be Cleveland cops, and a few of them did.

Much of Cleveland was not only skeptical of the ongoing protests, but also horrified that the city was in the midst of a crime wave. Things were getting even more dangerous for their officers; who was looking out for them?

"There has been so much negative publicity, we wanted our officers to know that the community is behind them," Mary Jo Graves, a police dispatcher in Cleveland, who also lived in Old Brooklyn, told me. Dismayed by what she saw as antipolice rhetoric, Graves put out a call on Facebook, asking people to meet her in downtown Cleveland for a rally in support of police. She had hoped for a hundred people; more than four thousand showed up. "I think people are finally fed up," said Graves, whose "Sea of Blue" rally was one of dozens of similar events that popped up in the months after Ferguson. "Our officers are good people who go out there to do good. Are there some things that need to be changed in law enforcement? Maybe. But it's important that our officers know they have their community's support."

Not long after I finished interviewing the council president in City Hall, I found his colleague councilman Zack Reed holed up in his cluttered third-floor office in City Hall. Just moments after I entered his office, he pointed to a map laid out across one corner of his desk. It's a simple enough setup, a white poster board with the city's seventeen districts outlined and dozens of red pushpins inserted, each representing a homicide this year. The council members get an email each Monday, tallying every homicide in the preceding week and telling them how it compares to that point in each of the four previous years. And for each new homicide, Reed inserts a red push-pin at the corresponding location on the map.

Reed described it as a step toward thawing the numbness that many in Cleveland, including members of the council, have felt toward the violence that for years has been prevalent here. Violence both by police and by residents. "It's in the DNA of not only the residents, but also the police," Reed told me. "If we don't change that mind-set, that it's us against them, then we're never going to fix this system."

Every Clevelander knows the long roster of names and cases in which either a resident was killed by police or a local crime story went national in part because it persisted due to residents' unwillingness to call officers.

The incident that most Clevelanders point to as their most horrifying anecdote of excessive force by police was the November 2012 shooting of Timothy Russell and Malissa Williams, whose miles-long police chase resulted in their death in a hail of 137 bullets fired by thirteen of the more than a hundred officers involved in the chase. The pursuit began when the two drove past a police officer who believed that they had fired a gun from their vehicle. He radioed for backup, and so began a chase that concluded with a sea of bullets in a school parking lot. One officer, Michael Brelo, emptied two separate sixteen-bullet clips and reloaded a third time before leaping onto the hood of the vehicle and firing bullets through the windshield and into Russell's and Williams's bodies. Both victims, it turned out, were unarmed. They had never fired the alleged gunshot that prompted the chase. Their car had backfired.

Brelo would be charged with murder in the 137 bullets case, but a judge would ultimately rule that because it was impossible to say for sure that it was one of the bullets from his gun that had killed Russell and Williams, he could not be convicted.

It is cases like the 137 bullets shooting that community leaders say have led to a deterioration of what little trust remained between the Cleveland community and the police. My dad would mention the case every single time I was home from school or back visiting after I had begun my career.

"A hundred and thirty-seven bullets!" he'd exclaim as he read the paper. "And the one guy jumped up on the hood of the car," he'd say with exasperation, crafting a gun with his fingers and mimicking the *pow pow* of the fatal gunfire.

Meanwhile, the DOJ concluded, the police department has in many parts of Cleveland abandoned the community policing that once was prevalent throughout this city; on page fifty of the report, the DOJ stated: "During our tours, we additionally observed that neither command staff nor line officers were able to accurately or uniformly describe what community policing is...."

Several current and former law enforcement officials insist that it hasn't always been this way—pointing to the 1990s, when, thanks to Clinton administration grants for community policing, police departments in Cleveland and its surrounding suburbs had more officers devoted to foot and bike patrols and neighborhood beats. But when federal money dried up and the local police departments were hit with round after round of layoffs and budget cuts as the national, state, and local economies tanked in the mid-2000s, the community policing model became more stated policy than practice.

"A lot of times, the officers begin to believe that the citizens of color are the enemy, and at this point many of them aren't getting out of their cars to get to know them," said James Copeland, a retired police commander who spent twenty-seven years working in East Cleveland, a majority-black community that borders the city. "The departments aren't representative of the community, so they don't understand the community."

While 53 percent of Cleveland's almost 400,000 residents are black, only about 387 of the department's 1,551 officers are, about

25 percent. Compounding the perception of the Cleveland police as an occupying force was the decision in 2009 by the Ohio Supreme Court to rule unconstitutional Cleveland's "home rule" policy. Passed by voters in 1982, "home rule" had required police officers and firefighters, as well as other city employees, to reside within the city limits. While it had long been a point of contention with the police and fire unions, many observers credited the policy with keeping a valuable working-class tax base in the city even as other Midwestern metropolises saw their employees flee to the suburbs in the 1970s and 1980s. While a still-recovering housing market has prevented mass exodus in the years since Cleveland's home rule was overturned, many officers who had been living within the city limits have since made the move out of the city where they work.

"The Supreme Court said that you don't have to live in the community, but if you're working in that community then you're a resident of that community, you need to treat it that way," said Copeland. "We know all about the blue code, but we need to let the people vent and then explain to the citizens about why we do what we do. We've got to talk to them first. We need to be transparent. That's called blue courage."

In the meantime, pain continues to flow throughout Cleveland's streets as gun violence claims the lives of more residents. As Reed and the other council members prepared for the upcoming Monday-night meeting, they got their weekly homicide update. By this point in the previous year, the first week of December, there had been eighty-three murders.

But this year, as the city was consumed in a fury of discussion about shootings and policing, three Clevelanders had been killed in the past week, including Amir Cotton, a twenty-six-year-old black male and the city's hundredth homicide of the year. By the end of 2014, homicides would number 102, an uptick from the previous year. And in 2015, homicides went up again, to 118.

"It's time for us all to wake up," Reed told me at the end of our meeting as he placed his poster board behind his desk. "We've all got to wake up."

Cleveland would remain one of the primary battlegrounds of the Movement for Black Lives—terminology organizers adopted to describe the protest movement—throughout 2015, with demonstrations breaking out at various points during the year. It was one of a dozen locations where, during the Martin Luther King Jr. Day weekend, organizers gathered to "reclaim" the holiday—traditionally considered a day of service—in light of the failure to achieve the justice they had demanded in New York and Ferguson. Activists wanted to transform a day known for reflection into a day of disruption.

Thousands were marching throughout the country, but only a few dozen were here in a musty church basement on Cleveland's East Side when the poet began. His words cut the air, his message clear: police killings were a genocide, and despite the promises of well-intentioned leaders, they were far from stopping.

The performance was one of several that took place as protesters prepared signs for the second of two marches in Cleveland on the holiday. In total, somewhere between a hundred and two hundred would participate.

But the gathering, though small in number and a bit more white than may have been expected, marked an important milestone for the still-budding protest efforts in Cleveland. Young and old had come together to coordinate the day's actions—a march, this lunch and performance, and then a second march.

Every social movement must grapple with the generational and tactical divides that arise between varying groups and factions that comprise the ground troops. In Cleveland, a city with a rich history of civil rights activism, there are not only black activist groups that have been around for decades, tracing their births to the last civil rights movement, but there is also a robust black political establishment.

"As an African-American guy trying to make a difference, I am fighting the white establishment, and I'm also fighting the black establishment," said Alonzo Mitchell, a fixture among the world of twenty- and thirtysomething Cleveland, who hosts a local radio show and emcees the city's New Year's Eve bash.

I'd caught up with Mitchell, a towering figure punctuated by his tightly picked Afro, a day earlier. Mitchell is the definition of outgoing, quickly rattling off half a dozen names of people in DC who must be mutual acquaintances of ours; he was right about at least half of them. He'd moved back here a few years earlier, after doing a stint in DC himself; he'd missed home. More young professionals, he believes, should move back to Cleveland, a wave of immigration he maintains would revitalize this at times struggling Rust Belt metropolis.

Mitchell hit Cleveland like a whirlwind, deciding he would attend every single City Council meeting. Once he began to ask questions, he soon took over his own public affairs radio show. Then he launched a concert and performance art series: Ohio Homecoming. His goal was to showcase the talent in his hometown.

He dreamed of one day entering politics himself, perhaps crafting a ticket of all young people to run for various city positions, so he reached out to several city officials, proposing that they set up a mentorship program for young adults hoping to enter public service. He got a hard no.

"No one is going to teach you," he recalled being told by one prominent official. "Power is never given, it's taken." It is an open secret that there exists a conflict between a new generation of young black leadership and a black establishment reluctant to give up the power they spent decades fighting to secure. Activists young and old, as well as some local elected officials and other observers of local politics, all acknowledge that perhaps one of the things holding this Midwestern city back is the ongoing tension between different generations of black leadership.

"We've had a history of black political leadership at the highest level; there has always been a high level of black political engagement here," Ronnie Dunn, a criminal justice professor at Cleveland State University who has for years studied the Cleveland police department, told me as I sat in his office. "There is certainly a group of us, myself included, who fall into what is short of a black managerial class, who in some way or another are part of the system."

According to journalist Ari Berman, whose book *Give Us the Ballot* tracks the battle for voting rights in the five decades after the Voting Rights Act, the percentage of black registered voters in the South more than doubled—skyrocketing from 31 percent to 73 percent—between 1965 and 2005. When the legislation became law in 1965, there were fewer than 500 black elected officials in the nation. By 2015, there were more than 10,500. The number of black members of Congress had grown from 5 to 43. And there was no victory brought about by the Voting Rights Act bigger, or more consequential, than the 2008 election of Barack Obama. The civil rights generation had fought for equality at the ballot box, rightly recognizing that the right to vote was an essential tool in the broader fight for equality of experience.

In fifty years America had gone from being a country in which a black man named Barack Obama would likely have been unable to cast a ballot for president to a country in which he was elected president.

"Obama's unprecedented election gave rise to the hope that America had become a postracial society," historian Gary May wrote in *Bending Toward Justice,* his 2013 history of the Voting Rights Act. "But the nation is not as different as it may seem. History reveals that improved conditions come less from a revolution in white attitudes toward African-Americans than from the [Voting Rights Act's] effectiveness in altering electoral conditions. In other words, if the Act had never existed, there is no guarantee that Mississippi would have so many black public officials or, for that matter, any at all....

"...And ironically it was Obama's election itself that indicated that race, for many, remained a divisive issue."

In the early days after Ferguson, many asked when the young activists would begin holding voter registration drives, but that question in and of itself betrayed an old way of thinking. "Why vote?" I remember one young activist asking me. "Having a black president didn't keep the police from killing Mike Brown."

During a forum moderated by PBS's Gwen Ifill not long after the shooting, local rap artist and activist Tef Poe rejected the suggestion by Senator Claire McCaskill, a Democrat, that getting out the vote was the first step toward fixing Ferguson's systemic issues. "The lack of trust that is so palpable right now ... the way to fix that is to make the government look more like them," McCaskill said, prompting Tef Poe to ask, "What do you say to those of us who are" involved in the political process already?

In a post-Ferguson world, young black activists were eager to work outside the system. "I voted for Barack Obama twice," Tef Poe said that evening. "And still got teargassed." A seat at the table, the new generation of black activists reasons, isn't worth much if your fellow diners still refuse to pass you a plate.

In the months after Tamir Rice was killed, some bridges had been built between the young activists and the established political class — both black and white. Among those meeting most frequently with the young protest organizers were several black city councilors, as well as prominent local professors, including Dunn, who readily self-identify as part of that black managerial class.

"All of us are trying to push for real reform," said Jason Eugene, a thirty-six-year-old organizer who was a key bridge between the various protest and activist factions in Cleveland. "We all want Cleveland to break this cycle." And that spirit flowed throughout the small church basement where several dozen had gathered on the afternoon of Martin Luther King Jr. Day.

As a group of three young Hispanic men, brothers, performed a rap song they had written about police brutality, several older organizers in the audience nodded along. Minutes later, a city councilman walked in to join the gathering.

"I never would have imagined that we would have had this much unity, and this many people, come together around addressing these issues," said Al Porter, a veteran organizer who has worked on organizing protests around police brutality issues in Cleveland for decades. "I just wish it hadn't taken us this long."

As the year came to a close, Cleveland still had a demon hovering over it: Would the officer who shot and killed Tamir Rice be charged with a crime?

I figured the local prosecutor, Timothy McGinty, who had a reputation for being tough and who had proved willing to take on cases that others might not have prosecuted, would announce near the end of the year that there would be no charges. The bad news would be sandwiched sometime between Thanksgiving and Christmas, when lake-effect snow might make it impossible for protests to swell to uncontrollable levels. And that's exactly what happened.

The case had been initially investigated by the Cuyahoga County Sheriff's Department, which turned its findings over to McGinty's office. As the investigation stretched from weeks to months and eventually past the one-year mark, the Rice family and civil rights activists grew increasingly agitated, convinced that no charges for the officers were forthcoming. Why would they think otherwise?

Most painful for the activists, even more so than the financial peril faced by the Rice family, had been the extended video of Tamir's death, released on January 7, 2015, which showed not only the split-second shooting that took his life, but also a scene minutes later, when his sister realized that he had been hurt and raced to him, only to be tackled into the snow by one of the officers.

"I'm sick. I'm crying," DeRay Mckesson, the protester from Ferguson, texted me on the day the extended video footage was released. By this point, DeRay, too, had amassed tens of thousands of followers on Twitter, and sent dozens of tweets each day publicizing the latest police shooting news. "I just keep thinking about what if that was my sister running to me. It's too much."

McGinty fueled their frustration by simultaneously releasing witness statements and other evidence to the press and the grand jury—an unusual move that he said was intended to provide transparency. The attorneys for Tamir's family insisted that this move telegraphed McGinty's intention to let the officers walk free. In the meantime, Tamir's mother and sister found themselves in dire financial straits. "The incident has shattered the life of the Rice family," the family's attorneys wrote in one court filing. "In particular, Samaria Rice, Tamir Rice's mother, has since been forced to move to a homeless shelter because she could no longer live next door to the killing field of her son."

Providing for the Rice family quickly became a priority for many of the young activists associated with the broader protest movement, not just in Cleveland, but across the country. Among those who most aggressively sought to intervene on their behalf was Shaun King, an author and life coach turned activist who, during the early days of Ferguson, built an online following of hundreds of thousands.

King had long seen himself as a racial justice activist, involved in both politics and activism since his days in student government at Morehouse College in the late 1990s. But, he recalled for me later, it was the death of Michael Brown that awakened him to the extent of police violence.

"If you asked me before Ferguson where the two poles of police brutality were, I would have told you Los Angeles and New York. I knew about Rodney King, and Amadou Diallo, and Abner Louima and Sean Bell," King told me. "These stories from New York and LA, even before social media, always got told. It created in me an impression that police brutality was at its worst in those two places. I didn't know how bad it was in other places because I wasn't reading the newspaper in St. Louis."

In 2014 King was working as the social media director for an environmental charity when someone emailed him a link to the video of Eric Garner's death in New York.

"I made up my mind right there at my desk...that I was going to share this video everywhere, and that somebody was going to be arrested," King told me. "I was posting it on Facebook and Twitter....I was so obsessed with it that I thought I was going to lose my actual job; all I was doing was researching this case."

Then, several weeks later, King got a private message on Twitter. A young black man had been killed by the police in a town called Ferguson.

"I typed 'Ferguson' in my search box and sure as hell there are photos of a kid lying in the street," King said. "I was like: oh my gosh, the police are killing folks everywhere."

King partnered with Feminista Jones, a social worker, activist, and feminist writer, to raise more than sixty thousand dollars to give to the Rice family soon after Tamir's death. The fundraiser was signed off on by an uncle, but there was a miscommunication, leading some to publicly question whether or not King and Jones had the authorization of the family.

Timothy Kucharski had been one of two attorneys representing the Rice family for several weeks when he got a call from a friend in early December, asking about an online fundraiser in the Rice name. As the funds raised surpassed twenty-seven thousand dollars, Kucharski contacted law enforcement as well as YouCaring.com, the site being used to raise the money, asking that assets donated to the fund be seized and held for the Rice family. He contacted King, who has previously used his social media following to raise money for victims of police shootings and natural disasters, and who insisted that his plan was always to give the money to the family. As they went back and forth, a number of Twitter users began insisting that the fundraiser was a scam and demanding it be halted.

It didn't help that King had become one of the most frequent targets of vitriol among political opponents of the protest movement. The backlash was in part his own doing. He had a complicated work history, which included time as a pastor, a motivational speaker, and a fundraiser. His posts on Twitter and Facebook were emotionally and rhetorically charged. He leveraged his presence to drive attention to overlooked cases and to disseminate small but important updates about the best-known police shootings. But King also had a propensity to play a bit fast and loose with facts and to fall into profane, aggressive arguments with media personalities, other activists, and political enemies. Here was the darker side of the immediacy and expedience afforded by social media.

In the hands of the movement's political enemies, legitimate criticisms about King and others snowballed into a barrage of personal attacks and hate. While many had "raised questions," the worst accusations ever substantiated against King related to inaccuracies in his online dispatches and irregularities in the financials of the nonprofit organizations he had previously led. While some argued that he had stolen money he had raised for the families of victims of police violence, several investigations into those allegations found nothing of substance.

When professional attacks didn't silence King, conservative blogs and writers began to attack him personally—culminating in a sustained weeklong effort to prove that King, a biracial man, was in fact white and had been lying about his race for his entire adult life.

After a week of constant articles and tweets from conservative websites like Breitbart and the Daily Caller, King was forced to publicly acknowledge that he was born as the result of his white mother's decades-earlier affair with a black man.

"The reports about my race, about my past, and about the pain I've endured are all lies. My mother is a senior citizen. I refuse to speak in detail about the nature of my mother's past, or her sexual partners, and I am gravely embarrassed to even be saying this now, but I have been told for most of my life that the white man on my birth certificate is not my biological father and that my actual biological father is a light-skinned black man," King wrote in a piece that he published online at the Daily Kos, encouraged by me and others. "This has been my lived reality for nearly thirty of my thirty-five years on earth. I am not ashamed of it, or of who I am—never that—but I was advised by my pastor nearly twenty years ago that this was not a mess of my doing and it was not my responsibility to fix it. It is horrifying to me that my most personal information, for the most nefarious reasons, has been forced out into the open and that my private past and pain have been used as jokes and fodder to discredit me and the greater movement for justice in America."

Even as the confusion spread over whether or not King's pledge drive for Rice was legitimate, the fundraiser for the Rice family presented yet another example of the power of his online fundraising prowess. He and Jones ended up netting almost sixty thousand dollars—money that, at the request of the Rice family attorneys, was then seized by the court. The court set up a trustee to manage the funds, placing all the money in Tamir Rice's estate, meaning any withdrawal would require a judge's ruling. Rather than being given the money directly, the Rice family would now have to apply for each disbursement. After attorneys' and administrative fees had been paid, more than twenty thousand dollars remained in Tamir Rice's estate, and the family had no means of accessing it. After I wrote about this financial drama in May 2015, King announced another fundraiser—this time with the publicly stated support of the Rice family and their attorneys—and raised another twenty thousand dollars.

"When I started that fundraiser it was all under the assumption that this is a good thing for the family....I had grown to feel like, giving money to these families would give them the freedom to be their own advocates," King told me later. "It still frustrates me to no end...that people were saying that I'd taken the money for Eric Garner's and Tamir Rice's families."

The controversy was crafted in part due to the media's unique discomfort with activists who cross into journalism, as well as the public's deep skepticism about online fundraising—a realm fraught with frauds and fakes looking to score a quick dollar in the name of those who are suffering. That skepticism was sometimes encouraged by King's own statements and behavior. But it was also, no doubt, further emboldened by the prejudicial thinking that tells us that this bold black man yelling to the crowds must be lying—about something.

King would ultimately take a job as a columnist for the *New York Daily News*, where he remains a controversial lightning rod. Detractors continue to raise questions about his past endeavors, and he continues to insist that these are coordinated smears to silence him. He remains one of the most consistent voices in the media writing and talking about police violence against black and brown bodies.

"At the end of the day, I have a small measure of satisfaction in this sea of ugliness in that I've been able to tell families' stories from the perspective of an activist, from a perspective that has been compassionate to them," King told me. "If I've moved the needle even just a little bit, then it's all been worth it."

On December 27, 2015, more than a year after activists had first seen the video of the young boy's death, prosecutor McGinty's office announced that it was calling a press conference on the Tamir Rice case. I was in DC, following along via a live stream of the press conference when McGinty came to the podium.

"The outcome will not cheer anyone, nor should it," McGinty

said. "The death of Tamir Rice was an absolute tragedy. But it was not, by the law that binds us, a crime.... If we put ourselves in the victim's shoes, as prosecutors and detectives try to do, it is likely that Tamir—whose size made him look much older and who had been warned that his pellet gun might get him into trouble that day—either intended to hand it to the officers or to show them it wasn't a real gun. But there was no way for the officers to know that, because they saw the events rapidly unfolding in front of them from a very different perspective."

McGinty called the shooting "this perfect storm of human error, mistakes, and miscommunications by all involved." But, he said, he had told the members of the grand jury that he did not believe they should bring charges. When they took their final vote, they agreed.

For activists in Cleveland and around the nation, the decision was a balled fist to the gut. Tamir Rice's death had been the most emotional and painful of the police shootings that had gained national attention to date. Whether you faulted the officer or not, you had to accept that this was the killing of a boy, playing with a toy, in a park.

"I don't want my child to have died for nothing and I refuse to let his legacy or his name be ignored," Tamir's mother, Samaria Rice, said in a statement that landed in my in-box that day. "As the video shows, Officer Loehmann shot my son in less than a second. All I wanted was someone to be held accountable."

And now, after making everyone wait for more than a year, the prosecutors were saying that under the letter of the law Tamir's death was not a crime, and that no one would be prosecuted. It would only be a matter of time before people were taking to the streets in Cleveland. As I started frantically writing and updating our online piece on the announcement, I knew we'd need to hire a freelance reporter in Cleveland to go to the protests and monitor the situation on the ground.

As I racked my brain, my editor came up to me: Had I thought of anyone? We really needed someone on the ground in Cleveland. I texted Teddy Cahill, a baseball writer, a former high school classmate of mine, and another of my closest friends in Cleveland. He was home, and I thought he might know of some freelancers with breaking news experience. He didn't, so I made an impulsive decision and gave Teddy's number to my editor. "Call this guy, say you got his info from me, and ask him if he'll go down to the protest. He's good, he can handle it." As I made my way back to my desk, I sent Teddy another text: "might have just given my editor your contact info."

Within the hour, Teddy was headed to the protest—his first news reporting assignment in years, possibly since our high school days, when he ran the sports page and I was one of the coeditors. He was nervous but had cleared it with his editors at Baseball America, and started filling his notebook with quotes from the crowd of demonstrators gathering in the park where Tamir Rice had been killed.

About three dozen demonstrators gathered that night in the park. They joined hands in the rain for a moment of silence, then began chanting, "No justice, no peace," as they marched across town toward the Justice Center.

The decision not to indict was "a burden on the family and the community. But at the same time, it's a burden on the police department," Angel Arroyo, an activist with the Cleveland Peacemakers Alliance, told Teddy. The officer who killed Tamir, Arroyo added, is "going to have to live for the rest of his life knowing that a twelve-year-old boy lost his life. So it's just pain all the way around for our community."

The night came and went with no violence. Teddy spent a few hours snagging quotes before we sent him home. The next day the piece, written by the two of us and another *Post* reporter, ran on the front page. We made copies for our mothers.

CHAPTER THREE

=====

North Charleston: Caught on Camera

A March morning had just turned to afternoon when my phone vibrated across my desk. At the time, I was screening my calls, deep into the reporting of our next big piece on police shootings. After Mike Brown, Eric Garner, and Tamir Rice, several reporters and researchers at the *Post* decided to spend a year tracking every on-duty police shooting in the country.

As 2014 gave way to 2015, I had hoped that I might be able to negotiate some time off—by that point I had banked close to a month off that the paper owed me after my nearly three-month stint in Ferguson. I was exhausted, beyond burned out. But instead of vacation, I found myself with even more work than before.

While we had all been in Ferguson, we constantly found ourselves running into the same frustrating dilemma. The civil rights groups and activists who had flocked to Ferguson were insistent that black men and women were being gunned down in the streets daily. The local police union and a routine stable of law enforcement talking heads insisted that these shootings almost never happened, and when they did, they were almost never unarmed black men (and besides, they usually added for good measure, Michael Brown had it coming for attacking an officer).

As a team of half a dozen *Post* reporters working in Ferguson through the grand jury decision, we continually fielded the same inquiry from our editors back in Washington: Who is right—the police unions or the activists? How many people are killed by police officers and how many of them are unarmed black men? These were vitally important questions. And, it turned out, no one really knew the answer.

Policing in the United States is a deeply decentralized institution, with more than eighteen thousand police agencies spread throughout the nation and accountable to no one but the local communities they serve. Despite the fact that police officers are the only people in our society given the near-unilateral right to kill other citizens, the federal government holds meager, and in some cases almost nonexistent, regulatory controls over them—local police departments are instead governed by state laws, municipal codes, and union contracts almost always negotiated well outside the public view and any scrutiny.

Because they are governed drastically differently depending on which state or local jurisdiction they serve, police departments also have very few standardized requirements in terms of what data they are required to report; as a result, at the time of Michael Brown's death, there was no comprehensive accurate national data on how many police shootings occurred each year and who, exactly, was being killed.

We weren't the first to notice this. For several years independent trackers—academics, criminal justice junkies, and a few police reform groups—had attempted to chronicle fatal police shootings, consistently finding that the number was northwards of a thousand people killed by the police each year (a figure more than double that which the FBI said occurred each year, based on a voluntary, self-reported survey it conducts of police departments).

At the time of Michael Brown's death, the most robust effort to keep track of police shootings was that of D. Brian Burghart, the editor and publisher of the 29,000-circulation *Reno News & Review,* who launched his Fatal Encounters project in 2012. Working with an army of volunteers, Burghart built a database of news clips and coverage going back several years, tracking thousands of fatal police shootings. His effort relied on searching Google each day, recording each new police shooting, and following up later as more details were published or made publicly available through the individual police department. The effort, a herculean attempt at amassing data, was not a real-time, public-facing one. The closest attempt at such a thing was Killed By Police, a website that listed the names, ages, and dates of anyone who news clips revealed had been killed by a police officer. The website was invaluable, but the data wasn't sortable and often included people who died of natural causes while in police custody or who were killed by off-duty officers.

"Don't you find it spooky? This is information, this is the government's job," Burghart told me when I called him in October 2014. "One of the government's major jobs is to protect us. How can it protect us if it doesn't know what the best practices are? If it doesn't know if one local department is killing people at a higher rate than others? When it can't make decisions based on real numbers to come up with best practices? That to me is an abdication of responsibilities."

I wrote a piece with the headline, "How Many Police Shootings a Year? No One Knows," and after it was published, I stood with two of my *Post* editors, Vince Bzdek and Marcia Davis, and excitedly discussed how insane I thought this was. Burghart himself had suggested that perhaps the *Post* could undertake a similar effort. I thought he had a point, so I continued to survey the existing databases and made my initial pitch. "Can't we do it? Couldn't we count the shootings? And create the data?" I exclaimed with a level of earnest yet righteously indignant excitement that could only be channeled by a young newspaper reporter. "We should do it."

Soon afterward, led by our national editor, Cameron Barr, editors and researchers at the paper began discussing how we might track fatal shootings, and how that would fit into a yearlong effort by the *Post* to hold police to account in response to the high-profile police killings and the protest movement they had sparked.

The first piece of the year was by my colleagues Kimberly Kindy and Kimbriell Kelly and examined every police shooting in the previous decade for which an officer had been charged with a crime. The piece, "Thousands Dead, Few Prosecuted," revealed the specific set of circumstances required for an officer to be charged in connection with a fatal shooting—there had to be video, evidence of a cover-up (perhaps a missing or planted weapon), or fellow officers needed to have turned on the shooter and contradicted his or her story. Darren Wilson was never going to have been indicted. There was no video, no clear evidence of a cover-up; just the word of the officer against the legacy of a dead kid.

To follow up on that piece, we began combing through hundreds of police shootings that had so far been recorded in 2015, with researchers Julie Tate and Jen Jenkins methodically checking Google News each day for reports of new shootings and then confirming the facts with firsthand reporting. We were looking for trends. Who were these people being killed? Were they mostly career criminals? Teens? The elderly? Gang members? Or just people who were in the wrong place at the wrong time?

My job was to weed through all the armed white men—the largest subcategory of people killed by the police—to spot the story in the numbers. I was shocked at how many of these men were mentally ill or explicitly suicidal.

My buzzing phone nonetheless seized my attention.

At the other end of the line was Ryan Julison, a public relations guru who often finds himself close to the center of the stories I cover. Julison's specialty is working as a PR consultant for attorneys and law firms, shepherding the stories of their clients into the scoop-hungry hands of national reporters. Often, local media becomes jaded or insensitive to police killings or incidents that may have racial implications. At other times, shrinking local newsrooms are just overextended. Perhaps they've got two police reporters tasked with covering dozens of major crimes a week, in addition to the police department budget and the broader politics of crime and justice. But if any case can be connected to a large theme or narrative—racial profiling, insensitivity, or the disproportionate number of deaths of unarmed black people at the hands of police—then the attorneys for the family can often interest a national reporter. Julison and others like him are the key step in the process that takes a death like Trayvon Martin's from being a small blurb in the local daily paper to being the lead story on the national news.

Julison had been instrumental in turning the eyes of the nation to the death of Trayvon Martin, guiding the story to reporters who back then knew little of "Stand Your Ground" laws, helping reacquaint those reporters and by extension the public with these policies, which gave legal latitude to people who commit homicides in self-defense. I had worked with Julison a handful of times; he had been working with the attorneys who initially represented the family of Tamir Rice and had a month or two earlier pitched me the story of Mikel Neal, a black firefighter in Marion, Indiana, who alleged that one of his supervisors had tossed a noose at him.

But the story Julison had for me today was the biggest he would ever bring to me—and it wasn't even an exclusive.

The weekend before, a white police officer in North Charleston, South Carolina, had attempted to pull over a car with a missing taillight. As the officer ran the license and registration of the black man he had pulled over, the man bolted from the driver's seat and ran toward a field about half a block away.

The officer, Michael Slager, first attempted to use a stun gun on the man, but for some reason, it didn't work. The two men struggled over the stun gun, and then the black man made another run for it—a limp-jog that didn't get him very far. Slager drew his weapon, lined up a shot, and put multiple bullets in the man's back. Then Slager picked up the stun gun and set it near the dying man's body.

The expiring black body belonged to Walter Scott, a fifty-year-old Marine Corps veteran who was behind on his child support and didn't want to be taken to jail. Slager, a five-year officer, married with a child on the way, told his superiors that Scott had taken his stun gun and was about to deploy it on him. In fear for his life, Slager said, he opened fire.

Neither man knew at the time that Feidin Santana had been standing just feet away, recording the struggle between Scott and Slager on his cell phone.

"Before I started recording, they were down on the floor. I remember the police [officer] had control of the situation," Santana would later tell NBC. "He had control of Scott. And Scott was trying just to get away from the Taser. But like I said, he never used the Taser against the cop. As you can see in the video, the police officer just shot him in the back.

"I knew right away, I had something on my hands."

Santana waited a few days. He wanted to see how the police would explain the shooting. When he saw that the department was advancing a narrative directly contradicted by his own video, he reached out to an attorney who had been working with Scott's family and gave it over.

"I can't give you the video," Julison told me excitedly. It had already been promised to the *New York Times* and ABC's World News Tonight under embargo, to be published and aired that evening. "But I like you, and don't want you to be screwed. Learn everything you can about a man named Walter Scott, and North Charleston." Julison added before he hung up, "This video is even worse than Eric Garner."

It was just after 4 p.m., so I had three hours.

I ran over to Mark Berman, who runs the *Post*'s national news blog. Within minutes we were both working the phones. The North Charleston police department wouldn't give us much of anything, just the press release that they had sent out a few days earlier. But they promised to keep us informed.

As we kept scrambling, the department sent out a news release announcing a 5 p.m. press conference. We watched the live stream, and our jaws dropped as the North Charleston mayor and police chief announced that Officer Slager had been fired and would be charged with murder. The video wasn't even out yet. Even though the *New York Times* had the video, they were still committed to their 7 p.m. embargo and didn't immediately jump on the news that the officer had been fired. By a stroke of luck, Berman and I had gone from waiting to be scooped on a huge story to being the reporters who broke the news that the officer had been charged with a crime, and the first national news outlet to publish Walter Scott's name. When 7 p.m. hit, the video immediately became one of the most viewed things that the *New York Times* published all year.

The preceding hours, frantic as we chased and updated the news, had been in many ways surreal. The impact of so many of the police shootings and other deaths at the hands of officers in 2014 and 2015 was derived in large part from the organic nature of the outrage. You would be going about your normal day when suddenly you were confronted by the image of Mike Brown lying on the concrete. It was another day at the office until suddenly someone tweeted at you the video of Eric Garner's dying words: "I can't breathe!"

But in this case I had been given a heads-up: I knew the name that was going to trend nationally hours before it did. I looked at the images of Walter Scott (just a handful were available at the time online), knowing that soon enough his face would be plastered across every news outlet in the nation.

Walter Scott was, in many ways, the "perfect victim," as far as proving police impunity was concerned. He had committed a minor infraction, ran knowing he was going to face the heavy hand of the legal system, and was then shot in the back by a white officer—all of it caught on tape. While Slager, who as of this writing is still awaiting trial, said a violent struggle occurred before the video recording began, most who viewed the video of Walter Scott's death could not fathom a context in which the shooting they were watching did not amount to murder. The response of the nation was once again outrage.

As I tweeted out more details as we knew them, an outraged tone began to overtake my language. While the video showed Slager setting the stun gun next to Scott's body, I used the word "plant." For the average person reacting to the video, it would have been a reasonable description. But coming from someone charged with providing fair coverage both to Scott's family and to Slager's, it was too charged a verb, ascribing motive and denying Slager the chance to provide his version of events. It was a mistake.

For months, for the most part, I thought, I had held it together. I had sent hundreds if not thousands of tweets since Ferguson began, and had been the constant target of online harassment for my reporting. But with a few exceptions (like the time I tweeted that an anarchist protester who pulled a knife as I attempted to report on a night of looting during the Ferguson protests was a "white punk"), I had tried to keep my personal reactions to the stories I was covering out of my Twitter timeline. If the facts of a case were compelling enough, the story would take off whether I relayed it emotionally or not.

I got called into an editor's office, and rightfully chided.

"The more emotional the story," he told me, "the less emotional the reporter." He was right, I knew, but I still walked out of his office in a huff.

In reality, it wasn't about the tweet. I was acting out, having a tantrum, because I didn't want to get on a plane to South Carolina. I was tired. The last seven months of my life had been a constant stream of black death. I spent my days cold-calling the families of those killed by police officers, and my evenings catching up on the hashtags and viral videos of police killings that I had somehow missed during the work day. The dead looked like my father, my younger brothers, and me. The way they were dehumanized by cable news talking heads stung me sharply, piercing the layer of emotional detachment I had learned to acquire since being thrust into the story in Ferguson.

I booked my flight for first thing the next morning and met a close friend and mentor, who was then an editor for a different section at the *Post,* at a hotel bar not far from our newsroom. I had yet to pack, but I also needed to eat something, even just a bite, to hold me over until morning.

As we sat at the bar, I was close to tears. I didn't want to get on this plane, I didn't want to spend days telling yet another story of a black man gunned down. Each story had drained me emotionally, and I wasn't sure how much I had left.

"You'll go," my friend told me after listening intently. "Because you have to."

I didn't go home. I doubled back to the newsroom. It wasn't that late yet, and I knew I could still get some valuable reporting done in the hours before my early-morning flight.

One of the lessons of Ferguson was that the story is never about the specifics of the shooting—in Missouri, the protests and community unrest were just as much about a long history of perceived and actual acts of injustice and discrimination as they were about the death of Michael Brown and whether his hands were raised in the air in surrender. In New York, thousands poured into the streets because Eric Garner's dying gasps of "I can't breathe" gave voice to their anger at the harassment of stop, question, and frisk, and resurrected the pain inflicted years before by shootings like that of Amadou Diallo. The crowds in Cleveland gathered and screamed not only in an attempt to earn justice for Tamir Rice and Tanisha Anderson, but also to awaken their city, so deep in its slumber, so encased in the numbness of Midwestern gloom, that even the most dramatic and horrific violence—the 137-bullet police shooting of Timothy Russell and Malissa Williams or the homicidal terror of serial killer Anthony Sowell—passed with barely a public whimper.

Knowing that I'd likely be on the ground for several days,

responsible for a front-page piece each day, I started making calls to find out the story behind the story. What was the deal with North Charleston?

First, I always reach out to the family, the attorneys for the family, and the police. This is largely a matter of obligation and typically isn't particularly fruitful. The police are most likely just going to add you to a media list and send you the updates they give everyone via press release, which are important to receive but don't do much in terms of advancing the story. An interview with the police chief, or the officer involved in the shooting, would be ideal, but in the days, weeks, and months after a shooting, as a national reporter without local ties, you've got better luck camping outside the chief's house than going through official channels to try to secure one.

The family, likely still grieving and now inundated with media calls, is another long shot. Typically, I don't even try to contact them directly if I can avoid it. Instead, I approach their attorneys, who then become long term sources related to the legal updates in the shooting, which will likely trickle out slowly over the course of the upcoming year. Eventually, the family is going to sit down for full-length interviews, and the legal team almost always decides which outlet will get the scoop.

But after putting in a round of calls to all of the above, I try to pivot as quickly as possible to peripheral players: local civil rights leaders, neighborhood associations, the police union, the town's former mayor or police chief, defense attorneys with long histories in the region, and local elected officials. Almost all of these folks, at some point, will either be formally briefed on the investigation or will acquire vital gossip about the status and details of the investigation. The key is becoming their media friend before some local reporter or pesky producer for CNN gets to them first.

It was close to 9 p.m., but I knew it was now or never. If I waited until I landed in South Carolina the next day, someone else might have sussed out the vivid insider details, or gotten the fruitful tip that, on a story leading every newscast, can set your coverage far above the rest. I kicked my feet up onto my desk and began working the phones.

The first person I was able to get on the phone was James Johnson, a local minister who ran the local chapter of the National Action Network, Al Sharpton's national civil rights organization. His diagnosis was what I expected it to be.

"North Charleston has a history of shooting and killing black men," he told me. "So I applaud the mayor and the police chief for coming out and quickly firing this policeman, but the community is a little skeptical. There is a lot that is going to have to happen, and it's going to have to happen quickly because this community is very angry and we don't want another Ferguson."

Johnson, who had spoken with members of Scott's family, said he was convinced the shooting was a result of racial profiling. Walter Scott had been driving a late-model Mercedes, which he had purchased three days earlier and on which he had installed big spinning silver rims. The traffic stop was allegedly for a missing middle brake light, which in South Carolina is not a moving violation.

State data showed that in a city whose residents were a near fifty-fifty split between black and white, North Charleston police stopped black residents twice as often as white drivers. "Do I get harassed? Do I? Do I?" Virgil Delesline, a twenty-eight-year-old North Charleston resident who works at a Chipotle restaurant, said sarcastically a few days later when I asked him about racial profiling during a protest held outside City Hall.

"It's 'cause I've got a Crown Vic with tinted windows, so they automatically see that as a dope boy car," Delesline said, adding that he gets pulled over almost weekly—at times having his car searched for drugs—even though he has never been charged with a drug crime.

"There have been lingering concerns for years about racial profiling, things like broken tail lamps or license plates or mirrors not there. People have been intercepted because they happen to be driving nice cars," local minister Reverend Joseph Darby, Jr., told me.

"The bigger context is just as American as apple pie. The Justice Department recently came out with a scathing indictment of what's happening in Ferguson. But if they looked at any number of police departments across the nation they could come out with the same kind of indictment."

Next on my call list that night was Wendell Gilliard, the state representative for the district that includes North Charleston. The call went straight to voice mail, so I left a message and kept dialing.

Next came each of the city council members—prioritizing the councilman whose district the shooting occurred in, those who were part of the "public safety" committee, and those with a history of speaking publicly on civil rights issues (in most cases, that means the black council members). But the few I got on the phone didn't have much to say; it was clear that the city—adamant that it did not want to become "another Ferguson"—was closing ranks and controlling the message.

"This incident just occurred and I'm sure the community is happy that the officer has been fired. Justice is going to be done," Michael Brown, who had been a member of the North Charleston council for eight years, told me when I got ahold of him on his home phone. He had just arrived home from church and had yet to see the video. "What happened in Ferguson is totally different from what happened here. It took so long for any measures of justice, there wasn't any video. We had video, and we've taken quick action."

He was right—the speed with which local authorities responded to the bystander video of Walter Scott's shooting was remarkable. But what remained to be seen was what, if any, the broader fallout would be. What would Walter Scott's death mean for the state of South Carolina? For the nation?

As I was packing my things to leave, a ring burst from my desk phone.

"This is Representative Gilliard," the aged Southern voice on the other end of the line declared. "You called?" Once we got talking, the representative barely came up for air. He was outraged by the shooting but was now praying it would provide a crucial opening for movement on two body camera proposals that had for months been stalled in the South Carolina statehouse.

"It reminds me of the Rodney King case," he declared about Scott's death. "The person who took this video should be seen as a hero. If they had not videotaped that moment, we would have just had the police officer justifying why he took another black man's life. We have a real problem in this country, it's just an all-out war on young black, unarmed men. And we've got to get real about this situation."

Like most who follow police policy, Gilliard could rattle off the agreed-upon antidotes—body cameras, more transparency, retraining officers in de-escalation. Perhaps, he said with just a sprinkle of hope at the end of an otherwise demoralizing conversation, Walter Scott would force the change in policing that for years the nation had been discussing.

"We have too many people who are talking loud and doing nothing," he told me before hanging up. "Now is the time, in South Carolina. We need to put up or shut up."

It was my second or third day in North Charleston, most of which had been spent interviewing demonstrators and local elected officials about the shooting and its aftermath. The speed with which the local elected officials had acted in firing and charging Slager had taken the wind out of some of the protests, one of several factors in South Carolina that kept the demonstrations there from ever swelling to the levels seen in St. Louis and Baltimore. "We're *not* going to be another Ferguson," city officials kept repeating to any reporter who would listen, as they had since those first interviews on the first night of the story.

But—just as the resident in Ferguson had forcefully alleged—the men and women who had taken to the streets in North Charleston, often in dozens as opposed to the crowds of hundreds that I had navigated in Missouri, said they were being overpoliced. Specifically, they noted, through traffic stops.

That day I had gotten a text from Ryan Julison, who had traveled to North Charleston to help the family handle the media storm. He gave me the Scott family's address and told me to come over. After I had stood for about half an hour outside the family's home, Walter Scott's mother emerged from a side door.

The TV types, who had for the last twenty-four hours or so anchored their news vans in the parking lot outside the North Charleston police department as well as here, on the side street where the Scott house sat, were preoccupied. It was just a handful of us print reporters—myself and colleagues from the *New York Times* and *Los Angeles Times*—who spotted Mrs. Scott's reluctant presence. I glanced over at Julison, who responded with a nod, encouraging the pack of us to move forward with our notebooks and recorders to speak to the distraught woman.

There's no "right" way to approach these interviews. In the moment, you are very literally walking up to a heartbroken human, someone struggling to avoid becoming completely engulfed by a wave of pain and confusion, and asking them to find words to express those feelings and thoughts. And the twenty-four-hour news cycle doesn't help, because it so often prompts reporters to ask either clichéd, leading sound-bite bait or process questions to which the response of the dead man or woman's family really adds little:

Do you think you can get justice?
Do you think there should be a special prosecutor appointed?
What do you think about those protesting? You would want
      them to be peaceful, right?

Now, all of those questions are fine; I've asked them all at some point or another. But it's hard, standing across from a mother whose son has just been stolen from her, or a father whose daughter will be buried next week, to justify asking about legal minutiae. Instead, at the advice of a veteran reporter I once found myself standing beside at the crime tape, my questions to the grieving center on the life lost — a memory, a character trait of the life lived, not a rehashing of the details of how that life was lost.

It always starts awkwardly, typically with me stammering through a preamble that is as much an apology for the fact that I'm in this person's face asking questions at a time like this as it is a setup for the questions themselves. Can you tell me about Walter? What will you remember about him?

Judy Scott paused. And then sighed. Walter was fifty, but he was still a mama's boy. He called her every day, his sharp "Hey, Mommy!" flowing into her ear, usually sometime in the afternoon. And at the conclusion of each call, he'd tease her.

"You know you're my Smurf, right?" Scott would say to his aging mom with the kind of loving tone that can be known only between a mother and her son. *"Love you."*

"I don't know why, but he gave me that nickname: his Smurf," Judy Scott told us, standing in the driveway of the Charleston home where for the last forty-seven years she had raised her now-slain son. And even now, as a man with children of his own, he spent every Sunday afternoon laid out on her couch, joking around with his siblings and cousins while she worked to prepare their after-church meal. It was a scene that had played out week after week in this home for five decades. Next Sunday, the mother knew, someone, something would be missing from it.

Just two weeks earlier Walter and his siblings had gathered the entire extended family here, for a surprise party for Judy and her husband in honor of their fiftieth wedding anniversary. It was a joyous evening, full of photo albums, cake, and laughs. And for Judy, it was a night full of tears, because it provided her with everything she had wanted: all of her family, grown but together again.

As Judy Scott spoke, I couldn't help but imagine my own mother, standing on the lawn in front of our family home in suburban Cleveland, being pestered with questions about me or one of my brothers. I couldn't help but think about how much Scott's family sounded like my own: the Sunday-afternoon dinners after church and the all-hands-on-deck gatherings to celebrate an anniversary or holiday.

There is nothing that can prepare a family for the heart-clenching shock of losing one of their own. And time and time again, those left behind described to me how so suddenly a normal, mundane week-day had become the worst day of their lives—a black hole of time permanently etched in the video feed of their minds.

When a police officer in Palm Beach Gardens, Florida, shot and killed Corey Jones, his parents were in Jamaica—having taken a trip to clear their minds after the death of another loved one, Corey's grandmother. But then one of their kids called them. They needed to get back to Florida. Corey was dead.

In Memphis, Henry Williams was sleeping on the night his son took his final breath and spoke his final words, uttered to a para-medic between desperate gasps.

I need some water. I'm about to die.

Williams's son, Darrius Stewart, had been riding in the backseat of a vehicle that was pulled over for a missing headlight. Officer Connor Schilling decided to ask everyone in the car for photo ID, not just the driver, and found two outstanding warrants for Stewart. He pulled the boy out of the car and set him in the backseat of the squad car. Eventually, the two ended up struggling on the grass after Stewart tried to run. Then Schilling pulled and fired his gun.

For the family of Deven Guilford, a white seventeen-year-old who was shot and killed by an officer after a February 2015 traffic stop, the shooting threatened their security and faith in law enforcement.

The teen was on his way to see his girlfriend, after a pickup game at his church gym, when he flashed his headlights to signal to an oncoming driver that his high beams were on. That driver, it turned out, was Eaton County Sheriff's Sergeant Jonathan Frost, who pulled a U-turn and signaled for Deven to pull over.

The two had an exchange, during which the officer insisted that his high beams had not been on and Deven refused to produce his driver's license, which he didn't have with him. Eventually, Frost ordered the teen out of the car and used a stun gun on him. Frost said Deven got up and attacked him. Attorneys for Deven's family said he tried to run away. Photos taken soon after the incident show Frost apparently bleeding from the forehead.

In June, prosecutors announced that Frost would not be charged with a crime, and they released the video of the encounter. Deven Guilford's parents initially accepted the decision not to charge the officer, citing their Christian faith and long-held trust in law enforcement. But that had changed by the time I first spoke with their attorney, sometime in October or November.

I called Hugh Davis late one night, on a Tuesday or Wednesday when I was trying to play catch-up. Our database project had shown that more than one out of ten fatal police shootings began with a traffic stop. And while shootings like Scott's had gained national attention, many of the others were relatively unknown stories. I figured I ought to try to tell some of them.

It was probably close to 8 p.m. when I punched in the number of Davis's law office, a libertarian-leaning civil rights shop in Michigan, expecting to leave a voice mail that he'd return sometime later in the week—so I was surprised when a jolly voice burst from the other end of the line.

"They thought Deven must have done something egregiously wrong for this to have happened," Davis told me. "And then they saw the video."

The same was true of Judy Scott, who had just a day earlier been among the first to watch the bystander video of her son's death that by now had been seen by millions. Judy Scott had taught her children to respect the police because she did. And she trusted them. The idea that one of these officers had killed one of her children, her son, by shooting him in the back, was too much for her to fathom.

"We're talking about cameras on the policemen. It's a shame that you have to do that, because the policemen are supposed to protect us, we're supposed to be able to trust them," the mother told us through tears.

"When I saw my son run . . . I just didn't want to believe it. I was broken, I was upset. I mean it, that really hurt."

Judy Scott could only bear to speak with us for a few minutes—which was many more minutes than we deserved. But she did invite a handful of us into the family home, where some other loved ones might be able to give us more details about Walter.

As I entered, the family members paused their conversations, wondering for a moment who this intruder was, before deciding it didn't matter. Nothing I could take from them, be it time or information, could compare to what had so freshly been stripped from their security and comfort. Seated in the kitchen, I found Anthony Scott, the slain man's brother.

"Come on over and have a seat!" he implored me, prompting my practiced shtick.

Anthony told me that he and his brother had bonded, like many brothers do, over sports. Specifically, he told me as his sisters and nieces scurried throughout the room arranging dishes and platters brought by friends and neighbors, his brother Walter loved football.

The brothers would play pickup ball late into the night on the gravel street out in front of the house, a cream and green two-story in which they had both been raised, as evidenced by the time capsule of photographs lining the walls and mantel—elementary school pictures, middle school sports team photos, the smiling sons reaching adulthood, Anthony in a cap and gown and Walter in his marine blues.

As they got older, Anthony and Walter began growing families of their own, but they never missed watching a Dallas Cowboys game. Even if they weren't at the same television, Walter would call his brother and the two would provide each other with real-time commentary until the final down, screaming into the phone in response to each big tackle or touchdown toss.

"'Did you see that!' He would be yelling it at the phone," Anthony told me, leaning back in his chair for a moment of reflection. "Man, I'm really gonna miss that."

The family gathered again on Wednesday night, April 8, 2015, in the living room to watch the national news, at times gasping and sighing as the video of Scott's death flashed on their television. Before long NBC flashed that they had an exclusive interview with Feidin Santana, the young man who had taken the video of Scott's death.

Lester Holt, one of the nation's top anchors—and one of the nation's most esteemed black journalists—had flown to North Charleston for the interview, which was being conducted on the Scott family's front lawn.

"Mr. Scott didn't deserve this," Santana said that day, prompting a round of applause from the Scott family, who along with me were watching the interview live from a living room just fifty feet away from where it was being conducted.

As soon as it had concluded, the family got up and began putting on their coats. I turned to Ryan Julison, who had joined the group to watch the interview, and earnestly asked him where the Scott family could possibly be headed.

"To finalize Walter's burial plot," he responded.

CHAPTER FOUR

Baltimore:
Life Pre-Indictment

What first caught my eye in Oliver Baines's office was the fading blue jacket with a bright yellow star patch that declared FRESNO POLICE embroidered on the arm. Baines was an energetic young man when he first joined the police force in 2000 after finishing college. He went into policing to make a difference, and to be the type of officer he wishes he had encountered as a kid.

"I had a very distorted perspective of police," he told me during an April 2015 meeting in his office. "I just saw awful things."

He grew up near Los Angeles in Windsor Hills, where police were a constant presence and hindrance. He and his friends were stopped, patted down, and questioned as a matter of course. Back in those days, the only good interaction with a police officer was one that Baines managed to avoid. During high school, he worked as a shoe salesman at a department store in the Fox Hills Mall, and nearly every weekend as he commuted to work he would find himself being pulled over to the side of the road by an officer. Usually by white cops, although sometimes it was black officers.

"They would pull me over, they would pull me out of the car, they would handcuff me, sit me on the curb, and just search my car," Baines recalled. "The funny thing is I didn't even realize there was anything odd about that or wrong...the experience of African-Americans and law enforcement, very different than that of whites and law enforcement. I grew up like that thinking it was pretty normal until I got to college and was like 'Oh, wait a minute, Fourth Amendment rights. So every weekend my rights were violated for no reason?'"

So, even though he'd spent more than a decade with a gun and a badge, Baines told me he understood the anger in the streets in places like Ferguson and the dozens of cities where protests had broken out in late 2014 and early 2015. Too often, officers were blind to how deeply torn their relationship with the community really was. Many of his fellow officers, especially the white ones, had grown up in a world in which cops were always the good guys, protecting the neighborhood from the thugs and criminals. As a young black man, Baines knew better.

After college, Baines went to the police academy in November 1998, and he was on the Fresno police force by the following January. While he was still a rookie patrol officer, he joined the department's newly created community policing unit, charged with building relationships in the Southwest district, a black and Hispanic stretch of town plagued by gang violence. Soon, as part of their efforts, they began hosting block parties to better get to know the residents there.

After eleven years on the Fresno police force, Baines gave up his badge to enter politics, getting elected to the city council in 2011. By the time I met him four years later, he had ascended to the role of council president. I visited Fresno desperate for an uplifting story after months of writing about death and depression. An old source of mine had given me a tip that the police in this dusty central California city had been holding block parties each weekend for twelve years, and that it had helped spur a drop in gang crime in some of their worst districts. Here, I thought, was a police force doing what they were supposed to do: connecting with the community, using relationships to curb crime.

One consequence of covering police shooting is being perceived as "antipolice." It wasn't just personal: in those early days after

Ferguson, anyone who asked questions of police officers or who believed they should be held accountable must be against them. Those criticisms were flawed, but they stung. Journalists are often unyielding optimists cloaked in the costumes of cynics. Often readers assume that with scrutiny comes disdain, but in my experience, many of the reporters who are the most likely to probe institutions—whether government or law enforcement or banks—are those who believe most firmly and fundamentally in their vitality.

As my few days in Fresno were wrapping up, I began writing an uplifting piece about a community policing program that officials there said worked. I interviewed the mayor, several other council members, and dozens of police officers, in addition to community members, primarily those who had come out to block parties.

It wasn't long after the story ran that I started getting reactions along the lines of those of a group of local ministers and activists who were angered at the version of Fresno I portrayed—a tight-knit community where police and former gangbangers cooked hamburgers and hot dogs together. Clearly, the world of friendly relations between the police and the community was not recognizable to all. It was almost as if it didn't exist. Instead of being accused of being antipolice, I was accused of boosterism, of failing to see that racial profiling, surveillance of activist groups, and allegations of corruption among some of the department's top officers were the way many Fresno residents knew their police force.

"When we heard that you were in Fresno writing about FPD, we community activists got extremely excited. We thought that someone finally saw what was going on here with Fresno PD and City Hall," one of the more prominent activists in the community wrote me. "We were completely wrong." While I hadn't claimed the Fresno police department was perfect, in my search for a counterexample to all the poor policing I had been documenting in Ferguson, Cleveland, Charleston, and elsewhere, I had overreached, committing to print a description of the Fresno police department that was too generous in its handling of the department's failings and also numb to the very real concerns of the activist community in Fresno. While I had reached out to some of them, I hadn't spent enough time seeking their critical feedback on the boasts made by the police.

By this point, I'd come to know distraught mothers and distraught police officers. I wanted the totality of my coverage to be able to reflect the difficult day-to-day reality of police. But in that search for a false balance, I ended up inadvertently lionizing a department that by many accounts was far from the shining example of community policing it aspired to be.

For more than a year after that piece ran, I still fielded regular complaints online from activists in Fresno. I knew that, to some extent, their qualms were valid. I'd sought a "positive" story on my beat to counterbalance the many critical pieces I had written. Instead, I ended up hurting my own credibility by treating a police department with kid gloves.

The time to harbor these kinds of regrets wouldn't come until later. At the moment, I was happy to have found an uplifting angle, a piece not about black death but rather about steps being taken to value black life and to restore to heavily policed neighborhoods some of the respect that had been lost. Perhaps, I thought, Fresno could be a blueprint for the type of world we want to live in. I wrote my piece, left Fresno for a weekend trip to San Francisco, and then boarded a plane back to Washington.

As I made my way back to DC, the images flashing across CNN on one of the airport TV screens caught my eye. They were reporting live from Baltimore, where, over the weekend, a man named Freddie Gray had died. Rumor had it that he had been beaten to death by the police, and crowds were starting to gather.

It was 8:39 a.m. on April 12 when three police officers on bike patrol spotted Freddie Gray on the street near the Gilmor Homes housing project in Baltimore's Sandtown-Winchester neighborhood—a ten-thousand-person community on the outskirts of West Baltimore that serves as perhaps one of the nation's most striking examples of urban decay.

More than a quarter of the buildings here—mixed among the slabs of row houses that fill many of the neighborhoods in Baltimore and Washington, DC—are vacant, with decades-old lead paint still peeling from the aging walls. Those that are occupied are almost exclusively liquor stores and bad takeout places.

African-Americans in Baltimore are arrested, per capita, at more than three times the rate of residents of other races, according to an analysis conducted by *USA Today* after the uprising in Ferguson. And many of those black men and women being cuffed were from the blighted blocks of Sandtown-Winchester, which at the time Freddie Gray was killed boasted the complementary honors of having an unemployment rate twice that of the average in the rest of the city and of producing more inmates than any other neighborhood in the state of Maryland.

Twenty-five-year-old Freddie Gray had a Sandtown résumé—a smattering of drug possession charges, minor crimes, and the court appearances they produce. When he saw the police that morning, he and another man ran.

The officers gave chase, eventually catching Gray and handcuffing him. They arrested him forcefully and found a switchblade in his pocket. Two bystander videos showed Gray being moved to a police transport van, screaming in pain as officers dragged him toward the vehicle. Once placed inside, Gray was not strapped into a seat. Over the course of the next half hour, the van made at least four stops, and by the time it stopped at the West District police station, Gray was losing responsiveness. By 9:45 a.m., Gray had been taken to a local trauma center. He was in a coma. A week later, on April 19, Freddie Gray died.

Hundreds took to the streets of West Baltimore, rallying and marching and crying the same insistent slogans heard on the streets of Ferguson and New York and Cleveland and Charleston. Officials with the local police union began comparing the protests to a "lynch mob," racial rhetoric that only further inflamed tensions. As day gave way to night on Saturday, April 25, the peaceful demonstrations became violent, with residents throwing rocks and setting several small fires. On Monday, the day of Freddie Gray's funeral, full-scale rioting and looting broke out throughout Sandtown.

I watched in horror from ninety minutes south in Washington, eager to get there. But unlike most of the incidents of police violence that year, Baltimore wasn't my story. I was a reporter for the *Post*'s national desk, so a story in Maryland would fall not to me but to our local desk, which was staffed with a number of veteran reporters with deep sourcing and connections in Charm City. After months of being dispatched on less than a moment's notice to shooting sites across the country, I was trapped at my desk while an American city just up the road burned.

In the months and years after the unrest in Ferguson, when the police elsewhere have killed someone, city officials have often been quick to declare "This is no Ferguson" or "We are not Ferguson." But Ferguson is not some faraway story. In a country where police kill more than a thousand people each year, Ferguson is in all places a local story. We live in a country where police violence is a pervasive fixture of daily life, not a problem plaguing some distant locale.

Finally, on Tuesday morning, I got a note from my editors—get in a car to Baltimore. The local staff was still calling the shots on the story; in fact, I'd only been called in because several of the *Post*'s top digital editors had an upcoming meeting with Snapchat, a new image-sharing mobile app that, at the moment, news outlets were convinced was the next big thing. The *Post* wanted to establish a formal news partnership with the company, especially in view of the upcoming presidential election, and saw the unrest in Baltimore as the perfect opportunity to show how we'd use the platform to cover news.

For months I'd been one of the paper's guinea pigs when it came to using social media for breaking news coverage. In Ferguson, it had been by using Twitter to document with both words and photos the minute-by-minute details of the protests. In Charleston, I used the newly minted live streaming app Periscope to share video from the ground, conducting a walk-through tour of the place where Walter Scott had been killed. And for the last few months, I'd been dabbling in Snapchat. I'd experimented with using it for news when I had traveled south earlier that year, first to Selma for the fiftieth anniversary of the Bloody Sunday march, and then to Mississippi when I toured the Delta as I wrote about the fiftieth anniversary of the lynching of Emmett Till. Knowing I was frustrated by being elbowed out of the Freddie Gray coverage, a few of the *Post*'s digital editors asked to send me, if only to help anchor our social media coverage. It was a back door into the story, but it was my way in.

By the time I arrived on Tuesday afternoon, the streets of West Baltimore were full of familiar faces. Yamiche Alcindor, then with *USA Today*, and Jon Swaine of the *Guardian*, both of whom I'd spent weeks competing with in Ferguson, were working the crowds. So were TV One's Roland Martin and MSNBC's Chris Hayes, television hosts who had devoted countless hours on their respective shows to chronicling the infancy of the protest movement. Reuniting with others who had tracked this story was both comforting and grating, almost as if we'd become a morbid fraternal order.

"It shouldn't take buildings burned for the people here to have a voice," said Shauley McCray, an eighteen-year-old Baltimore woman who came out early that morning to help clean up West Baltimore after the rioting and then spent most of the day joining the peaceful protests and demonstrations. "Baltimore has been broken, it's been broken all of my life. I'm not saying that all of our cops are bad, I'm not saying that everyone who was out here at night during the rioting is a criminal. I'm saying that this is a wake-up call." Moments later, as I leaned against a street sign interviewing a young college woman who had driven six hours to join the protests after seeing photos and videos on Twitter, a spectacle about half a block away caught my eye.

The first thing I saw was the perfect hair, gliding atop a head a few inches higher than most in the crowd, as the crisply dressed white man made his way through the scrum, the unmistakably familiar smile of a politician taped to his face. I quickly ended the interview and jogged to catch up with the man, now encircled by media cameras and residents alike as he grabbed the phones out of the hands of several and then posed for photos that he himself took.

"You have to be present when we're living through the pain," former Baltimore mayor Martin O'Malley, who also served as Maryland governor from 2007 to 2015, told me and several other reporters as he weaved his way through the blocks that just hours before had seen violence. "Everyone's needed right now in the city. Everyone needs to step up."

O'Malley displayed a wide smile as he shook hands and posed for selfies with residents, while a team of aides worked to keep both reporters and residents from questioning the man whose administration's aggressive policing policies had led to hundreds of thousands of arrests that many believe disproportionately affected black and low-income residents.

He only spoke to us reporters for a few minutes, instead working his way up and down the sidewalk and shaking the hands of the Baltimoreans who stood holding protest signs and bottles of water. When he did acknowledge the group of more than a dozen reporters trailing him, he refused to directly engage the sea of questions being thrown at him about his record on crime and policing while mayor.

"Every mayor does their very best to strike the right balance, to save as many lives as we possibly can," O'Malley said. "And every mayor since my time there has tried to do that as well. We're a safer city than we were, but we still have a lot of work to do, you know?"

Suddenly, another voice, this one as angry as O'Malley's practiced speech was soothing, broke through the air.

"Fuck that, this is his fault!" screamed a man who followed along on a red motorcycle as O'Malley and the mob that surrounded him moved down the street. "Do you know who he is? Why would you shake his hand?" Many of the protesters who have taken to the streets point to O'Malley's "zero tolerance" policing policy as the root of the community's distrust of the police. Under the program, arrests skyrocketed, in many cases for minor crime or no crime at all—at one point topping a hundred thousand arrests in a single year.

O'Malley declined, when asked directly, to discuss the aggressive arrest policy under his mayoral administration.

"What we had zero tolerance for was police misconduct," he said. "We worked at it every day. When we had the long hot summer and talked about taking back our open-air drug markets—"

O'Malley was interrupted as two of his handlers got into a shoving match with a television reporter attempting to keep up with the candidate and the gaggle of other reporters and community members that surrounded him. The cameraman had been chasing after the pack and had stumbled, bumping into one of the aides walking with O'Malley. The two men ended up shouting at each other, then seemed to square up, bracing to fight just inches behind where the fledgling presidential candidate was taking questions. The back-and-forth became so loud that O'Malley couldn't ignore it any longer, and the former mayor let out an "Oh come on, guys" as he extended his arm between two of his aides and the journalist, breaking up what seemed about to become a fistfight.

"I mean, we had a long summer," O'Malley continued. "And we talked about the fact that we have to police our corners and police our police."

Not long after O'Malley departed I got a call from former Baltimore police officer Neill Franklin. Born and raised in Baltimore, Franklin spent decades as a Maryland State Police officer and a Baltimore police officer, including stints as an undercover officer working drug stings in the 1980s and as the department's head of training and human resources from 2000 to 2004. Now he works as a police reform advocate, specifically focused on ending the drug war and many of the policies he was responsible for enforcing when he worked as an officer.

"To be surprised that we ended up with this type of community unrest over the last week? It shouldn't be a surprise," Franklin told me. "It was just a matter of when."

"The goal was to go out there and make as many low-level drug arrests as possible. These were people who needed treatment instead of jails," he said. "And in these searches, we were stopping and searching anyone who might look like they fit the bill of a drug user...and now we're seeing arrests for failure to obey, and for disorderly conduct because they didn't want to be frisked...officers did whatever they had to do to lock up as many people as they could to satisfy police headquarters."

Franklin and several other former officers whom I interviewed in the days after the riots pointed specifically to two things: the end of community policing programs such as police athletic leagues, and "zero tolerance" policing. While they're not a fix-all for a policing system in dire need of reform—Fresno had taught me as much— the officers I spoke with in Baltimore were quick to note that the loss of their community policing programs only deepened the deficit of trust in neighborhoods where their sole interactions with citizens were now patdowns and arrests.

"The first order of leadership is providing a safe place to live, work, and raise a family. Without civil order and accountability, other well-intended policy issues fail. Trust is the foundational issue many around the country are struggling with....At the very core we are dealing with the foundation issue of trust, and that's trust between the community and its police department," said Rob Weinhold, who spent years as a Baltimore police officer, including as the department's top spokesman, before leaving for a job with the Justice Department in 2000.

"Which, by the way, yielded terrific results from a crime stand-point," Weinhold noted. "But what I know is this: you can't arrest your way out of the drug problem.... When a department begins to arrest everyone for any infraction, the first thing that happens is your criminal justice system becomes overwhelmed, and then it creates a lot of anger within the community."

In fact, a 2013 strategic plan prepared by the Baltimore police commissioner focused heavily on community policing, declaring that having more foot patrols and stronger relationships between officers and citizens, especially in heavily policed areas, was the best way to cut crime. Yet in 2014, a thorough probe by the *Baltimore Sun* found that even as new city leaders were touting community policing, the city was continuing to pay out millions in settlements and lawsuits related to police brutality—poisoning already-fragile community relationships.

"I interact with law enforcement every day, and what I'm seeing on a daily basis, the way that the young men and women in our community are being treated is unacceptable," said Charmaine Slade, a twenty-four-year-old Baltimore native who works for the city as a probation agent. "I've got clients who are arrested twelve or thirteen times a year. Their charges are dismissed but they're still sitting in jails. That's why there is no trust for law enforcement."

In a survey conducted by the Baltimore Police Department in 2013, 53 percent of residents described their perception of their police force as very or somewhat favorable. However, 31 percent of the respondents described their perception of the Baltimore PD as unfavorable, and another 16 percent did not respond to the question.

And the shaky relationship cuts both ways. In a 2013 survey of Baltimore police officers, just 19 percent of officers said they believed the community supported the department and only 9 percent described the department's morale as good. Meanwhile, some observers have noted that while the police force is relatively diverse—roughly

47 percent of the force is black, in a city that is 64 percent black—many of the department's officers live outside the city.

"I don't think you have to live in the city, but I want you to have lived in the city. I want you to have invested. I want you to understand what makes a city tick, I want you to have ridden a city bus," Peter Moskos, an assistant professor at the John Jay College of Criminal Justice and a former Baltimore police officer, told me. "There is something [sic] really rubs me the wrong way when you get some white guy who had never lived in Baltimore before out policing these majority-black neighborhoods."

As Martin O'Malley made his way down the block that Tuesday afternoon in Baltimore, he approached a street musician and community resident. The resident asked if O'Malley wanted to really work to solve the problem of police brutality, and when the former mayor said yes, the man asked how he could get in touch. O'Malley fiddled for a few seconds—he didn't have any business cards on him, and neither did any of his aides. The candidate had walked himself into a trap: Was he willing to recite the ten digits of his cell phone number to this man on the street and risk the television cameras catching it?

As reporters offered him both pens and paper to write down his number for the resident, O'Malley smiled awkwardly, hemming and hawing in a last-ditch effort to avoid having to give his direct contact information to his former constituent. Finally, after a minute that felt like five, one of his aides located a campaign business card and handed it to the man.

Satisfied that he had saved the photo op, O'Malley was guided into the passenger seat of a black SUV that had pulled up at the end of the block and was whisked away.

With the former mayor gone, several of the remaining reporters approached the man on the motorcycle, who was still sitting just several feet away from the scrum.

"He had his chance to fix this," said Wayne Grady, who described himself as a housing developer, as he continued to sit on his motorcycle. He said he couldn't help himself when he saw O'Malley touring the riot-damaged neighborhood and posing for pictures: after spending all of his forty-seven years in Baltimore, Grady believed he had earned the right to call a spade a spade.

"He's part of the frustrations that are built up in these black young men…that's why central booking was so crowded, because he started the policies."

Later that night, a longtime local reporter put it even more bluntly.

"Just look around at this place," the reporter told me, pointing to abandoned and deteriorated buildings. "This is his legacy. And now he wants to run the whole country?"

With just an hour until the city-imposed curfew, large crowds of people remained at the intersection of Pennsylvania Avenue and North Avenue in West Baltimore. Demonstrators stood face-to-face with lines of police officers. Soon after 9 p.m., dozens of volunteers, some in clergy clothes, and some young men who described themselves as gang members, pushed their way through the crowd. As they reached the police line, they locked arms and insisted the crowds move back and away from the police.

"Bet you never thought you'd see the Bloods and the Crips do this," declared one volunteer, a red bandana covering his face.

But after they had moved the crowd back a few feet, a single water bottle was thrown over their heads and landed at the feet of the officers, who immediately raised their shields and prepared to respond.

"No, no, no!" shouted several of the volunteers as they rushed back to the police line, insisting the officers not engage.

When the officers listened, the volunteers again locked arms and pushed the crowd and media back more than a block from the police line, urging everyone to go home.

"Let's show America that we don't need police to police us, we can disperse ourselves," urged then–State Senator Catherine Pugh, whose voice came from a loudspeaker just behind the police line. "Let's disperse peacefully."

After violence starts to gain momentum, a curfew is one of the first steps taken to regain control of a city. The line between day and night becomes the way to identify and detain those few among the crowds who are bent on violence.

But the curfew also furthers the media spectacle. Once a deadline is set, cameras have to stay *at least* that late, to see what happens. So the standoff begins. The residents are watching the police and the media. The media are watching the residents and the police. The police are standing there, waiting for a water bottle or a rock to land at their feet; then they'll teargas whoever they find.

By 9:40 p.m., there were still more than a hundred people in the street in West Baltimore. And at least a hundred reporters, photographers, and videographers.

"We had to come to show that black lives matter, that this is about more than Freddie Gray," LaKeisha Shuey, an eighteen-year-old who drove from Harrisburg, Pennsylvania, to join the demonstration, told me as we waited to see what would happen at the 10 p.m. deadline. "Ninety-nine percent of these protests have been peaceful, so it's important to be out here highlighting and showing that."

As 10 p.m. arrived, there was peaceful silence. No tear gas, no rubber bullets, no sudden aggressiveness from either the demonstrators or the police.

About five minutes after the curfew, the booming voice of Congressman Elijah Cummings emerged from a loudspeaker, urging the crowd to leave and go home.

"There is nothing wrong with peaceful protest," he said. "We all need to go home."

Then I heard shouting, a singular, strong voice cutting through the air and prompting the chatter of a crowd in response.

As I moved toward the noise, I saw cameras encircling two

men — an older, silver-haired media type and a young black man in a backward baseball cap and a black hoodie.

"Is that Geraldo?" I asked myself. It was, in fact, Geraldo.

Geraldo Rivera, the former broadcast journalist turned talk show host turned conservative political talking head, had been working the streets for a few hours, followed by a bodyguard and a cameraman. The men would approach a group of protesters, asking them to condemn the violence of the night before.

It was typical of much of the cable news coverage of the unrest both in Ferguson and in Baltimore. Of course the peaceful protesters carrying homemade signs and leading the chants didn't agree with the violence: they were the true victims of it. Trapped as they were in neighborhoods where businesses and economic opportunities were few and far between, one less CVS or gas station was a major blow to their quality of life. But the habit of cable news anchors and reporters of insisting that each person on the streets answer, repeatedly, the question of whether they condemned rioting, served only to highlight the truth: that the majority of protesters were peaceful, and that violence was being carried out without the consent or sanction of the majority of those on the street.

"All we want is Fox News and every other white media outlet to leave Baltimore until they are going to report the real story!" shouted the young man as Geraldo moved on to interview other protesters around him. The young man, and many who were part of the protests, believed the police had purposely facilitated the rioting with the hope of discrediting the demonstrations. Why hadn't officers stopped the looting, they asked?

"You really think a bunch of high school students really took down Baltimore city yesterday?" the man in the baseball cap and black hoodie shouted. "And y'all couldn't do nothing? . . . We want the mayor to resign, we want Anthony Batts [then the police commissioner], we want the police out. We want the police gone."

As Geraldo stood, speaking live on Fox News, the man stepped in front of him.

"We want you gone!" he shouted.

"Don't touch my camera!" Geraldo responded.

"This is our city!" the young activist shot back.

The sharp-tongued, quick-witted young man was the then-twenty-year-old Darius "Kwame Rose" Rosebrough.

Rose had grown up in Baltimore, but in another Baltimore than the one where Freddie Gray and many of the black men who call this city home lived. Rose's parents weren't drug addicts or drifters; they were both college-educated professionals who raised their kids on the more affluent east side of the city, homeschooling them until fourth grade and then sending them to private schools. "But privilege didn't necessarily protect me from racism or white supremacy," Rose later told me.

Rose told me his transition into private school was tough, full of fights with fellow students—white classmates who teased him for his brown skin, and black classmates who called him bougie and stuck-up, envious of his comfortable family life.

"Freddie Gray's death helped me fully grasp for the first time that I wasn't really free, even with my privilege. We were all under attack. Black lives and black bodies were all imperiled."

After high school, Rose went to the University of Texas at San Antonio, where he had a scholarship and a place on the speech and debate team. It was fitting: the energy bursts from his voice when he debates, a flurry of well-crafted sentences carrying soaring rhetoric from his lips.

"College debate is definitely a white activity, and here I was trying to project my blackness, and probably overdoing it," Rose told me later. "I was that Farrakhan kid who was trying to assert his blackness in every space, purposely making people uncomfortable."

But he only stayed on campus for a year, before moving back home, where he took a series of odd jobs, joined a band, became a regular in the city nightlife circuit, and got involved in the local activist scene — helping to start a youth mentorship program in one of Baltimore's worst-performing middle schools.

"We went into one of the most underperforming places in Baltimore City and tried to be big brothers to the young men there," Rose said. "These boys, because of where they live, are forced to grow up more quickly. Knowing that, we tried to instill in them leadership qualities."

It wasn't college, but it was a comfortable life for a twentysomething. Rose would spend his days working his job as a bellboy at the Inner Harbor Marriott, his afternoons running the mentorship program, and his nights on the dance floors and barstools of the city's hip-hop clubs.

Rose was at work when he first heard the name Freddie Gray, as coworkers discussed the young man who lived not far from him, and who was apparently in the hospital after being arrested. He was also at work when he first heard of Freddie Gray's death, after a colleague saw it on social media and pointed it out to him; Rose quickly decided to join the infant protests.

"I got off work at eleven p.m. and was out in the streets until six a.m.," Rose recalled about that first night. "The police didn't take any of it seriously at first. They were all just sitting around, eating pizza and telling jokes. The whole thing was a joke to them. They thought Freddie was just another drug-dealing knucklehead who didn't matter."

You can understand what drove Kwame Rose to the streets in protest, but what about so many other young people? As was the case in Ferguson, the media became as much a motivating factor as the death itself. While cable news talking heads often declare that the media is to blame for mass protests — arguing that if the cameras would go away, so would the demonstrators — the logic is only partially correct, and it diagnoses the wrong root cause. Many of those who take to the street and demand justice do emerge in response to the media, but it's not necessarily because they want to get on camera (although many of the protesters happily embrace the chance to step under the bright lights and speak their piece). Rather, many in these communities show up in the streets because they do not recognize the way their home is being depicted on their television sets. They are upset and offended by what they are hearing and reading about their community. They emerge to serve as ombudsmen, correct the record, tell their own stories. The people who took to the streets were, in many ways, protesting not only the death of Freddie Gray, but also the way his life and death had been portrayed in the media.

"What hit me was they were reporting thugs and criminals are taking to the streets, but when I looked at the TV, I saw kids who were just let out of school and who were angry about Freddie Gray's death," Rose said. "The media was serving no other purpose than to instill fear in people. For the first time ever, I was seeing firsthand that the media was not explaining to people what was going on. It was just telling white audiences, essentially, that they should be afraid of black people.

"This was a moment for me. I had always gotten in trouble growing up, for being argumentative and for yelling at people," Rose said. "Now I was able to use that to fight for a real change. To do the real work to make my city a better place for people who look like me. None of us activists planned any protests, there were no 'organizers,' there were just thousands of people who poured out into the streets, which is beautiful because that means there are thousands of people who care about justice."

As Rose and Geraldo went back and forth, a police helicopter overhead warned that the curfew was in place and everyone must leave.

"All news media please clear the area," the helicopter's message said. "You must go home or you are subject to arrest."

At 10:15 p.m. the police moved forward about ten steps, prompting dozens of young people still in the street to scatter. As volunteers ran to protect the residents, several bottles and rocks flew at the officers, hitting their riot shields. The officers responded by firing smoke canisters, one of which landed next to a trash can, sparking a fire.

As the clock struck 11 p.m., there was a thorough, if almost disappointing, silence. There were no sirens, no helicopters. No gunshots or hissing tear gas canisters. No shattering glass.

Much of the media would stay out there for several more hours—we were largely exempt from the curfew, as long as we stayed in a few designated areas—but my eyes had tired of the riot porn. I had begun walking toward the car I had rented to drive back to DC when I heard a familiar voice call out in the night.

"Missster Low-er-ry!"

I turned and saw a familiar blue vest.

The first time I saw that vest, and the lanky, toned body that wore it, was in October 2014, outside a Walmart in St. Louis.

I had only spoken to DeRay Mckesson a handful of times at that point, and frankly, I was more than a little skeptical.

DeRay, as he would soon be known nationally—I'm always amused by the number of people who can recall for me their four favorite tweets of his but can't remember or pronounce his first name—had gotten to Ferguson after I left. He'd seen the tweets and the media coverage, had driven, from his then-home in Minneapolis, more than five hundred miles to Ferguson.

The burned QuikTrip and the growing memorial covering the stains of Michael Brown's blood on Canfield Drive had become a mecca for progressive and black America. By now a cliché, but also impossible to overstate: Ferguson had birthed a new movement. Caravans of college students, reporters, and activists pulled in every day for weeks. On any given night there were as many demonstrators from Texas and New York and California as there were from

Greater St. Louis. Dave Chappelle was there. Talib Kweli was there. Jesse Jackson and Al Sharpton were there.

And by the end of August, so was the school administrator from Minneapolis who would soon become the most singular presence linked to the Black Lives Matter movement.

DeRay Mckesson was born on July 9, 1985, in Baltimore, not far from the neighborhood where, just a few years later, in a run-down row house, an infant Freddie Gray would learn to crawl and then stand. Both of DeRay's parents were drug addicts, his mom leaving the family while he was still just a young child. His father pledged to get clean, got himself a job with a local seafood distributor, and, with the help of a grandmother, raised DeRay and his sister.

The chaos of DeRay's early upbringing created a young man who thrived in structure and with control. He excelled in school, prompted by his desire to achieve and to please. Of his many unique qualities, it is DeRay's uncanny ability to craft the deepest of intimacies with people he has just met that has lent a crucial binding force to the protest movement.

"There is a touching earnestness to Mckesson that makes you want to believe everything he says," wrote Jay Caspian Kang in a profile of Mckesson and Johnetta Elzie for the *New York Times Magazine*. Kang's description was right—Mckesson speaks with a soft authority, calmly asserting confidence so unwavering that, before you realize it, you've been intoxicated by his message.

To know DeRay is to be DeRay's friend—he will have it no other way. He has kept the phone number of almost every person he has ever met. He name-drops, not in the grating way of a Capitol Hill intern or a career-climbing Beltway reporter, but with the earnestness of someone who can't fathom that you, too, don't know every person imaginable.

He was elected to student government every year from sixth grade through his senior year at Bowdoin College, where he served as both senior class president and student body president. After college he took a series of jobs in education, beginning with a two-year stint as a middle school math teacher in Brooklyn through Teach for America. He later moved back to Baltimore to start an after-school program for fifth-through-eighth-grade students on the city's west side before taking jobs as a human resources administrator, first with the Baltimore City Schools and later with the Minneapolis Public Schools.

Mckesson told me it was that background in education that drove him to Ferguson. Education had been his own means of creating a life of stability after he'd been handed a deeply disadvantaging slate of circumstances. He'd gone from the housing projects to one of the nation's finest private colleges, giving campus tours and dining with the college president. As a teacher in New York, then as an administrator in Baltimore and Minneapolis, he wanted that same escape valve for the young children who stormed through the front doors of his schools each day. But he realized after Ferguson that those children could never make it to the dream of a better reality if their lives were being extinguished in the streets.

It was a troubling revelation for the soon-to-be activist, whose outlook on life was largely predicated on the belief that the system, with some exceptions, worked. That if he could get his children in front of better teachers, in more functional school systems, with better and more culturally sensitive and responsive curriculums, he reasoned, he could improve their circumstances and save their lives. He might bristle at the description, but DeRay Mckesson was an institutionalist. He believed that power could be modified and tailored to uplift the oppressed.

The death of Michael Brown, and the way peaceful protesters were treated by responding officers—encased in clouds of tear gas and chaos—broke that worldview.

Once Mckesson arrived in Ferguson, he injected his activism with the academic rigor and attention to detail that had brought him professional success. In a medic training—one of the dozens of such sessions held by activists to prepare for the ongoing protests—he met Netta

Elzie, who at the time was still the most prominent voice on the ground in Ferguson. She was equal parts brash and brief in her introduction—"I'm one of the big tweeters here." Days later, they found themselves side by side again, this time in a church pew at Greater St. Mark's, which hosted the bulk of activist trainings, strategy sessions, and services during the early days of the Ferguson protests.

Mckesson had an idea, spurred in part by the way he had watched Elzie's tweets and, to a lesser extent, his own, go viral night after night. There was a clear hunger for content from the ground—people around the country could sense that there was something just short of a revolution breaking out in the streets in suburban St. Louis—but there was also so much news that was just inaccurate, portraying Michael Brown as a thug, unquestioningly passing on police accounts justifying the use of tear gas and rubber bullets, not to mention the commentary that borrowed from well-worn racial tropes. In other words, there was little real news, not to mention nuance and context, coming out of Ferguson.

Mckesson and Elzie decided together that instead of letting the media control the narrative, they would curate media content—circulating the pieces that got it right and calling out the outlets that got it wrong. Partnering with Brittney Packnett and Justin Hansford, they started the *Ferguson Protester Newsletter*. Among its most powerful features was the day counter near the top of each edition:

> # of days since Darren Wilson has remained free: 50
> # of apologies from the Mayor of Ferguson: 0
> # of protesters arrested last night: 24

By the time the grand jury declined to indict Wilson in November 2014, the newsletter had more than twenty thousand subscribers.

Mckesson and Elzie played a crucial role as the de facto communications team for the ongoing Ferguson protests. Among the links, they included information about planned demonstrations by St.

Louis activist groups, as well as Black Lives Matter–affiliated groups across the country. They would then promote positive coverage that the demonstrations had received. The newsletter's subscribers, and the robust online followings that Mckesson and Elzie amassed while publishing it, grew by the hundreds each day, keeping the protests in the headlines and near the front of the nation's collective consciousness during the months between Michael Brown's death and the grand jury decision—a crucial three-month period when a diversion of the nation's attention could have forever muted the growing movement.

The work they were doing was certainly impressive, but I couldn't help but view Mckesson as a bit of an interloper—someone who, like me, had parachuted into Ferguson and suddenly was granted a measure of legitimacy by his newfound proximity to the chaos. Aided by the fact that I had been arrested and thus had an outsized platform and following, I had developed a steady stable of sources within the upper ranks of the protesters, and talked regularly with at least half a dozen of them. Mckesson arrived late in the game, after the protests were already in full swing. Often, both in the media and in activist spaces, we assign credibility based on proximity to trauma. That manifested itself in the pride many on the ground in St. Louis took in being "day one" protesters. It shows up in the us-versus-them mind-set local reporters and outlets sometimes project toward national correspondents who drop into a story. The theory is that legitimacy can only be earned through a long-suffering and constant presence. But that view is limiting in that it forecloses on the possibility that at times change is most effectively spurred by a fresh set of critical eyes.

Yet as August and September gave way to October, Mckesson became an indispensable source. While activist groups continued daily protests outside the police station, with groups like Tribe X and the Lost Voices, as well as individuals like Tony Rice and Heather DeMian, serving as essential foot soldiers, the media and national attention had largely shifted away from Ferguson. The *Ferguson Protester Newsletter* provided a daily reminder and tip sheet for the media, still eager to cover the developments but now geographically far from the action.

On the second weekend in October, activist groups convened Ferguson October, which would prove the most successful collaboration among the organic protest groups, individual actors like Mckesson and Netta Elzie, and the broader Black Lives Matter network, including Alicia Garza, Patrisse Cullors, and Opal Tometi, the three women regarded as founders of the hashtag, and their various allies. The efforts of all these individuals would be amplified by public relations work spearheaded by Mervyn Marcano and the Advancement Project, a national civil rights group that for months provided crucial support to the young organizers. Thousands of college students, clergy, and activists traveled to Ferguson for the weekend.

The movement had found a new name to rally around while they awaited the Darren Wilson grand jury decision: just one night before Ferguson October was set to begin, another young black man, Vonderrit "Drup" Myers, had been shot and killed in St. Louis. That night, more than a hundred demonstrators gathered at the spot where Myers had been killed and set out to march through St. Louis, ending outside a QuikTrip gas station, where they staged a sit-in in front of the glass doors.

The plans for the late-night march were closely held by organizers — with only several dozen of the local activists most active in Ferguson aware that the group would be led to the gas station and that an act of civil disobedience would take place. Organizers remained tight-lipped about their destination, going as far as tweeting inaccurate information about when they were embarking on the march and in which direction they were walking.

Chanting "No justice, no peace" and "The whole damn system is guilty as hell," the marchers were on the move for close to half an hour. Blocks from the QuikTrip, officers in cruisers, trucks, and large tactical vehicles began to catch up.

When the protest reached the gas station, leaders yelled through the loudspeakers: "Do not cause any destruction, this is a peaceful protest." Then volunteers stood guard at the gas station's entrances to make sure no one entered or harmed the building.

Responding officers ordered them to disperse, but the protesters locked arms and remained seated as the officers used batons to try to break their arms apart and deployed pepper spray. At least fourteen people were arrested; the rest of the crowd dispersed into the night.

The arrests and disruption, a departure from the rest of the Ferguson October schedule, were only the first signal of what was to come for the rest of the weekend.

Two days later, on Sunday evening, the demonstrators again gathered in the Shaw neighborhood. The media was growing impatient. All that had been said was that we should show up here, and then something big was going to happen. Were they going to march? Where were they going? This tension was present at many of the protests, with journalists demanding information from the protesters, who in turn told them where they could shove their cameras.

"You're shooting yourselves in the foot," the slighted reporters would respond. "You need us."

There is a fundamental arrogance among reporters when it comes to assessing our own role in the creation of social movements — aided by the fact that we seem to have trained a generation of us to believe that we were somehow responsible for the success of the civil rights movement.

That's not to say that the press did not play a vital role, as outlined exhaustively in Gene Roberts and Hank Klibanoff's *The Race Beat*. Their book reveals that the reporters, who traveled deep into the heart of the Jim Crow South, relayed dispatches to their audiences in New York, Chicago, and Washington, DC, that played a crucial role in spurring change.

"Without the media the civil rights movement would have been a bird without wings," John Lewis, who was beaten close to death on Bloody Sunday, has said often, this version from a 2005 address to Congress. "I am not certain where we would be today as a nation, if the American public had not been made to acknowledge the struggles we faced in the American South.... Without the media's willingness to stand in harm's way and starkly portray events of the Movement as they saw them unfold, Americans may never have understood or even believed the horrors that African Americans faced in the Deep South."

The role of the press in the civil rights movement also points to our larger failure as a nation to validate and trust the black experience. Why did it take white reporters writing for white audiences to finally address the inequities that black communities had for decades been fighting? Was the lens of whiteness required for the nation to accurately recognize the black experience?

Why did it take gripping images of police dogs and fire hoses for us to recognize the righteousness of the civil rights struggle of the 1950s and 1960s? Why must a black man or woman's death be captured on video, and played on a loop on cable news, for us to finally give credence to decades of declarations by black Americans that they were being brutalized by the police?

In recent years, it's been hard not to notice the tendency of media outlets and reporters to overstate our own importance in the role of social movements. From Occupy Wall Street to the conservative Tea Party to Black Lives Matter — the three movements that have most prominently defined the Obama years — the media has anointed itself the kingmaker. "Without us, no one would hear your message," enraged cameramen and television anchors declared to groups of hundreds of protesters who had amassed an immeasurable online following and had already brought the city of St. Louis to a near-standstill. These arguments, fundamentally, were about access to power. The media was pointing out to these young activists that they still lacked power; only via the media's cameras and their pens would the struggle be recognized or acknowledged.

As the arguments between activists and journalists continued, I found Netta Elzie, who whisked me off to a rental car where a group of the night's organizers were sitting. There was Alexis Templeton, who led the chanting on most nights in Ferguson, and Kayla Reed, who would soon join the Organization for Black Struggle, a local organizing group that had been in the area for decades, and DeRay Mckesson, who had flown in from Minneapolis—at this point he was basically living in St. Louis on the weekend. Also there were Cherrell Brown, of Justice League NYC, who had been instrumental in planning the protests after Eric Garner's death, and Charles Wade, who during those first few months was perhaps the most crucial fundraiser for a protest movement struggling to survive its chaotic infancy. Tonight, they told me, would be a night to remember. Then they kicked me out of the car so they could continue planning.

The protesters split into two groups, walking in different directions to an undisclosed location. The first group departed just after 11 p.m., marching to a nearby intersection and shutting down traffic by playing hopscotch, jumping rope, and tossing footballs. The demonstration was a play on what had become one of the most popular chants during the protests: "They think it's a game. They think it's a joke."

The second group departed about forty-five minutes later, marching silently on the sidewalk to meet up with the first group. As the groups converged, they were met by officers in riot gear who held cans of pepper spray and smacked their shin guards. The methodical thumping, an intimidating show of force, radiated through the night air.

The officers stood both on the sidewalk and in the street and threatened to make arrests. Protest leaders said they had the right to proceed on the sidewalk.

"This is an unlawful assembly!" an officer yelled.

"No. It's not," responded Dhoruba Shakur, one of the protest organizers who stood at the front of the group. "This is a peaceful group of people silently walking on the sidewalk."

The scene played out on a bridge leading toward the Saint Louis University campus, with the protesters standing on the sidewalk, shoulder to shoulder. The riot officers fanned out in front of them, refusing to allow the group to continue marching forward, in a scene nearly identical to depictions of the Bloody Sunday standoff between voting rights activists and Alabama state troopers that had occurred in Selma nearly five decades earlier.

"Can you please stop beating your sticks and talk to the people you protect?" Derrick Robinson, a local minister who had been heavily involved in the protests, asked the officers.

After about twenty minutes, officers allowed the march to continue up the sidewalk toward Saint Louis University. The university's security and police officers tried to stop the protest from entering the campus.

"I am a student, I have my ID, and I have a lot of guests," a protest leader said into the megaphone.

The security officers stepped aside, and the crowd kept moving. Participants then gathered at the campus center, chanting "Out of the dorms and into the streets" as students rushed out of buildings. Some joined the protesters, others took photos or brought out bottles of water.

The "occupation" of the university, which took local officials completely by surprise, lasted until the following morning.

On the last day of Ferguson October, clergy members, led by Cornel West and Jim Wallis, conducted a planned mass arrest demonstration at the Ferguson Police Department. Officers lined the parking lot, blocking them from entering. After saying a prayer, the clergy members walked forward into the police line, in some spots breaking it, before being taken into custody.

Later that night, it was again the young activists' turn, as they spread out in various parts of the city to host disruptive protests.

Some went downtown to the site of a St. Louis Rams game, others blocked traffic in and out of a fundraiser being held by Senator Claire McCaskill, with whom the activists had been deeply frustrated after her vocal support for prosecutor McCulloch. Others went from Walmart to Walmart—the department store chain where, in Ohio, months earlier, John Crawford had been shot and killed—linking arms before dropping to their knees.

"I've got my hands up on my head, please don't shoot me dead!" they chanted at the officers standing guard beneath the bright blue letters above the entrance. Moments later, police announced that the store was closed for the night. As I made my way back to the car, I spotted Mckesson, who was off to the side of the dwindling demonstration, tweeting.

Mckesson felt as if he was everywhere during those days in October and November, an ever-present force at the site of the action. He'd post images of the protest signs and videos of the long lines of police officers who showed up in riot gear.

"Wild!" he would declare.

"The movement lives," he would add.

After the protests in Ferguson largely ended in November, he took the work on the road, traveling to New York and to Selma, and then to McKinney, Texas, where an officer was caught on tape manhandling a young woman at a pool party, and then to Charleston after the killing of Walter Scott. Then the police in Baltimore killed Freddie Gray.

Armed with a deep Rolodex of media contacts built during the Ferguson protests—there are likely few national reporters or television producers without one of his several cell phone numbers—Mckesson became a go-to interview during the unrest in Baltimore, plastered on cable news as a representative of those who had taken to the streets. Because he had grown up there, Mckesson now spoke with an authority he had lacked during the Ferguson uprising. He pushed back at cable news hosts and spoke with expansive rhetoric.

For media looking to anoint a leader on behalf of the leaderless protest movement, he was the easy choice.

In an April 28, 2015, exchange that quickly went viral, Mckesson grew visibly frustrated with CNN anchor Wolf Blitzer, who spent most of the interview asking the activist, repeatedly, to condemn the riots. "There's no excuse for that kind of violence, right?" Blitzer asked Mckesson after listing statistics on the property damage during the rioting. "There's no excuse for the seven people that the Baltimore City Police Department has killed in the past year, either, right?" Mckesson, who earlier in the exchange had said he hoped to see nothing but peaceful protests, jabbed back.

Mckesson and the newsletter team transitioned from "We the Protesters" to "Campaign Zero," a policy-oriented activist arm that pledged to put forth recommendations for how "we can live in a world where the police don't kill people." The efforts first consisted of ten recommendations, spanning from body cameras to new police union contracts, but eventually expanded to include detailed proposals, earning the group sit-down meetings with the White House, as well as Democratic presidential candidates Hillary Clinton and Bernie Sanders.

Meanwhile, Mckesson continued to milk his humongous social media following for access—to business leaders, political figures, and celebrities. It's been rumored that when music superstar Beyoncé began to consider financially supporting the protest movement—which her music had frequently referenced in the months since Ferguson—she secretly met with Mckesson in her New York offices. Months later, she and her husband, rap mogul Jay Z, gave a six-figure donation to Black Lives Matter–affiliated groups.

But by summer 2015 the nation's mood was shifting, or had already shifted. For the first year after Ferguson, the focus of many of the activists had remained urgent awareness—the battle to convince the rest of the country that the police killings of black men and women were a crisis. This had been largely accomplished. Now, new questions were being raised: How would these newly identified leaders continue the work, and how, if at all, should they interact with the ongoing presidential campaign?

It was around that time that I got a text from Mckesson. He's a creature of habit, so most of our conversations begin with a three-word message from him. "Can you talk?" he asked, using one of half a dozen phrases he recycles through dozens of times a day.

A few minutes later we were on the phone, talking off the record, as we often did when I wasn't working on a specific story. He was thinking of running for mayor, he told me, and wanted to know what I thought.

"Mckesson has already inspired thousands around the country to protest police brutality," Greg Howard would later write for the *New York Times Magazine*. "But the viability of any civil rights movement lies in its ability to move from the street to the places where governance happens."

I don't remember what I told Mckesson that day, other than that he'd better let me break the story if and when he actually decided to run, but I do remember being struck by his audacity. Here was a thirty-year-old with no real political experience, currently crashing on the couch of a family friend in Baltimore, who was willing to boldly dream of being elected to lead the city in which he grew up. He had already examined the residency laws and the eligibility requirements. He could win, he assured me. But the question that mattered was what impact his run would have on the protest movement—would it help or hurt the greater cause, and what would this mean to his digital platform?

He made dozens of phone calls, bouncing the idea off activists—both local and national—as well as at least half a dozen reporters, another half dozen political consultants, a prominent pollster, and people like Twitter CEO Jack Dorsey and David Simon, the former *Baltimore Sun* writer whose work on *The Wire* has defined the city in the minds of most millennial Americans.

In early January, I traveled to Baltimore for his not-yet campaign's first planning meeting. There were apples, pizza, tins of holiday popcorn, and freshly brewed coffee spread across a conference room table inside the Charles Fish Building, a historic storefront once home to a white-owned clothing and furniture store known locally for nondiscriminatory practices toward black customers long before the civil rights movement.

Mckesson had called me two days before, offering to let me sit in on the meeting as long as I didn't report anything from it until after he made a decision about whether or not he was going to run. This type of access reporting—agreeing to a set of terms, no matter how logistical, in exchange for an exclusive reporting opportunity being denied to your peers from other media outlets—always makes me uneasy. It is how, too often, powerful people are able to craft the media narratives that ensure that they maintain that power, doling out morsels of news and information to news outlets in the knowledge that it will discourage hard questions or any degree of skepticism.

When I covered city politics in Boston and Congress for the *Post,* access reporting was the bread and butter of almost anyone who was working either beat successfully, with both the reporters and the politicians knowing that they were being used. But since I had moved to covering issues of race and justice, there had been much less need for that access. The young activists knew me and, it seemed, for the most part trusted me—even when I covered them critically or wrote things they wished I hadn't. They knew I was talking to most of the other young activists; they all felt they should be talking to me, too. There was a fundamental honesty in our interactions, lacking the quid pro quo of so many of my past source relationships. These activists knew I cared about getting the story right, and because of that, they trusted me. At times Mckesson was the exception. His professional background led him to conduct himself as a deliberate operator, working the media and strategically giving out kernels of information and perspective to keep himself and, by extension, the protest movement in reporters' good graces.

Mckesson had always been particularly forthcoming with me, willing to clue me in to behind-the-scenes details about intermovement drama and fights, as well as strategy as it related to the upcoming presidential contest. He was, and is, a valuable source. But his popularity quickly made him a polarizing figure within the ranks of activists. He got into high-profile Twitter spats with activists like dream hampton and Shaun King. Others posted thinly veiled slights at him and his style of activism on their Facebook pages. Some of the hate was due to jealousy—Mckesson was becoming legitimately famous, an outsized media presence in a movement that had for months insisted it had no central charismatic leader. But some of his critics had more grounded qualms. Mckesson could be thin-skinned and could, at times, occupy so much space that others were shut out of discussion. Even as he insisted he didn't speak for the entire movement, the media often spent so much time either propping him up or attempting to tear him down that it missed others doing valuable work.

Mckesson's tactics were tethered to his fundamental belief that the system could be fixed—something that, in a movement that spanned from current elected officials to actual anarchists, and everyone in between, earned him scorn from some BLM-affiliated groups. Meanwhile, conservative media outlets chose him as the person they would attack; they were hyperbolically outraged when he was invited by the Yale Divinity School to give a two-day lecture series. A writer for *National Review* declared him a "next-generation race-baiter." Tucker Carlson, the conservative pundit, told a Fox News audience that Mckesson was "not an impressive guy. Just kind of a race hustler."

I decided early on that I would go out of my way not to use him as an official, on-the-record source when I could avoid it. It wasn't meant to shield him—one of the reasons we clicked almost immediately is that we both speak matter-of-factly, with a layer of bluntness that is equal parts obnoxious and endearing. But I knew that

Mckesson's value to me as a reporter came from my ability to keep him speaking freely with me as often as possible — providing me with a sounding board for my story ideas and an analysis of the protest movement, challenging my thesis while also giving me information. That's not to say I never quoted him, but I also wanted to be sensitive to the insistence of the activists that there was no one leader of the movement. Just because Mckesson would always answer the phone didn't mean I should always call or quote him.

Still, if he was going to run for mayor, I knew I was going to have to cover it to some extent. His entrance into electoral politics would mark the beginning of a new chapter in the protest movement one way or the other.

"The question is," Mckesson asked the assembled advisers, "what is the world we want to live in? What does that world look like?"

Netta Elzie was there, and so was the rest of Campaign Zero: Samuel Sinyangwe and Brittany Packnett (who phoned in via conference call). Sitting next to me was Donnie O'Callaghan, an education policy analyst and Mckesson's best friend — the two talked nearly constantly, with Mckesson often calling O'Callaghan to talk through the strategy for a meeting with an elected official or activist group, or even to go over the wording of a tweet he was about to send.

Around the rest of the table were Baltimore residents, primarily worker bees in the school district who had gotten to know Mckesson during his time working for the city schools, as well as a handful of activists who had known him during his teenage years when he was involved in local youth programs.

Mckesson would bank on his celebrity to mobilize the electorate, a Donald Trump–esque strategy that was always partially flawed. A municipal electorate, much more so than a statewide or national one, votes less on its hopes and aspirations than on its daily necessities. Few candidates could match the inspiring life story of DeRay Mckesson. But they didn't have to — instead, they could lean on electoral or city government experience. Voters in city elections want to know if you can fill the potholes out in front of their home, and whether you're going to promise that, unlike that last time, the roads will be plowed in a timely fashion after a crippling snowstorm. Mckesson couldn't guarantee them any of those things—he would have been the first political outsider elected to the corner office of Baltimore City Hall in modern history.

In the early 2000s, Jelani Cobb wrote this about the long-shot presidential bid embarked upon by the Reverend Al Sharpton:

> Sleep if you want to, but beneath the comic appearance, the self-deprecating one-liners and the deliberately Ebonic dictation is a political rationality that Sharpton has parlayed into his present standing as the most influential nonelected black Democrat in the party. Never mind the snickers from the wine-n-cheese set, because Al Sharpton knows he can't win. He also knows he doesn't have to win—all he needs to do is not lose.

The mayoral run made the nation's most prominent protester even more famous. It gave him an opportunity to flex and strengthen his policy chops on issues other than police and education. It forced him to build expansive fundraising and email lists that, no matter what direction his public life takes next, will help ensure his powerful reach long after others have called it quits.

DeRay Mckesson was not going to be the mayor of Baltimore. But success isn't always defined by victory.

Just after 10:41 a.m. on Friday, May 1, 2015, a *Washington Post* colleague shouted out for my attention.

"She's coming on!" he yelled. "Turn on CNN."

The pearl necklace around her neck poked out near the top of the white button-down blouse that state's attorney Marilyn Mosby wore beneath a tailored black blazer that day. The podium was crowded with microphones, but her head boldly stuck out above them and into the camera shot.

"I had the opportunity to meet with Mr. Gray's family," Mosby said. "I assured his family that no one is above the law and that I would pursue justice on their behalf."

In a city looking for a leader, they seemed to have found one in Mosby. She praised the peaceful protests and the crowds who had called for justice. And she decried the acts of violence, with strokes of support for law enforcement.

"My administration is committed to creating a fair and equitable justice system for all, no matter what your occupation, your age, your race, your color, or your creed," she said.

The wife of city councilman Nick Mosby, who represented the neighborhood where Freddie Gray lived and where the bulk of the demonstrations were being held, went on to announce that six officers involved in taking Gray into custody would be charged in connection with his death.

"We have probable cause to file criminal charges," Mosby declared.

"Yes! Yes!" some in the crowd could be heard shouting.

In an instant, she became a polarizing national figure—a long-awaited savior to the scores of activists and protest movement sympathizers who had for months craved a prosecutor with the audacity to charge officers in connection with the deaths of unarmed black men, and an anticop villain to police sympathizers and police unions, who largely believe that officers should never be charged with crimes when they kill people on the job.

Within hours, the local Fraternal Order of Police was calling for Mosby to recuse herself from the case. But she had no plans to step aside. These officers would see their day in court.

In many ways, Marilyn Mosby was born and bred for this case. Her family tree was built of branches full of law enforcement, primarily in Boston, where she had been raised. She thrived under pressure and in front of the camera. In announcing the charges, she spoke with the deep and even sweeping conviction of an activist and the prophetic fire of a preacher whose message was a lifetime in the making.

Marilyn Mosby was just fourteen years old when her cousin was shot and killed as he sat on his bike in the driveway of their grand-parents' Boston home on a Friday night in August 1994. Like Mosby, the slain boy, Diron Spence, had grown up in Dorchester, a racially diverse working-class section of the city, in a family of police officers. His stepfather, grandfather, and several aunts and uncles were veteran Boston police officers, and the family's connections to the department traced back at least five generations.

The shooting was a case of mistaken identity. Spence's bike, borrowed from a cousin, had a satchel attached to it, not unlike the kind used at the time by some neighborhood drug runners to traffic their product. Family members concluded that the shooter must have assumed Spence was a dope boy, approached him, and attempted to rob him.

The slaying captivated Boston, which at the time was dealing with a spike in crime and wrestling with issues of law enforcement, gangs, race, and drugs.

It was a turning point for Mosby, who watched her family members become characters in a gritty city's tabloid story of the month.

"She says that to this day, that murder was a factor in her having the initiative to become an attorney," Linda Thompson, Mosby's mother and a former twenty-one-year Boston police officer, told me when I got her on the phone the same day her daughter announced the charges against the six officers. "It was very hard for the whole family.... But she was very close to him, they were just a few years apart, and to have him murdered so senselessly, it really shook her."

While police initially said they knew of no motive in the slaying, the *Boston Herald*—one of the city's two major daily newspapers, which despite its conservative leanings is widely read in the black community—speculated that the killing might have been a drug deal gone wrong or an attempt by eighteen-year-old Kevin Denis to rob Spence of his shoes.

"I want to know why," demanded Preston Thompson, Spence's stepfather and Mosby's uncle, who was a Boston police officer, during an impassioned press conference at the family home, according to coverage that ran in the *Boston Globe,* "every time a black boy is killed in Dorchester you have to mention drugs? My son was a good boy. He wasn't involved in drugs or any crime. He was a good student and I'm very proud of my son."

The slain boy's father had been working his beat at the time of the shooting, and found out through the Boston PD radio dispatch that his son had been shot twice in the chest.

"It was such a tough, sad time in all of our lives," said Linda Thompson.

Kevin Denis was immediately arrested and charged with the killing. Prosecutors alleged that he had demanded money from Spence, having mistaken him for a drug dealer. In 1996, Denis was convicted and sentenced to life in prison.

The media speculation that the slaying involved drugs prompted an aggressive campaign by Spence's family and friends to redefine the narrative of his death, with many granting interviews to highlight the fact that he was an honor student and varsity basketball player just months from graduation.

According to the *Globe,* more than 450 people showed up for Spence's funeral—including more than a dozen Boston police officers.

"It shouldn't have happened to him," then-seventeen-year-old Rob Legrow told the *Globe* on the day of Spence's burial. "More people have got to see this. This shouldn't happen to anyone."

The incident helped solidify for the young Mosby what the rest of her life would bring. She would work in the legal system, and she would seek justice for people like her cousin.

"[Mosby] had always said she wanted to be an attorney, or a judge," said Linda Thompson, "but her cousin's murder made her determined to seek justice by doing what she could to be a part of the legal system."

But the burst of hope that greeted Mosby's audacious decision to charge the officers involved in Freddie Gray's death would eventually abate. Even more rare than an officer being charged, it turns out, is an officer being convicted.

The six officers involved each faced separate trials, and as of this writing, none of the four officers who had been tried so far had been convicted. It seems unlikely that any of them will be.

"What we see after four trials—including last year's mistrial in the case against Officer William Porter—is that Freddie Gray's death was tragic, senseless, and unnecessary, yet in key respects still somewhat mysterious. We know that if Gray had been standing on a street corner in another part of town he probably would not have been chased by police, would not have been handcuffed and frisked, would not have been placed facedown with feet shackled in the back of a police van, and would not ultimately have suffered a fatal spinal cord injury," the editorial board of the *Baltimore Sun* wrote in mid-July 2016. "But we don't know precisely when or how he was injured, and we know nothing about what was going through the heads of the officers who encountered him along the way—critical information to sustain the kinds of charges they faced. Gray was treated horribly and unjustly, but there's a big gulf between 'someone must have done something' and 'guilty beyond a reasonable doubt.'"

Mosby, the newspaper wrote, should drop the remaining charges against the other officers. Days later, Mosby did just that.

CHAPTER FIVE

Charleston: Black Death Is Black Death

On election night 2008, as he took a Chicago stage to give his first address as president-elect, Obama credited the scores of young volunteers who were the backbone of his campaign, declaring that his efforts "grew strength from the young people who rejected the myth of their generation's apathy, who left their homes and their families for jobs that offered little pay and less sleep.

"This is your victory," said the man who two months later would be inaugurated as the nation's first black president.

The 2008 campaign by then-senator Barack Obama inspired a generation of political activists and operatives on the left, mobilizing energetic and hungry young people who happily made "Change We Can Believe In" the first political rallying cry behind which they had ever aligned. That was especially true in battleground states like Ohio, Florida, and North Carolina, and among the ranks of young black political operatives who saw in the Obama campaign an opportunity for a milestone in the nation's civil rights history.

"The young black activists we now know, a lot of them began organizing through the Obama campaign," Bree Newsome told me in early 2016. "You're talking about an entire generation of political participants that started out very enthusiastic about the process, and then who by the time you get to Ferguson, had completely soured on the process."

Born in Durham, Newsome was raised in North Carolina and Columbia, Maryland, where she was class president at Oakland Mills High School three of her four years there. Next she went off to film school at New York University. Of the most prominent Black Lives Matter activists, she is among those who most vocally proclaim their faith. Her father, Clarence Newsome, has for years served as dean of Howard University's School of Divinity. And as with many of the other post–Joshua Generation activists who became the steady heartbeat of the Black Lives Matter movement, it wasn't until after the election of Barack Obama that Newsome became truly politically active.

"To understand it, you have to go back to the election of Barack Obama in terms of what that symbolized in terms of the hope. We saw that as us turning a corner in the country," Newsome told me. "And then what we saw through the Trayvon Martin case was that we haven't actually turned that corner. Honestly, Trayvon was the turning point.

"Trayvon Martin just had so many echoes of Emmett Till. It felt like something out of 1955."

By the time of the protests and riots in Ferguson and Baltimore, Newsome told me, the movement had matured beyond the stage at which activists believed they had the luxury of working within the system, of coloring inside the lines. Black America had peacefully made its demands for justice after Trayvon Martin. And those cries had gone unheard.

"Now we talk about indicting the whole system. But back with Trayvon, a lot of people truly believed in the process," Newsome recalled. "A lot of the protests back in 2012 were just about getting George Zimmerman arrested and tried. In 2012 it was about 'let the system work.' The demand was for him to be arrested and tried. Well, he was arrested and tried—and then he was acquitted."

Zimmerman's acquittal further fanned the fires of protest. The Dream Defenders led a thirty-one-day sit-in at Florida governor Rick Scott's office, and Newsome was one of the dozens who traveled to Florida to join them. Million Hoodies began a national campaign aimed at media representation of black men. And a new group, #BlackLivesMatter, began holding discussions about what coalition-based, intersectional activism around the unique, systemic threat to black bodies could look like.

The year 2012 represented a turning point for Newsome, and for her faith. She'd been raised in the church, but her personal commitment as an adult began manifesting itself through activism, which she saw as part of her Christian charge to work on behalf of others.

In 2013, the year after George Zimmerman was acquitted, Newsome moved back to North Carolina to help take care of her grandmother in Charlotte. What she found brewing in her home state was a historic voting rights battle that would consume her. She had no intention of becoming an activist, but to hear her tell it, she had little choice.

In the wake of President Obama's reelection and the Tea Party movement that his presidency had sparked, North Carolina was in the midst of one of the most intense battles over voting restrictions that had played out in any state since the passage of the Voting Rights Act. Republican legislators, under the leadership of State House Speaker Thom Tillis, passed legislation requiring photo ID to vote, ending same-day voter registration, and limiting the number of days allotted for early voting. In response, local activist groups led by the NAACP and Reverend William Barber II held massive protests throughout the state and at the statehouse, declaring the new North Carolina law "the worst voter suppression law in the country and the worst one since Jim Crow."

"It was surreal," Newsome recalled. "What struck me was that we were having this massive debate about the Voting Rights Act, something that I thought was written in stone, that I thought was settled history.

"Maybe I had taken my rights too much for granted," she went on. "If there is one thing I've always felt passionate about, it is access to voting. America—for all of its problems, I've always believed in our ability to vote and change our problems that way."

Newsome joined the Moral Monday protests, which convened each week for rallies, sit-ins, and marches in opposition to recent state legislation that, the activists argued, was meant to do little other than make it harder for the state's black residents to vote. The battle, in a state with a Republican governor and a GOP-run statehouse, was always uphill. When it became clear that, at least for now, they were going to lose, many of the activists who had joined the coalition were forced to grapple with a brutal truth: generations of voter registration drives and get-out-the-vote efforts made little difference if access to the ballot box could be restricted or restructured so easily and in such a politically partisan manner. It's a long way from electing the first black president to having your very right to vote placed in jeopardy by Tea Party–inspired legislative bodies.

And then, the following year, came Eric Garner, Michael Brown, John Crawford, and Tamir Rice.

"It was not just the killing of Michael Brown, it was the reaction from the police. It was seeing the police dogs, and knowing the history there," Newsome said.

Newsome knew of Rodney King, and of the long-ago allegations of brutality by the New York Police Department. But Ferguson opened a new possibility in her mind—that the American problem of policing could in fact be as pervasive as the nation is broad and diverse. That if the police in Ferguson, Missouri, were gunning down unarmed black men, this must also be happening everywhere else.

That possibility was only reinforced in Newsome's mind as she watched incident after incident play out on the national stage—the death of Freddie Gray and the riots in Baltimore, the traffic stop of Sandra Bland and her death in a Texas jail cell, the viral video of an aggressive officer in McKinney, Texas, manhandling a black girl in a bikini and then pulling his gun on two boys who attempted to intervene.

While these were almost always presented in the media as isolated, unrelated incidents, Newsome couldn't help but link each to the other, and connect them to her knowledge of the black struggle for justice and liberation that in America dates back to 1619.

"It's a modern iteration of a struggle that has existed for hundreds of years," Newsome said.

Around Easter 2015, Newsome and her family traveled to South Carolina, where generations before, her family had been enslaved. They visited Rafting Creek Baptist Church, the congregation in Rembert, South Carolina, that her great-great-great-grandfather Theodore Diggs, a former slave who could read and write, founded in 1864, near the end of the Civil War, along with twenty-five original members, primarily former slaves.

"It was a deeply spiritual experience for me," Newsome said, recalling the pain and perspective she found by tracing the lives of her ancestors. "It was almost like I was being pulled there in anticipation of what was coming."

Three months later, on June 17, 2015, Newsome was at home, watching the local news, when she saw a breaking news alert flash across the bottom of the television screen. An active shooter was being reported at Emanuel African Methodist Episcopal Church in Charleston, South Carolina. Later, an update: several people who had been attending a prayer meeting were dead, and the shooter was still at large.

"I was devastated, not just from the standpoint of my work as an activist or an organizer, but as a Christian," Newsome later told me. "This was a prayer meeting, someone had knocked on the door and they had let him in. He prayed with them, and then massacred them."

Newsome couldn't stop thinking of the uncountable number of times her own family had gathered in a church sanctuary or meeting room for a Bible study led by her father, of the refuge they had found in the confines of their church. She imagined the abiding feeling of safety that must have filled these worshippers, and how in an instant it would have been overcome with unthinkable terror. In tears, she called her older sister.

"I was up until midnight, reading every update I could find," Newsome recalled. "I was just caught in this period of time, since I was awake at that late hour, where I was aware that everyone was going to wake up the next morning, and everything was going to be different."

Ron Davis walked into the *Washington Post*'s building carrying three folded newspapers under his arm.

For three years, Ron Davis and Lucia McBath had traveled the country telling the story of their slain son, Jordan Davis, the black teen who was killed by a white man in a 2012 shooting in Jacksonville, Florida. Jordan's parents joined what became a traveling tour of families mourning young black men and women killed by police or by white vigilantes.

They were in DC that day promoting a documentary about their son's death. Their next stop would be Charleston.

"Can you believe it?" Davis asked me as he laid the newspapers on a conference room table and pointed at the images and headlines of horror and grief from Charleston. "I'm headed down there later today," he said. "It's just so heartbreaking."

I couldn't believe it. Even though it had been several days since the massacre—nine black Americans gunned down as they sat around a Bible study table at the historic Emanuel African Methodist Episcopal Church—the gravity and consequence of the shooting were evident, yet at the same time not yet fully revealed.

Unlike Bree Newsome, I'd had my phone turned to silent that night so hadn't seen the news of the massacre until the following day. When I finally looked at social media that morning, I learned that the lives of nine black Americans had been extinguished by a troubled traveler they had lovingly invited into their midst.

There was Sharonda Coleman-Singleton, forty-five, whose son teased her that she went to church too much. DePayne Middleton Doctor, forty-nine, whose powerful voice was known to fill the church rafters during hymns. And Cynthia Hurd, the local librarian who at fifty-four years old was described as being a stylish lady with a "fierce shoe game." The oldest of the slain was Susie Jackson, eighty-seven, who just two weeks earlier had visited her grandkids in Euclid, Ohio, near Cleveland. The youngest was Tywanza Sanders, a twenty-six-year-old barber who had posted photos from the prayer meeting to Snapchat just moments before the terror began. Ethel Lance, seventy, was one of those church ladies who were a constant presence at Emanuel AME. She showed up on weekdays to clean the church grounds. She was among several of those killed who were Emanuel's most faithful members— Daniel Simmons, seventy-four, was a retired pastor himself, and Myra Thompson, fifty-nine, was a church trustee and the wife of the minister of another nearby congregation.

Then there was Reverend Clementa C. Pinckney, the forty-one-year-old minister, the shepherd who died doing what he did every Wednesday night: leading his flock.

"He was a preacher, he was a teacher. He was about service, peace and taking action," his grieving wife, Jennifer Pinckney, recalled during a speech memorializing her slain husband. "He was a voice for the voiceless."

Equally shattering was how familiar each of these names, faces, and stories was.

On my last night there, a reporter friend from the local newspaper convinced me to head out for a walk into historic Charleston. As we made our way down uneven brick streets, I couldn't pull my eyes from stone statues and other relics that dot White Point Garden, a park near the southernmost tip of the city. We passed a monument to Lucius Mendel Rivers, a congressman and ardent segregationist who routinely voted against civil rights and voting rights legislation. Next came the Daughters of the Confederacy hall, which appeared to be a public meeting space that, according to the paper signs posted, still hosted farmers' markets and other public gatherings. As we walked deeper into the park, there were the cannons, placed near the water's edge, whose plaques declared they were used by the Confederates to defend Fort Sumter. And off in one corner stood a massive monument, which seemed to depict a Greek soldier whose shield featured the South Carolina state seal. Behind the soldier stood a guardian angel. At the monument's base, an inscription: TO THE CONFEDERATE DEFENDERS OF CHARLESTON—FORT SUMTER 1861–1865.

As a young man who had grown up almost entirely in the North, the pride with which the Confederacy still seemed to be so publicly celebrated gave me pause. "How do you stand in front of a statue," I had written to a group of writer friends that night, "and reconcile that it stands in honor of a man who died fighting to keep you considered less than human?"

On the first Sunday after the shooting, Emanuel was filled to capacity. In one row sat Rick Santorum, a staunch conservative who at the time was hoping to win the GOP presidential nomination in 2016. Next to him sat DeRay Mckesson, one of dozens of activists who had flooded this city in solidarity with those slain. Ron Davis was there, too.

While there are stark differences—the Charleston killings were a premeditated massacre, while Jordan Davis's death was a sudden violent act—Davis's parents were struck by the underlying theme of white supremacy that ran through both incidents, as well as many of the other racial incidents that had made headlines in the years between. Michael Dunn, then a forty-five-year-old software developer in town for a wedding, told jurors he was scared of Jordan Davis because he listened to "rap crap," and his fiancée testified that when the two pulled into the gas station the first words Dunn said were "I hate that thug music." (At one point during a jailhouse phone call, Dunn declared that he had to kill Davis before the teen killed someone himself.)

Dylann Roof, who faces the death penalty as the alleged shooter in Charleston, has told law enforcement that he walked into the Charleston church with the intention of targeting black worshippers. He said he hoped the shooting would prompt a race war, decrying black Americans as a plague that needed to be dealt with.

"He somewhere got into his head that he hates black people, and he wants to kill them. Where do you get that, at twenty-one, in your head?" said Ron Davis. "I told Jordan that there are people out there like that; I don't think our kids really believe that this world is so messed up that there are people really like that. And unfortunately he had to learn the hard way that there are people really like that."

Ron Davis and Lucia McBath hadn't planned to be in Charleston; in fact, they were in the midst of a national tour to promote the documentary *3-1/2 minutes, 10 Bullets,* which follows the two trials it took to put Dunn behind bars for their son's death. But the tragedy in Charleston rocked them to their cores. They knew where they needed to be.

"Our story is just one of the many threads that thread through the larger problem of how we view race, guns, violence, bias," McBath said. "Every one of these stories, they're all so completely relevant for what we have to deal with in this country; every time there is a story, that's another thread. For so long these have been our stories...and they've never been told outside of our communities."

The tie that binds Trayvon Martin to Jordan Davis to Michael Brown to Tamir Rice to Clementa Pinckney is the hazard of black skin. In each case an innocuous behavior—walking home in the rain carrying a packet of Skittles, sitting at a gas station listening to music, jaywalking on a suburban side street, playing with a toy gun in a park, or sitting around a church table for a prayer meeting— suddenly leads to a fatal encounter, seemingly only because the person involved was black.

While some have argued that the Charleston shootings should be viewed in isolation — separate from the police shootings that have prompted protest during 2014 and 2015 and the vigilante shootings of Trayvon Martin and Jordan Davis before them — others have argued that they're all undeniably linked. "Our stories represent a whole magnitude of stories that have never been told in this country — all of people, of black people, who didn't get justice," McBath said. The nation would again turn its eyes to Emanuel AME Church the following week, when President Obama traveled to Charleston to deliver the eulogy at Reverend Pinckney's funeral.

"The Bible calls us to hope. To persevere, and have faith in things not seen," President Obama began, standing flanked by black clergy cloaked in purple.

" 'They were still living by faith when they died,' Scripture tells us. 'They did not receive the things promised; they only saw them and welcomed them from a distance, admitting that they were foreigners and strangers on Earth.'

"We are here today to remember a man of God who lived by faith. A man who believed in things not seen. A man who believed there were better days ahead, off in the distance. A man of service who persevered, knowing full well he would not receive all those things he was promised, because he believed his efforts would deliver a better life for those who followed."

Most striking in Obama's words that day were their dual meaning. They told the story of the slain Reverend Pinckney, who by age thirteen was preaching behind a pulpit and by twenty-three had begun serving in public office, serving as a state representative and later a state senator. They told the story of the reverend who was remembered as a fierce advocate for his flock, who fought for access to health care and new resources for the poor despite the political winds blowing in opposition. But the president was also speaking of himself, telling the story of the young, idealistic politician who had ascended to the democratic perch of the presidency on the promise of hope and change. He was speaking of himself as a man who had sold the country on the promise of a better America to come, who in the face of radicalized attacks not only on his policies but also on his very legitimacy—as an American, and as a Christian—had dared a nation to look into the future, toward even better days.

In his speech to the mourners in Charleston, Obama drew the same parallels Jordan Davis's parents have. These slayings were, in fact, linked to the centuries-long assault on the black body. "For too long, we've been blind to the way past injustices continue to shape the present," Obama said. "Perhaps it causes us to examine what we're doing to cause some of our children to hate. Perhaps it softens hearts towards those lost young men, tens and tens of thousands caught up in the criminal justice system, and leads us to make sure that that system is not infected with bias; that we embrace changes in how we train and equip our police so that the bonds of trust between law enforcement and the communities they serve make us all safer and more secure."

But Obama has never described America as fundamentally broken, or as a country that will forever pay the wages of its original sin. Obama has consistently preached an ideology of American exceptionalism that holds that this nation's greatness is derived not from its present state, but rather from the promise of what is to come. Unlike politicians who through rhetoric pine for some alleged greatness of years past, Obama keeps his belief in American greatness rooted in the reality of the shortcomings and injustices of generations past, and premises it on the hope of a greater America yet to come. On election night 2008, he declared that "that's the true genius of America: that America can change." Four years later, having been reelected after a vitriolic campaign in which his citizenship and faith were again questioned, he invoked the doctrine once more: "Tonight, in this election, you, the American people, reminded us that while our road has been hard, while our journey has been long, we have picked ourselves up, we have fought our way back, and we know in our hearts that for the United States of America the best is yet to come."

It's an ideology that has often been critiqued by the young Black Lives Matter activists who came to prominence toward the end of Obama's term in office. They heard in Obama's words the condescending moralizing and equivocating of a politician who had long abandoned his activist roots.

President Obama's time in office would never see the postracial America that so many had assumed his presidency would usher into existence. And he knew that. On that first election night, in 2008, he declared, "This victory alone is not the change we seek. It is only the chance for us to make that change."

In his eulogy in Charleston, Obama said, "More than any particular policy or analysis, is what's called upon right now, I think — what a friend of mine, the writer Marilynne Robinson, calls 'that reservoir of goodness, beyond, and of another kind, that we are able to do each other in the ordinary cause of things.'

" 'That reservoir of goodness,' " Obama repeated. "If we can find that grace, anything is possible. If we can tap that grace, everything can change." And as applause broke out, the president of the United States transitioned into a hymn: "Amazing Grace."

"Clementa Pinckney found that grace," Obama declared when he had finished singing. He went on to again list the name of each of those killed by hatred's bullets that evening in Charleston. "Through the example of their lives, they've now passed it on to us. May we find ourselves worthy of that precious and extraordinary gift, as long as our lives endure. May grace now lead them home."

As Obama concluded, Bree Newsome, several hours north in Charlotte, turned off her television and headed to her car. The themes of forgiveness and God's amazing grace had resonated with her. As had the faces of those slain, which reminded her of her own church family. And she believed in the audacious hope in each line of the president's plea.

But if that day was one for hope, the next would be a day for action.

Earlier that week, on Tuesday, Bree Newsome had been one of about ten activists who hatched a plan at a meeting convened in a Charlotte living room by Todd Zimmer, an environmental activist who had previously protested in Charlotte. The group was a mixture of racial justice activists and several local environmental activists. They all agreed that they had to do something—the shootings of the Charleston nine had rocked them each to the core. And the fact that Reverend Pinckney's body was lying in state in a building that proudly displayed the Confederate battle flag on its grounds, they felt, was a deranged insult to the slain minister's humanity. By honoring a flag flown by an army that had fought to keep his ancestors enslaved, South Carolina was making an unspoken declaration of how little it valued Reverend Pinckney's life.

The flag had first been placed above the South Carolina statehouse in 1961, as the nation began an intense, decade-long debate about desegregation and civil rights; allegedly, the flag honored the hundredth anniversary of the start of the Civil War. For years, activists, led by the NAACP, have argued that the reinstatement of the flag in South Carolina, as well as a wave of Confederate memorials, flags, and markers that popped up in the 1960s, was little more than a racist backlash against the civil rights movement, and have demanded that they be removed.

"The fact that we were even having this conversation embodied why we were in the streets saying 'black lives matter,'" Newsome told me. "It shows why it's necessary to say it, it reinforces the truth that we live in a society built on devaluing black life."

Newsome speaks with the calm confidence of a grade school teacher going over her lesson in front of a class of eager pupils. Many of the activists who have found platforms during the Obama years overflow with the fire of the righteously indignant, speaking with the voice of an oppressed people who will no longer sit silent. But Bree Newsome speaks truth with a steadiness of temper and tone that attests to the veracity of what she says, enticing you not with soaring rhetoric or emotion but through thoughtful measure.

"What hit me was not just the massacre," said Newsome, who could still remember the feeling of disgust churning in her stomach when, after public debate, the Confederate battle flag was moved from atop the South Carolina statehouse to a monument just outside it. "It was the lack of leadership, the lack of moral leadership."

Each of the activists gathered that day in that Charlotte living room wanted the flag to come down and believed that a disruptive protest in which they forcibly took it down themselves could swing momentum in the ongoing debate about Confederate symbolism. Next came figuring out who would be the one to take the flag down, and how they would do it.

"We needed to raise morale, and to rally the movement. We were really devastated at that time, in those immediate days after the massacre. I remember being at the vigil the day after, there was just this absolute feeling of devastation and shock," Newsome recalled. "We felt that it was an important statement to make, that it would force a 'crisis moment,' forcing South Carolina at that moment to either leave it down or raise it back up."

Initially, they considered a covert, nighttime operation, with the hope of minimizing the likelihood that those who removed the flag would be accosted by onlookers or Confederate flag sympathizers, or harmed by the police who guard the statehouse. But ultimately, that wasn't the message they wanted to send.

"There was no reason to hide our action in darkness," Newsome said. "We're on the side of justice. We didn't need to be ashamed or hide our actions." The next tactical hurdle was more logistical: they had to figure out who in the group could afford to be arrested.

It's a conversation commonplace in activist circles as they plan direct action protests, figuring out who can afford—physically, financially—to be taken into custody for the cause. Mothers and fathers responsible for the daily care of children, those with prior legal records, and those employed at places that may not take kindly to one of their employees' acquiring a new mug shot will all be ruled out. In Ferguson, during the early protests, several of the activists with the largest social media followings—Netta Elzie and DeRay Mckesson among them—often deliberately avoided arrest, reasoning that they would serve a greater purpose by documenting the scenes of other protesters being shackled and teargassed than if they themselves were taken into custody. During Ferguson October, dozens of clergy members led by Cornel West and Jim Wallis crossed the police line in the parking lot of the Ferguson Police Department, an act of civil disobedience meant to prompt their arrests, while other activists—many of them young locals who might have had unpaid speeding tickets that could result in pending warrants or who were more likely to lack the funds to bail themselves out—continued the chanting behind them.

At the Charlotte meeting, several of the activists were immediately ruled out. Newsome had no hesitation. She'd studied the history of nonviolent disobedience, read the writings of Gandhi and Martin Luther King, Jr., and knew the value of disruptive protest. She'd also been arrested before—during the Moral Monday protests over voting rights.

If the State of South Carolina would not take down this flag, she would take it down for them.

Next began her preparation: Newsome and her partner, James Tyson, another Charlotte-based activist, began to train. An activist friend they knew in New York traveled down to North Carolina to teach Newsome how to climb. Next the pair found a local school and spent hours practicing on the flagpole out in front. When summer classes were in session during the day, they would find light posts on secluded side streets and resume practicing there.

"It's critically important that white people actually put some skin in the game," Tyson told *Democracy Now*, the nonprofit interview program, not long after the protest. "Racism is unacceptable, white supremacy is unacceptable."

The full group met at an IHOP near Charleston before dawn the morning after President Obama delivered Reverend Pinckney's eulogy. There was a KKK rally scheduled for the statehouse later in the day, so they decided the flag would need to come down early in the morning to protect Newsome from attack by any white supremacists who happened to arrive early. Fellow activists posing as joggers or sitting in cars pretending to read served as lookouts for police and other threats. Meanwhile, Newsome and Tyson remained at the restaurant. After forty-five minutes of waiting, they got word via text message: the coast was clear.

Another activist dropped them off near the statehouse, and Newsome and Tyson began to move toward it, at a pace somewhere between a walk and a jog. They knew Newsome would need to catapult herself at least fifteen feet up the pole to be safely out of the reach of the police.

They reached the flagpole, and Tyson carefully helped Newsome over the four-foot fence that surrounds it. That fence, installed by the statehouse after an attempt by activists years earlier to remove the flag, would serve as vital protection for Newsome; the police couldn't get to her without climbing over the fence themselves.

She shimmied higher, foot by foot.

With the lowest corner of the flag just out of her reach, she heard the voices of the police officers who had begun to respond.

"Ma'am, ma'am!" they yelled. "Get off the pole!"

"Ma'am, come down off the pole!"

But just moments later, she had reached the top, had unhooked the flag, and was holding it in her right hand, her left arm wrapped tight around the flagpole.

"It was personal to me, as a matter of faith, to show defiance in the face of fear," Newsome told me months later. "I was feeling the struggle, the struggle of millions of people over hundreds of years. And with James standing guard beneath me, I was feeling the racial solidarity of our white allies, from the abolitionists until now, in this fight. It was a reminder that we're not in this alone."

Moments later she descended the flagpole, reciting Scripture as she lowered herself into the arms of two officers, who placed her and Tyson in handcuffs.

As the two were taken to a patrol car, their fellow activists emerged, chanting the words of Assata Shakur, a former Black Panther, that were among the most commonplace rallying cries of the Black Lives Matter activists: "It is our duty to fight for our freedom. It is our duty to win. We must love each other and support each other. We have nothing to lose but our chains."

Just forty-five minutes later, the Confederate battle flag was again raised outside the statehouse. And even before much of the national media had taken note of Newsome's protest, its cameras would be focused on the dozens of angry white supremacists gathered in front of the statehouse. *"What was the point?"* skeptical commentators were quick to ask. *"They're just going to put that flag right back up,"* they argued. But Newsome had succeeded in creating that crisis moment. In a battle that at points had felt fruitless, the momentum had begun to shift.

The next week, when legislators began to debate a bill that would remove the flag from the statehouse grounds, the mood had clearly changed.

"Think about it for just a second. Our ancestors were literally fighting to continue to keep human beings as slaves, and continue the unimaginable acts that occur when someone is held against their will," declared State Senator Paul Thurmond, the son of famed segregationist Strom Thurmond, who had represented South Carolina for forty-eight years. "I am not proud of that heritage."

On July 10, 2015, the flag that Bree Newsome had removed again came down.

CHAPTER SIX

Ferguson, Again: A Year Later, the Protests Continue

Kayla Reed never intended to be an activist. In fact, on August 9, 2014, she was on the clock, at the first of her two jobs, as a pharmacy technician.

Reed was St. Louis–born and –bred, a proud graduate of Riverview Gardens High School, one of three public high schools in which Ferguson children may end up enrolled. Her graduating class, the Class of 2008, had been the last students to walk the stage before the school lost its accreditation.

Next up for Reed was Saint Louis University, where she had studied nursing—but it soon became clear to her that a medical career wasn't for her. She did fine in the classes but didn't enjoy them. Maybe she should pursue public service, she thought. In the meantime, she began volunteering with a program that mentored high school students and picked up two jobs, one at the pharmacy and the second at a furniture shop.

On that day in August 2014, a coworker arrived comically late, and when asked why, explained that all hell had broken loose. She lived in the Canfield Green apartment complex in Ferguson, and the police had shot someone.

Reed didn't go out to Canfield that day. Later that weekend, at the beckoning of her friend Tef Poe, the local rapper who would soon become one of the faces of the protests, she did. When she arrived, she stood stunned—staring at the same police dogs, armed officers, and tear gas that would soon mobilize thousands across the country.

As she stood watching the chaos that played out night after night on Ferguson's streets, Reed tried to think of ways she could help the people she saw, who were so hurt and so angry. Her curiosity ignited, she, too, kept coming out night after night.

"What kept bringing me out was that the police were just not letting people hold space—gather in the street and on the sidewalks— for a young man who had just lost his life," Reed recalled. "People were being teargassed, and people were running. There was that fear, and then also the determination not to back down. To show back up the next night. That was really inspiring for me."

A few weeks later, Reed was helping lead the chants outside the Ferguson Police Department each night.

"Indict, convict, send that killa cop to jail. The whole damn system is guilty as hell."

It was sometime before the grand jury decision, as she watched another night of protests end with arrests and confusion, when Reed decided it was time for her to become more formally involved.

"We need to do something more than just show up. We've got to get organized," Reed recalled thinking.

She began organizing meetings with other young protesters— Netta Elzie, DeRay Mckesson, Brittany Packnett, Tef Poe, Tory Russell, and others. They started sharing information about upcoming protests and comparing tactics. Essential, they all agreed, was not losing the momentum. But equally important, Reed knew, was finding ways to support the young people who had flooded the streets. Many were underemployed, underhoused, and underfed.

These young would-be activists, these black residents of Ferguson and St. Louis County who had been crucially responsible for her awakening, how might she now pay them back?

"In that moment I realized that I could do more than just be there and lead a chant. I could be a part of a bigger strategy. And I could be part of the group of people who were envisioning what this movement could be."

By the time the media descended on Ferguson again, one year later, in August 2015, Reed had become one of the enduring presences on the ground. She served as a primary point of contact for activists seeking housing and began working full-time with the Organization for Black Struggle, a local activist group that often charged her with representing the demands and the passions of the streets in meetings with nonprofits and elected officials — what she has described as the "nonromantic work behind policy change."

Activists titled the first-anniversary weekend United We Fight and planned massive marches and rallies to commemorate the day Michael Brown died. On the afternoon of August 9, 2015, thousands packed the street that snakes through the Canfield Green apartments, pausing with solemnly bowed heads for four and a half minutes to remember the four and a half hours during which Michael Brown's body had lain on the ground.

It was a moment of solidarity after what had been a year of anxiety, anger, and, among the activist ranks, internal discord. Several of the activists and activist groups who had been thrust to the forefront of the Ferguson unrest had one year later left the spotlight. Many who remained in St. Louis after the death of Mike Brown were angered as they watched the national media link them to #BlackLivesMatter. Many in Ferguson couldn't remember the activist network ever being a prominent presence on the ground. That conflation, and other tactical and rhetorical disagreements, caused infighting that often spilled over in public. For outside observers, it was not uncommon to perceive that the young people at the center of this activism had seized the spotlight only to get in a fistfight beneath it.

"One year later," Reed recalled, "St. Louis was exhausted. Meanwhile, people nationwide were looking to replicate what the people in Ferguson did. But there was no blueprint for it. It was an organic moment."

Standing near the front of the crowd that day on Canfield Drive was Tony Rice, who was perhaps Ferguson's most faithful protester. Since the early days of August 2014, Rice had been everywhere—at the protests, at the sites of police shootings, at the important meetings between activist groups—and constantly tweeting from his Search4Swag Twitter account. His omnipresence on the street continued for months after the cameras had left. How could he be everywhere (so much so that some journalists and fellow activists began joking that he must be the Feds) and also manage to be right in the center of the action, night after night? If and when something went down in Ferguson, Tony Rice's Twitter account was the first place to look for information.

As I spoke with him over the course of the year, Tony's enthusiasm gave way to dejected cynicism. He'd lived in Ferguson about twelve years, one of just a handful of local activists who actually lived within the city limits. When groups called marches, he would walk near the front, live streaming or posting video clips later. When the tactic changed to disrupting city council meetings, Rice was among the first to empty his pockets and walk through the newly installed Ferguson City Hall metal detector each night. When several activists began a petition to recall Ferguson mayor James Knowles III, Tony Rice hit the streets with them, walking door to door for days to collect signatures.

But as 2014 became 2015, Rice found himself lonely. The movement birthed in Ferguson soon left the small town behind.

Too often, it seems, the eyes of the nation can gaze in just one direction. Once the grand jury had finished its work, the Ferguson activists found that the country was no longer hanging on their every chant. The terrible march of black death that followed the decision not to charge Darren Wilson—the deaths of Tamir Rice, Sam DuBose, Sandra Bland, and Walter Scott—seized attention previously showered on those in Greater St. Louis, forcing newly minted activists and veteran activist groups alike to conduct their work in the shadows and without recognition.

Netta Elzie, DeRay Mckesson, and others like them had become national figures: they were giving talks around the country, sitting on discussion panels, and conducting media interviews, in addition to their work as activists. Brittany Packnett had been appointed to the state-level Ferguson Commission and the President's Task Force on 21st Century Policing. Others, like Reed, had joined legacy organizations in St. Louis, eagerly committing their professional lives to the same righteous indignation that had drawn them to the street protests. And others still were working to restabilize the lives they had upended to join the protests.

"Some days I want to quit this movement," Alexis Templeton told me on the phone one day late in 2015. "Well, a lot of days."

A year before the protests began, on July 6, 2013, Templeton had been a passenger in a deadly car crash that killed her father, her uncle, and her partner. The survivor's guilt was almost impossible to shake and led to a debilitating two-year depression fueled by constant flashbacks and a feeling of helplessness that comes with knowing that it's only by chance that you're still alive. "I didn't feel like I deserved to be here, and I didn't want to be here," Templeton said.

On August 13, 2014, Templeton sat in an empty bedroom with a loaded gun in one hand, tears streaming beneath the cold barrel pressed to her forehead. Even in that crucial moment, she couldn't shake the images of protest pouring out of Ferguson. A childhood friend, the rapper Thee Pharoah, had been among the first to tweet photos from the scene of Michael Brown's death. Templeton had watched intently, glued to her phone, as demonstrators were tear-gassed night after night. Next came the media coverage, and then more tear gas. By that point it had been going on for days.

Why not go outside, Templeton rationalized that day, *and see what this is all about? This gun will still be here tomorrow.*

"I went outside and I never came back in," Templeton later told me. Night after night, late into the night, she stayed out with the protesters, each passing hour further dispersing the demons left back in that bedroom. As the community of activists evolved into a de facto family, Templeton realized that these people, and this fight, were worth living for. Ultimately, Templeton met Brittany Ferrell, a fellow activist who cofounded Millennial Activists United. The two fell in love, and by the time the Ferguson anniversary came around, they were married.

"This movement saved so many lives," Templeton told me. Though jaded by the politics of organizing and frustrated by the infighting that had derailed what could have been many more alliances between prominent Ferguson protesters in the year since the unrest, Templeton saw the deaths of Michael Brown, Eric Garner, Tamir Rice, and Sandra Bland as a crucial awakening, one with the power to restore life to those who had forfeited it. Their deaths could never be in vain because they had forced others to live.

"If I had not been consumed, if I hadn't been so enraged by Mike Brown, I wouldn't be here," Templeton told me. "I attribute being alive to Mike Brown. Mike Brown saved my life."

For most of the year after Michael Brown's death, my reporting focused on policing policy—tactics, training, best practices, and reform—with race serving as an ever-present subplot. My goal was and is to pull back the veil over a profession that had become among the least accessible and least transparent corners of government.

The team I was with at the *Washington Post* worked daily to track police shootings—recording almost four hundred fatal shootings by police officers during the first five months of 2015. In the meantime, we reported what I considered a stunning finding, that nearly one in three of these fatal shootings included mental illness as a factor. Soon we'd dive into deeply reported pieces on body cameras, and on "repeaters"—officers who had previously been involved in fatal shootings who ended up shooting and killing again. But first, with the anniversary of Ferguson quickly approaching, we knew it was important to explore the role of race in police killings. After collecting data for half of a year, what could we say about the police shootings of black men and women—specifically when they were unarmed? Between January and August 2015, twenty-four unarmed black people had been shot and killed by police. While black men and women make up just 12 percent of the nation's population, they accounted for nearly 25 percent of those who were being shot and killed by the police.

At the same time, a national conversation had taken hold about the demonization of black youth in the media. Among the first hashtags to trend nationally during Ferguson was #iftheygunmedown, in which young people of color posted photos of their graduations, or with family members—photos that portrayed them in a positive light—next to photos that showed them partying or goofing off, the implication being that were they to be killed by the police, the media would certainly frame their life using the less flattering images. On the day of Michael Brown's funeral, the feature on his life on the front page of the *New York Times* included the declaration that Brown was "no angel."

Tanya Brown could have told you herself that her son Brandon was "no angel." It was one of the first things she said to me when I first spoke with her in July 2015.

Brandon Jones had always been big for his age and, according to his mother, had a learning disability, which resulted in some bullying in school from children intimidated by his size. As he got older, Brandon was embarrassed at how far behind he'd fallen in his classes. And as he approached high school age, he still lacked most advanced reading skills.

Soon he was no longer attending classes and was hanging around with the wrong types of kids from the neighborhood.

It was after two one morning in March 2015, just a week before what would have been Brandon's nineteenth birthday, when a woman dialed 911 and informed the Cleveland Division of Police that she was watching as Brandon broke into Parkwood Grocery, the corner store across the street.

Cleveland police said "a struggle ensued when the two officers attempted to take the suspect into custody" and that during the confrontation "one officer fired a shot from his weapon, striking the suspect."

"What he did was definitely wrong," Tanya Brown said. "I'll say it until I'm in my grave: hell no, he shouldn't have been there, coming out of that store hands full of cigarettes and change. But he should be incarcerated. My son shouldn't be in my dining room in an urn on the shelf."

The case, like most police shootings, never drew the national spotlight. In fact, only once did the shooting of Brandon Jones earn a significant round of media coverage: when the local police union announced it would auction off a gun to raise money for the officer involved.

"Because he committed a crime, it just seems like his death doesn't matter to anyone. You hear all of this talk about unarmed individuals shot by the police, but when I speak about my son those same people are like: who?" Jones's mother told me through tears. "A life is a life, and a death is a death. What my son did was wrong, but that doesn't justify taking his life."

Among the twenty-four black men shot by police in the first eight months of 2015 were several exceptional cases, such as that of Sam DuBose, the black man shot and killed by University of Cincinnati police officer Ray Tensing, who had pulled him over and then ordered him out of the car after DuBose admitted he didn't have his license with him. The man refused, the officer pulled his gun: seconds later, DuBose was dead.

Tensing was wearing a body camera. For weeks, as prosecutors considered charges, the public clamored to see the tape. Many in

Cincinnati felt as if they could still smell the smoke from the 2001 riots that engulfed parts of the city after a similar shooting there. But with video in hand, the local prosecutor announced he would charge the officer.

"I used to defend cops in these cases," Paul Cristallo, one of the attorneys working with the family of Brandon Jones, told me. "Without video, nobody believes you. If there hadn't been that videotape, none of us would even know Rodney King's name. In the absence of video, unfortunately, it's the officer's word against the unspoken tale of a dead person."

Sam DuBose's death was a rarity, not only in that it had been caught on camera but also in that Ray Tensing was charged with a crime. The shooting joined those of Walter Scott in South Carolina, Eric Harris in Oklahoma, William Chapman in Virginia, Anthony Hill in Georgia, and Corey Jones in Florida as one of only 6 out of the 248 cases of fatal shootings by police of black men in 2015 in which an officer was charged.

In other cases, critics are quick to note, protests erupted in support of the slain only to be undermined by details that surfaced during the investigation. That was the case after Tallahassee police officer David Stith shot and killed Jeremy Lett in February 2015.

The shooting immediately drew local outrage—largely from Florida State University students involved with Dream Defenders, a group formed after the 2012 shooting of Trayvon Martin, who stormed the state's attorney's office demanding that Stith be charged.

Protesters adopted the narrative that Lett, an assistant minister at a local church who had been standing outside an apartment building, had been racially profiled. Lett appeared to match the description of a burglary suspect when Stith approached him and a struggle ensued. Photos of Lett in a pinstriped suit and a clerical collar soon circulated on social media. Police had been called at 8:08 that fatal night by John Calman, who reported that Lett was knocking on his door repeatedly, demanding to see Calman's roommate, Denise Skipper.

Lett had first arrived an hour earlier, asking to speak with Skipper. But she was sleeping, so Calman told Lett to come back another time. Lett then went to Skipper's bedroom window, banging on the glass. When that didn't earn a response, he went back to the front door at least twice more, banging with his fist.

"He used to live in this complex, was always friendly but haven't seen him in around about a year," Skipper wrote in her witness statement. "This was totally unexpected — this visit from him."

When Officer Stith arrived at the apartment, he later told internal affairs investigators, he discovered Lett lying at the foot of the front stoop, seemingly drunk. He awoke Lett by shining a flashlight in his eyes.

As Stith backed up, he said, Lett leaped to his feet, let out three loud screams, and ran toward the officer, who sidestepped him at the last moment.

"It's almost as if he, he anticipated trying to tackle me," Stith told investigators. "He just bit it and went right into the grass."

Lett then got up to charge again, and Stith said he attempted to use his Taser but missed before again sidestepping Lett, who again fell to the ground. Stith tried once more to stun Lett with the Taser, but the man threw the officer off his back.

"I'm thinking this ain't working and then I realize that the Taser's Tasing me in my right hand because of the rain," Stith said.

As the officer reholstered his Taser and drew his gun, Lett gave one more scream and charged again, prompting the officer to fire one shot.

Then, according to Stith, Lett charged again. But this time, Stith fell to the ground as he backpedaled. He said he kicked his feet up, preventing Lett from mounting him on the ground, and began firing a series of shots into Lett's chest.

After his final shot, Stith said, he thrust with his legs, forcing Lett off him and flat onto his back on the ground.

Lett was dead, five bullets lodged in his body. The medical examiner later concluded that there was a significant amount of cocaine in his system. By the end of February, a Florida grand jury had concluded that Stith's actions were justified.

"I don't know what the fuck was wrong with this fucking guy, but he just started coming at me and coming at me," Stith told one of the first officers to arrive on the scene after the shooting. Later, while speaking to a commanding officer still at the scene, he got emotional.

"I just kept firing because he wouldn't stop fucking coming," he said.

For critics, cases like that of Jeremy Lett served as examples of the flaws in the ideology of the movement for black lives. Didn't this man, or others like him, deserve to die? Wasn't his fate sealed by his own poor decision-making?

But the protest chants were never meant to assert the innocence of every slain black man and woman. The protests were an assertion of their humanity and a demand for a system of policing and justice that was transparent, equitable, and fair.

Who is a perfect victim? Michael Brown? Kajieme Powell? Eric Garner? Sandra Bland? Freddie Gray? Young activists reframed the question: Does it matter?

For too long, many of the activists declared, black bodies had been extinguished by police officers without public accountability or explanation. For all the stories of police abuse, brutality, and impunity that had been shared at black dinner tables, barbershops, and barstools for generations, these basic facts went ignored or unacknowledged by the nation at large.

"It doesn't matter what race the cop is, it's about the culture of policing in America," Anthony Jordan, another of Tanya Brown's attorneys, told me. "It's unquestionably a race issue. But it's not this cartoon image we get in our heads, of police officers going home and putting on Klan garb. It's about a culture that's devaluing black men."

Unlike the civil rights generation before them, young activists on the front lines today refuse to poll-test their martyrs, a practice they see as yet another bastion of respectability politics. Insisting that the burden of proof rests with the body of the slain black man or woman is to argue that black life, on its own, does not matter.

Clifton Kinnie grew up in Spanish Lake, a neighborhood about three minutes from where Michael Brown was shot in Ferguson.

Kinnie's dad had worked at General Motors and was a brilliant man, he told me. But he was also an alcoholic, often emptying his wallet into the hands of bartenders and liquor store cashiers even as his family struggled through poverty. Kinnie is the third oldest of eight children.

On July 16, 2014, just a month before he was set to begin his senior year of high school, Kinnie's mother died. It was three weeks later, as the seventeen-year-old battled the depression and crippling anxiety that plagued him after his mother's death, that he first saw the Instagram posts.

He was sitting at home, scrolling through his phone, when he saw Michael Brown's body. At first he assumed it was a screenshot from a movie; there was no way a body would just be lying out in the street like that in real life. Then he saw the location: Canfield Drive. Soon text messages were pouring in from friends, asking if he knew Mike Brown (he didn't) and asking if he was going to see what happened.

"I don't know what it was, that force, a combination of anger and tiredness, it pulled me out there," Kinnie recalled. "I stood out on the street for an hour and a half and I witnessed everything: the police being aggressive toward the community, the dogs, the riot gear.

"Seeing his mother scream, seeing his body on the ground, it put me in a traumatized state again. It reminded me of my own mother," Kinnie said. "I had to drive home, to gather myself. I had to think."

Days later, Kinnie and a friend joined the now-bustling protests, only to be teargassed and struck with rubber bullets minutes after arriving.

"At first I'm thinking that it's smoke, that something is on fire. So I stopped, dropped, and rolled," Kinnie recalled with a laugh. "And then all of a sudden my body is beginning to sting. This smoke is burning my nostrils. I couldn't breathe, I started to throw up, and then I began to cry.

"I wasn't crying because I was in pain, I was crying because I didn't believe that something like this could happen in America. That the police would harm me this way in America, in 2014."

That was the day Kinnie became a protester.

"Hands up, don't shoot!" became his rallying cry — and not only because he believed that it had been among Michael Brown's final words. For the Ferguson protesters, it was as much a personal plea as a rhetorical declaration. Please, they were screaming to the officers who responded to each protest, do not shoot us, *our* hands are up.

Before she died, Kinnie's mother had fought to get him admitted to Lutheran High School North, a private Christian school not far from Ferguson. The public school he had been attending, Hazelwood East, had lost its accreditation.

"My mom always instilled in me that education came first," Kinnie recalled, noting that even as she battled several rounds of cancer, his mother returned to college to get a degree in social work. She was too sick to work full-time, but she would do "freelance social work," helping out friends and family members. "I don't know who else would think to do that but my mom. I guess she was just an angel."

As he sat in English class on August 13, 2014, the morning after he'd been teargassed, and as I sat on a plane tens of thousands of miles overhead en route to St. Louis, his teacher began to riff about the ongoing protests.

"I wish those people would stop looting and burning stuff," Kinnie recalled his teacher declaring.

Kinnie was stunned. He'd been at the protest the entire previous night. He had been hit with tear gas and rubber bullets as he stood peacefully chanting in a parking lot. But the condemnation he was hearing from a teacher was of the residents, not the police? The paralyzing shock he felt soon turned to mobilizing rage. He stood up and stormed out of the classroom.

When he got home, he sent a group text message to dozens of friends at his school and others. They needed to do something, he said. They needed to join the protests and make people understand. He asked twenty friends to come to his place for a planning meeting. Each spread the word, and more than fifty people showed up.

The coalition of high school students soon took the name Our Destiny STL and began cohosting protests, joining the evening marches and chants organized by the older protest groups, and holding voter registration drives at local high schools, hoping to get as many eighteen-year-old high school seniors registered as possible.

"The students, the young people, we had to take a stance. Here we are, in these schools right around Ferguson, and Mike Brown had just graduated from one, he was about to go to college," Kinnie told me later. "This case showed us that a high school degree wouldn't protect us from state violence."

In November, Kinnie organized a massive walkout—a larger form of his own personal protest—in which more than eight hundred students from St. Louis–area high schools agreed to leave class and campus on the Monday after the announcement that Darren Wilson would not be charged. This at a time when much of the media was speculating that activism in Ferguson would be coming to an end; after all, the wait for the grand jury decision was now over.

Most striking to me about Kinnie has always been his level of introspection—he speaks with poise, confidence, and a wisdom far beyond his experience. It's unclear if the tumult of his teen years forced him to acquire this maturity, or if it was always there. When he speaks about his life, and about Ferguson, he sprinkles in historical references, placing each rhetorical point in the context of racial justice leaders and movements of the past. What is clear with Kinnie, more so than with many of the other young leaders who emerged since Ferguson, is that he is first and foremost a student.

"I used to learn about all of those guys and women, and now we're here, in our own civil rights movement," Kinnie told me. "I really have to sit sometimes and think about the time and the moment that we're in right now. It can be unreal."

In February 2015, Kinnie's work to organize high school students near Ferguson was recognized with the Ambassador Andrew Young Distinguished Leader Award and, during his trip to accept the honor, the young organizer found himself seated next to Andrew Young, one of the civil rights giants he had studied so intensely.

"Thank you," Young would lean in to tell the young man.

"We're just continuing your fight, we're fighting your fight," Kinnie responded.

"No, no, no," Young replied. "This is all of our fight. You all are just the next ones up. You all are the next leaders."

Kinnie had decided, when his mother died, that he would make sure he attended college. That had been her dream for him, and in the short time since her death, he had vowed not to let down her legacy. Halfway through August 2015, I got a call from DeRay Mckesson: Kinnie had chosen to go to Howard University—the school had given him a prestigious scholarship, in part because of the organizing work he had done while in Ferguson—and a group of activists were going to help him move in.

I met Kinnie and the group on August 15 at Ben's Next Door, a bar and restaurant next to Ben's Chili Bowl on U Street in DC. At the table were Mckesson, Netta Elzie, Brittany Packnett, and Justin Hansford, who had spent the day treating Kinnie like their own child, making sure he filled out the move-in forms correctly, making runs to Target and Bed Bath & Beyond for bedding, amenities, and a dorm room's worth of snack food, and nudging him toward certain clubs and organizations that had booths set up near the center of campus.

In the year since Michael Brown had been killed, these young leaders had found fame, notoriety, influence, and each other. For months, Mckesson had preached to me that the power of protest is found in the communal space it creates—that by connecting marginalized people, the protests create a combined force that is powerful where singular voices would be weak.

As the group debated an upcoming congressional race in Missouri, Kinnie listened intently. At a pause in the conversation, he interjected—bursting with excitement as he detailed his plans for the upcoming year—that he was going to make sure he didn't lose the energy of Ferguson. He was going to find the right activist organization, he vowed, and would start his own if needed to ensure that this moment continued.

"The movement," he declared with youthful hubris to the rest of us at the table, "is coming to campus."

Martese Johnson wasn't supposed to succeed. He wasn't supposed to become one of the most recognized leaders on one of the nation's most storied, predominantly white college campuses. And he wasn't supposed to become one of the faces of the movement.

He grew up poor and black. He was raised by a single parent. And worst of all, he was from Chicago, the rough side.

Johnson moved at least a dozen times as a kid, bouncing from home to home with his mother and two of his brothers, almost always on the South Side of Chicago.

Those moves traced the struggles of a single mother, working as a social worker, who was trying against the odds to build a better life for her boys. The family moved from school district to school district, spending one semester in a predominantly Latino district in Chicago and the next in an almost-all-white school across the state line in Indiana. By the time Martese was in middle school, the annual move to a new apartment and a new school had become normal.

Nearly all the males he knew growing up were gang affiliated, from the boys playing dice on the corner to the man behind the counter selling bags of fruit chew candy for a dollar. For many, the neighborhood gang was little more than a cliché, a pack of friends, a means of finding camaraderie and belonging in a lonely and under-achieving sliver of the city. And with that affiliation came a code, a set of rules that extended beyond the roster of self-proclaimed members and into the minds and actions of the rest of the boys in the neighborhood.

"It was really hard being that close in proximity to constant gang activity; it means that the gang mentality is really big for you as a kid. And with that comes the idea that we hate the police, that they're an enemy," Johnson told me, reflecting on his childhood. "My mom would always tell me when I went out — no matter what the police said to me, don't say anything back and do exactly what they tell me to do, or I could lose my life."

Johnson never joined a gang, but he never felt much need to go out of his way to avoid his friends who were affiliated, either. The kids on the block now dealing on the side, now carrying a piece, were his friends, his playmates; staying cool with them didn't seem like something that would endanger him. If anything, he figured, the proximity might keep him safe.

When he was thirteen, just shy of high school, he was hanging out with one of these friends, a kid from the block who had been the standout in elementary and middle school for singing and the arts.

"He was a really good kid," Johnson recalled with a knowing chuckle. "That he was affiliated with the local gang, that part was just another facet to this kid."

What Johnson didn't know as he stood on the corner with his friend and several others was that earlier that summer day his friend had been involved in a drive-by shooting targeting a rival gang. As he and his friends stood outside their apartment building, the gang that had been targeted earlier had piled into a car and was searching for them.

Johnson can still see the car, with faded paint, pulling up slowly as he joked with his buddies. Almost in slow motion, the vehicle stopped, arms extended out the windows, and the silent stillness was shattered by the popping of gunfire.

"We all just scattered," Johnson recalled. "I ran into the apartment building and crouched down in one of the breezeways until the shooting stopped. Then I ran home.

"When you grow up in that environment, being in a gang feels so natural," said Johnson. "But getting shot at was another level. That was not natural. That was not the life I wanted.

"It was a pivotal moment for me, it alluded to what my future could be. I had always been a smart kid; that was the moment I decided to prioritize those smarts."

Johnson was ambitious and driven. He excelled at Kenwood Academy, where his mentors pushed him toward business school. The summer before his senior year, they signed him up for a summer business institute at the University of Virginia, a school the young man with the soothing baritone voice had never even heard of before. Unable to make the basketball team, he picked up volleyball, which soon became his chief adolescent passion. He loved volleyball because it required skill and precision, unlike basketball and football, which could be dominated by kids who had been blessed with an early growth spurt.

It was in high school that Johnson says his perception of the police began to slowly shift as well. To be clear, he still didn't completely trust them. But maybe they weren't the enemy. If he played by the rules and stayed out of trouble, he thought, they could be allies.

He recalled for me that one day, in either his junior or senior year, he was followed and taunted by a few of the guys from the block. As part of his business leadership program, he wore a shirt and tie, which made him an easy and obvious target of ridicule as he made his way home through some of the city's rougher neighborhoods. Johnson said he tried to ignore the kids, but they kept following him. He got scared and broke into a jog.

"These kids just kept following, and eventually they were all chasing me. I'm running for my life, and at that moment, a police officer comes out of nowhere." The officer flashed his lights and blared his sirens, and the crowd chasing Johnson dispersed. He waved to the officer and finished his walk home.

"Up to that point my only experience with the police was them coming up to me and my friends and harassing us — 'Why are you outside? Shouldn't you have someplace to be?' I had always experienced what I considered biased policing. And here was a moment in which a police officer was actually helping me. It was such a big moment for me because it had never happened before."

Johnson's dream was to go to the University of Southern California. During his high school years he had taken to rooting for USC in football and basketball, but when he visited campus he found himself intimidated by Los Angeles. The designer jeans and vanilla lattes made the campus feel like a world far different from the one he was used to. The bright lights of Hollywood can be a shining beacon, attracting those from afar, but for Johnson they were more like the flashing brights that catch your eye in the oncoming lane. After committing to USC, he decided he wasn't ready for a move to Los Angeles.

He had applied to and been accepted by more than two dozen schools, but there was only one other on his list that he thought would work: that grassy campus on the East Coast where he had stayed in a dorm during the business institute the previous summer. Johnson called the admissions office of UVA and told them he was headed to campus.

Freshman year is tough for most, and Johnson was no exception.

He was the only black male in his dorm of more than 150 students, and it was hard for him not to perceive slights and insensitivities from some of his classmates—some of whom, he soon became convinced, had never before encountered a black person. Some of them started teasingly calling him the Fresh Prince of Bel-Air.

"I'd walk into parties and everyone would be white; I'd stick out," Johnson said. "Everyone would stare from across the room and eventually someone would ask: 'Do you go to UVA?'" And those were just the parties he could get into; often he'd be greeted at the door of an all-white fraternity and told he wasn't welcome.

Things got better his sophomore year, when he decided to dive into the black organizations on campus with the hope of finding friends with whom he had more in common (or who at the very least wouldn't tease him with insensitive nicknames). He pledged a fraternity and joined the Black Student Alliance. By his senior year, he had been named to the Honor Committee, an elite student council that helps enforce the campus honor code and weighs in on student disciplinary matters. Of the twenty-seven members of the council, he was the sole black student.

Martese Johnson thought he was following all the rules. He had made it out of Chicago, he had been admitted to an elite school, and he was now among the most recognizable leaders on campus.

But as he'd soon learn, his individual accomplishment wouldn't keep his head from hitting the concrete or keep the sharp sting of an officer's knee from finding the small of his back during the late hours of St. Patrick's Day 2015.

He and a few friends had been hanging out on campus that night and decided to head to Trinity, a popular bar just off campus. As he approached the door, the owner asked for his ID. Johnson had lost his VA driver's license a week or two earlier but had a second ID card from Illinois. What he didn't realize was that because his Chicago ID was older, and given how often his family had moved, the zip code on that photo ID was different than that on his driver's license.

As the owner quizzed him, he gave the wrong zip code—so the bar owner turned him away.

"I walked away and immediately I was grabbed from behind by a police officer; it was less than a minute before it escalated into three officers slamming me to the ground," Johnson told me. The officers, he believed, assumed he had been turned away from the bar for being underage and using a fake ID. As the officers held him on the ground, a gash opened on his forehead and blood began to trickle down his face, mixing with perspiration and tears.

"I go to UVA! I go to UVA! How could this happen?" Johnson screamed to the officers, assuming they must have taken him for a local resident. "I go to UVA!"

He recalled, "I was just wondering how this could happen. I felt that I had done everything I was supposed to, I had checked all of the boxes. I came from a rough background but I had made it to somewhere better. I thought the police were here truly to protect us, and now at that moment I was surprised again. I never believed Charlottesville could be as bad as Chicago."

Johnson was handcuffed and shackled and taken by police to a local hospital, where ten stitches would be sewn into his head. He spent the night at the police station, unaware that his name had already become a national rallying cry.

As Johnson lay on the ground, the officers atop him, his friends had pulled out their cell phones and recorded video of his frantic screams. Once the video was posted online, it took just minutes for his shouts and pleas to go viral. Other students knew who he was and filled in the blanks for those following the story from afar— here was a campus leader, thrown to the ground and wounded for having misstated his zip code.

By the time he was released from jail the next morning, Johnson had twenty thousand new followers on Twitter and four hundred unread text messages in his phone. His name had been trending on Twitter overnight, with dozens of articles already written about the incident. He didn't want any of it. Frankly, he was embarrassed. He washed his face, put on fresh clothes, and went to an Honor Committee meeting, where he hoped to regain some anonymity. Instead, the other committee members immediately asked him what had happened, expressed their support, and sent him home to rest.

Johnson faced two misdemeanor charges—public intoxication and obstruction of justice. Eventually, they would both be dropped.

But Johnson's arrest—and the viral videos that captured his pain—prompted the next round of awakening. He had done everything right. And yet here he was, his head cracked open with two officers on his back. If this could happen to Martese Johnson, it could happen to any black college student. The incident served as a wake-up call to college students on campuses across the country—the privilege of education, and the disguise of respectability, can't protect you. Even on the nation's most elite campuses, your black body remains vulnerable.

"My situation was the one situation, of those that sparked protests, where the black man hadn't been killed. It shattered all aspects of respectability politics. I was a kid who did everything I was supposed to have done. I wasn't some weed-smoking gangster who didn't pull up his pants. I was a student, doing what I was supposed to do, and I still ended up being harmed by police."

It had been months since Martese Johnson's arrest. A summer had come and gone. But as black students flocked back to college campuses in the fall of 2015, they brought with them a renewed energy. That summer had included the anniversary of Ferguson, and the deaths of Sandra Bland and Samuel DuBose.

While dozens of campuses would see protests, the most memorable was, unsurprisingly, at the University of Missouri. About thirty football players, all black, crowded the multipurpose room near the back of the university's Gaines/Oldham Black Culture Center one Friday night in November 2014.

Across from them sat Jonathan Butler. It had been five days since the twenty-five-year-old graduate student had begun a hunger strike, and his fellow protest organizers were worried about him. The protest had drawn little notice initially, but as it approached its first weekend, national attention had slowly begun to shift to this university campus dropped between St. Louis and Kansas City. By the following Monday morning, it would be the biggest story in the nation.

Butler had been raised in Omaha, hailing from a prominent family of ministers and businessmen. Before Mizzou, he had gotten a degree in business administration, and now he was pursuing a master's in educational leadership. He had only recently become involved in campus activism and described himself as an unlikely protester.

Butler's demand was that university president Tim Wolfe resign or be removed from office. Butler, like many black students at Mizzou and their allies, believed Wolfe was derelict in his duty to ensure their safety in light of a spate of racial incidents.

The University of Missouri, a majority-white campus of thirty-five thousand with about twenty-five hundred black students, is a school at which, despite the small percentage of black students, racial activism has brewed for decades. Like many colleges in the Midwest, Mizzou features a student body that is a cocktail of races, political beliefs, and socioeconomic backgrounds. Overall, the campus is relatively liberal compared to the more conservative section of Missouri that surrounds it. A thick spirit of discontent had settled at the core of the black student body during the past year as they watched the unrest unfolding in the streets of Ferguson, just two hours away.

It took just two days from when Butler stopped eating for members of the football team to inquire about his protest. First they wanted to know why he was doing it, a question they asked fellow members of Concerned Student 1950, a small but growing activist group of which he was a member and which was named after the year when black students first successfully enrolled at the university. Then they wanted to know how they could help.

Like many Division I athletes, members of the football team were segregated on campus in special dorms and had special course schedules. They felt removed from the rest of the student body as a whole and from the rest of the black student body in particular, even though the majority of the team was black. If change was coming to Mizzou—where it seems nearly every black student knows of a friend, roommate, or professor confronted by racist taunts or slurs—they wanted to play a role.

"I got the text message that the football players wanted to meet and I ran to get there," said Reuben Faloughi, a Mizzou graduate student and one of the original eleven activists who founded Concerned Student 1950. This could be their chance, the activists knew. This would be their moment.

The movement's presence on Mizzou's campus had begun three months earlier, thanks to the work of three women, all University of Missouri seniors. The trio was gathered in Naomi Daugherty's campus apartment in August 2014 when they decided they had to do something. Daugherty, Ashley Bland, and Kailynd Beck were angered and hurt as they watched their Twitter and Instagram feeds flood with images of the spot in Ferguson where Michael Brown had been shot and killed by a police officer.

Like many of Mizzou's black students, Beck had grown up in St. Louis, and she was getting most of her updates not from media outlets but from the posts of high school friends and family members who had arrived in Ferguson to protest.

"A lot of my people were literally on the ground where it happened," Beck told me. "So I said: 'Why don't we start something together?'"

First the women started an "MU for Mike Brown" account on

Twitter and Facebook; then they set up an email address. Within an hour, more than sixty students had messaged them to say they wanted to join the protest group. The group caught fire as students returned to campus eager to do something about the unrest developing just an hour and a half away from their dorms.

The lack of an official statement from university officials on Michael Brown's death only stirred the discord. Enraged by the eighteen-year-old's death and by what they saw as inattentiveness by the university administration, MU for Mike Brown was soon hosting vigils, rallies, demonstrations, and, most crucially, weekly planning meetings for would-be activists.

Two die-ins, during which participants lie flat on the ground in public spaces, held on campus drew hundreds of participants. Many, including Butler, traveled to Ferguson to participate in the protests there. But the newfound racial activism came as the nation, and the state of Missouri, remained bitterly divided about the events in Ferguson. In November 2014, as the grand jury concluded that the evidence did not support indicting Officer Darren Wilson, a new round of riots began in Ferguson, and with them declarations of "we told you so" from those skeptical of the growing protest movement.

The president of the police union in Columbia, Missouri, organized a "Darren Wilson day" in honor of the police officer who killed Michael Brown. Dozens of students took to Yik Yak, an anonymous message board app popular on college campuses, to decry the protests. "They were calling us monkeys, and niggers," said Ashley Bland, one of the MU for Mike Brown founders. "It was blatant, it wasn't even hidden racism." In early December, after the grand jury's decision, a popular campus nightclub gave out wristbands that read HANDS UP, PANTS UP. The establishment said it was a play on their dress code, while activists saw it as a mockery of a popular protest chant. The following Friday, at least ninety students protested outside the nightclub, blocking traffic and chanting. The nightclub apologized in a Facebook post.

Those protest actions, the counterprotests, and the clashes between these two mobilized groups were symbolic of what was to come. As the daily vigils in Ferguson and Baltimore began to wane, the mantle was soon taken up on campuses across the country. Young men and women saw themselves in the protest leaders, and in the names and faces of the men and women who had been killed by police.

Mizzou student body president Payton Head, twenty-one, could barely remember what day it was, and his phone wouldn't stop ringing as he wandered into his office late on a Friday night in November 2015. The room was full of student government colleagues and campus activists. In the past week, they had successfully run out their university president and his boss, the chancellor, had come under vicious attack by political partisans, and in the process Head had become the new faces of black campus activism.

Sunk into his chair, Head picked at a Chipotle bowl before pausing to look up at the Albert Einstein quote he had written in Mizzou gold above his desk: "The world will not be destroyed by evil, but by those who watch without doing anything."

A week earlier, Head had been in Kansas City with activists as they confronted university president Tim Wolfe outside a fundraiser. Head had worked closely with Wolfe and liked him, and up until that point he had thought the president might be able to calm the anger of the black student body while retaining his job. When Wolfe tried, and failed, to explain to activists what systemic oppression was, Head changed his mind. If the university president could not adequately define and explain the role of systemic oppression, how would he effectively lead a university to address it? It was clear that Tim Wolfe hadn't been listening to his own students.

Head had been elected on a platform that emphasized inclusion, and most of his prior campus government work had centered around issues of diversity, social justice, and equity. A year after he had become the public spokesperson for the student body, his on-campus office was overflowing with university apparel, the walls and counters covered in pictures: one from his White House fellowship, one each from meetings with Senators Claire McCaskill and Roy Blunt, and the official photo from his run for student body president, which included his campaign slogan boldly across the top: BELIEVE WITH US: IGNITE MIZZOU.

The slogan was taken from a speech by the school's chancellor to mark the university's 175th anniversary, given near the historic columns that stand on campus, which that night were illuminated by bright lights resembling flames. "Keep the fire rolling," the chancellor implored. Head took the urging to heart.

Raised in Chicago, Head first visited Mizzou because his twin sister was interested in the journalism school. They both fell in love with the campus and were soon enrolled. Head loved his classmates and Columbia but found himself unnerved time and time again by the stories he heard from fellow black students. Many upperclassmen had tales of being confronted by drunken men with Confederate flags. A close friend of Head's showed up at a party at a fraternity house only to be told she couldn't come in — only white girls were welcome, they explained to her. She transferred.

In 2013, the spring of his sophomore year, Head was walking through Greektown, the stretch of fraternity and sorority houses near campus, when a group of white kids sitting in the back of a pickup truck began screaming the n-word at him. "At that moment, I didn't know what to do," Head said. "My high school was like eighty-seven percent black; I didn't know how to deal with racism blatantly being thrown in my face."

It's the kind of story that many of Mizzou's black students say that they too can tell. Dewy-eyed freshmen get the same warning from campus elders in Mizzou's black community: It's going to happen to you, just wait.

That fall at Mizzou, activists participated in a series of other, less race-based protests, against sexual assault on campus, the defunding of Planned Parenthood, and the decision by President Wolfe to cut health care for graduate students. But, above all, the semester-long protests were propelled by a series of racial incidents on campus that began when, in September, Head was again confronted by a pickup truck.

Head was walking with a friend late one night, on their way to the cookie shop in downtown Columbia, when a pickup truck drove up and the white men inside began screaming the n-word at them. "What made me most angry about that situation was the fact that I had been working on inclusion initiatives this entire year," Head said. "I'm getting to the end of my time in office and I'm still seeing the same things."

Head took to Facebook, writing an impassioned post about the incident, calling for change on campus. It was unacceptable, the student body president declared, that nearly every black student he knew on campus had a similar story. Something, he said, had to change. "I didn't realize the platform that was out there," Head said. Like Martese Johnson, he had ascended to roles of power and privilege on campus and realized his personal responsibility to speak up in the face of injustice.

"If Payton had posted this being a sophomore from Chicago, everybody would be like 'Okay, that's bad.' But Payton posting from the privilege of the MSA [Missouri Students Association] president's office, there's a platform where people actually listen," Head told me.

The post went viral; it was shared hundreds of times, prompting media coverage from both local and national outlets. But it still took six days before the campus administration addressed the incident, calling Head and asking him if he would help write the chancellor's statement.

The campus activists decided they'd had enough. Four days after Head's incident, three students, Ayanna Poole, DeShaunya Ware, and Jonathan Butler, issued a call to action to sixty student leaders.

Eight people responded, and the group of eleven decided they would confront Chancellor R. Bowen Loftin and President Wolfe at homecoming.

"We have this dangerous culture of apathy where things aren't being addressed," Butler said. "If leadership wasn't going to do something, we had to do something."

At the homecoming parade, the group surrounded Wolfe's car, linking arms and launching into speeches decrying the racial attacks and declaring they felt unsafe on campus. The university president didn't talk to the students, and police soon arrived to disperse them. The activists were shocked that the president hadn't gotten out of the car to speak with them.

In the days that followed, the activists assumed Wolfe would reach out to them to smooth things over and discuss what had happened. He didn't.

The inaction dismayed student leaders. Head called the president's office himself, privately urging Wolfe to reach out to the student group and make amends. His pleas were ignored. "Every day we had to wait for him to respond was another slap in the face," Reuben Faloughi said.

After more than a week, the students from the homecoming protest set up a meeting with members of the administration themselves. The protests earned the support of large swaths of the student body, but they certainly weren't without detractors. Several preexisting activist groups on campus didn't like the tactics of the eleven students, who then formed Concerned Student 1950. Even among the university's black student body, some thought (and still think) that everything was being blown out of proportion.

"I've heard of a couple of racial incidents, but I don't think it necessarily warrants a hunger strike," said Rodney McFaul, a junior at Mizzou, who is black and who, like me, grew up in Shaker Heights, Ohio. He reached out to me when he heard I was headed to campus to cover the unrest. "I'm not sure what removing the president of the university will do to combat racism on campus; no administrator is going to be able to convince students not to be racist."

To be clear, McFaul wasn't alone in his skepticism.

To critics and many white Americans, the campus push to oust President Wolfe represented what McFaul observed: an overreaction to a series of unrelated racial incidents that no administrator could have prevented, and which President Wolfe was under no obligation to respond to. To supporters and many black Americans, the protests became a decisive victory, a validation of the unsuccessful struggles undertaken by countless others before them.

And to organizers, activists, and observers of the ongoing Black Lives Matter social justice movement, the upending of the state's most prominent and beloved college campus represented the next chapter in the still-accruing legacy of Ferguson, Missouri. The taking up of the protest mantle on these campuses marked a new evolution for the movement, as black men and women who would have had the privilege of staying at home and off the streets were overcome with the urgency of the moment.

From Ferguson to Mizzou—it was fitting that Missouri played such a crucial role in the nation's new reckoning with race and justice. The state sits near the exact geographic center of the nation, pulled at one time between the free states to the north and its fellow slave states to the south. It was here that a court handed down the infamous Dred Scott decision, ruling that a black man was not, in fact, in the eyes of our nation a man with inalienable rights.

"It's been a long boil," said Scott Brooks, a Mizzou sociology professor who spoke at several of the 2014 rallies. "Students felt like they weren't being heard and the university wasn't taking them seriously. And in a post-Ferguson world, increasingly the students felt the mantra of 'all deliberate speed.'"

The headlines flowing out of Columbia reawoke and enraged many black alumni, who saw in these anecdotes an experience that was all too familiar.

"Many of us found ourselves protesting similar incidents on campus," a group of more than 780 black alumni wrote in an open letter in early November 2015. "We find it highly unacceptable that many of these issues are not only continuing, but have become more pervasive." The letter outlined a list of incidents dating back to 2004, when a student wrote a piece for the campus newspaper blaming black students for vandalism, and recalled an incident in 2010 when two white students threw cotton balls on the lawn of the Black Culture Center. After the cotton ball incident, and with university officials considering a proposal to end affirmative action policies at state universities, black leaders on campus desperately approached the athletic teams.

"The response was lackluster," recalled Anthony Martin, a Mizzou grad who said that after several attempts, the campus activists essentially gave up on trying to get football and basketball players to join their demonstrations. "There just wasn't at that time a lot of camaraderie between student organizations and athletes."

But as they walked graduation stages in the early 2010s, Martin's generation looked back at what they considered an opportunity missed, and passed along a message to fraternity brothers and sorority sisters, student government leaders, and campus activists who were coming up behind them. "If you can get the athletic department and the student body leadership together, that's a force to be reckoned with," Martin said to me, recalling conversations with Head, who is his fraternity brother, and others. "When you mess with someone's money, you mess with their livelihood. If you can get the athletes, the university can't ignore you."

Now, buoyed by the boycotting football team, Concerned Student 1950 doubled down on its demands, and the number of activists camped out on the university quad swelled to dozens. Would they be able to pull off the kind of campus shakeup in 2015 that campus activists had desired for more than a decade?

But they still weren't sure. President Wolfe had told them as recently as the Friday before that he was not going to step down, a sentiment he reiterated in a statement over the weekend. Late Sunday night, with his hunger strike about to enter its seventh day, Jonathan Butler said he had almost no confidence that Wolfe would resign.

The Mizzou activists, like many of the organizers in Ferguson and elsewhere, communicated constantly using a group-text app called GroupMe, firing off hundreds of messages a day in a group they titled We Gon Be Alright, after a hip-hop track by Kendrick Lamar that has become the unofficial anthem of this generation of black protesters.

Thus far, the victories of Concerned Student 1950 had been few. Butler's hunger strike had yet to gain much national attention. Some other campus activist groups were hesitant to cosign Concerned Student's tactics.

A message on Monday morning summoned the Concerned Student 1950 leaders to another meeting with the football team. The boycott had become the leading story in the nation, and now dozens of additional players—many of them white—wanted to hear from Butler directly.

They crowded into a small theater in the university's athletic complex, typically used to review game footage, and Butler took the microphone. "I shared with them my reasoning [for the hunger strike], why I was doing this. And I also shared with them my experience, going back to as an undergrad, in 2008, when I had the n-word written on my door, to . . . the cotton ball situation," Butler said. "I just explained that through my undergrad career and now as a graduate student, nothing has changed." As the meeting ended, the players decided they would join the protest. They would not play or practice until Butler's demands were met. They gathered around Butler and posed for a picture.

Just before noon the next morning, November 9, Butler met with the football team, and as Head dashed across campus in search of the Board of Curators meeting for which he was running desperately late, their phones buzzed with a new message in the group chat.

President Wolfe had resigned. They had won.

When Butler stepped to the microphone Monday afternoon to make his first public statement since Wolfe's resignation, his T-shirt declaring I LOVE MY BLACKNESS AND YOURS—a slogan made popular by several national Black Lives Matter activists—he declared his allegiance, loud and clear, to the movement birthed in Ferguson.

"When we look at what has been happening on campus in terms of activism with black students...it would be inappropriate if I did not acknowledge the people who got us here," Butler said. "When we look at post-Ferguson activism, the movement that was started in terms of igniting the fire with black students was ignited with three queer black women who started MU for Mike Brown."

By the time I arrived on campus, the Mizzou protesters were struggling to figure out what would happen next. They hadn't exactly been ready to win; they hadn't expected Wolfe to resign—at least not as quickly as he had. Now what?

What began as a last-ditch personal protest had become one of recent history's most significant victories for student activism. The throng of media who had come to cover a football team's boycott were instead now scrambling to contextualize a university coup d'état with roots tracing back through years of unaddressed campus racial tension endured by black students as reliably as the school's white leaders chose to ignore it. Here was a campus protest built to dismantle institutional racism whose organizers had first been emboldened by a police shooting in a small St. Louis suburb a year earlier.

A cloud of chaos would hover over campus for the following week, with the president's resignation prompting clashes between activists and the media about the framing of coverage, as well as about the right of reporters and photographers to access protests held in public space. New conversations started up about race on campus, not just at Mizzou, but at universities nationwide, as did a fresh spate of racial threats, primarily from the same anonymous online trolls who surface each time the nation begins to grapple with race. For at least one night, these threats thrust the school's black community into a state of traumatized paralysis.

Critics couldn't understand the abrupt resignations, or the grievances being voiced by the media-shy protest groups. In these young activists, they saw a group who were at best misguided, at worst liars and frauds; these critics demanded definitive proof that racist incidents had occurred. But even as questions were being raised in the national media about whether or not these actions had taken place, similar acts of racial hatred kept happening at Mizzou.

In the days after Wolfe's resignation, a drunken white man appeared in the middle of campus, yelling threats at students who walked past; Yik Yak message boards filled with violent threats toward black students that prompted hundreds to skip classes and avoid campus; and the sign outside the Black Culture Center was vandalized overnight, the word "black" covered in spray paint.

When that news broke out on the night of Tuesday, November 10, 2015, more than a hundred student leaders were assembled for a once-a-semester joint meeting of student organization heads. As they sat in a conference room, they quickly began spreading the word to their fraternities and sororities and other organizations. State troopers soon arrived at the meeting and escorted the entire group across campus to the Black Culture Center, which had been secured by police. Meanwhile, reports of drunken white students screaming racial slurs at black students had prompted social media hysteria. Most likely there were a handful of foolish, bigoted students out and about that night—but judging by social media, a reasonable person would have assumed that the entire campus was besieged by hooded terrorists.

By now, Head had heard from several students that white men

claiming to be KKK members were on campus. That was not confirmed, but in the heat of the moment, the rumors felt frightening. Head and others began reaching out to the various law enforcement and civil rights contacts they had gathered in the subsequent days—school administrators, Jesse Jackson, an official at the Department of Justice, and, of course, their parents. Head posted a Facebook status urging students to stay inside and away from windows.

Dozens of black students poured away from the school, crowding into off-campus apartments. Butler and other activists used their group texts to organize car pools. Worried mothers and fathers of black and white students frantically called their freshman and sophomore sons and daughters, who stayed holed up in their dorms if they couldn't find a ride off campus.

No one was hurt that night, but many were traumatized. Just hours after triumphant victory, it was a painful return to reality: the resignation of the president hadn't changed the culture of the campus and the state in which they lived.

One of the hardest things for many of the activists I interviewed on and off campus was figuring out what should come next. Should they continue to fight? Should they find "real" jobs? Should they become politicians? Gadflies? Full-time activists?

Equally hard was deciphering what, exactly, the victories they had earned would mean both in the short term and in the long term. They had run out the top university administrators and forced a campus to acknowledge a discontent it had long ignored among its black student body. But would things actually get better? And what would be the collateral consequences? The following fall, enrollment at Mizzou dropped by twenty-six hundred students, a clear cost of the stigma associated with the unrest.

A few days after Wolfe's resignation, Butler and the others led a march through campus. They chanted and cheered, danced and gyrated through campus buildings and the row of fraternity and sorority houses that make up Greektown. It was a defiant display of jubilation, a declaration to their campus that this fight, though seemingly settled, still wasn't over. There was still work left to be done.

The march that day ended in an auditorium, the kind that hosts plays and concerts on almost every college campus in America. Gathered by the stage, the fifty or so students who remained, almost all black, stood in a circle, holding hands or with arms over shoulders. Then someone turned on the sound system. For what may have been the millionth time, the beginning chords were heard of "Alright." The young activists were soon jumping and dancing to the declaration of perseverance that had become their battle hymn.

Alls my life I has to fight

I didn't yet know all of the details of the story's end, but as I listened to the jubilant chants and watched as dozens of students jumped and danced in unison, I could feel the truth emanating from the words echoing into the auditorium rafters.

We gon' be alright, we gon' be alright, we gon' be alright

Three Days in July

The Movement for Black Lives—as activists had begun calling the protest movement—and the national push for police reform had faded from the national consciousness during the first months of 2016, in stark contrast to its constant presence in 2014 and for most of 2015. There were bursts of attention—ongoing fallout in Chicago following the release in late 2015 of the video of Laquan McDonald being shot and killed, and the water crisis in Flint, Michigan, most significantly—but in each instance Americans' focus on race and justice landed like another strong wave, only to recede right back into the wide ocean.

Six months into 2016, I was fact-checking our latest piece. My colleague Kimberly Kindy and I had analyzed the number of Americans killed to date and discovered that even after more than a year of protests and outrage, police nationwide were on pace to take more lives in 2016 than they had in 2015. Yet none of the men and women killed by police in 2016 had received the same level of attention from the media or had galvanized activists as had those killed just months earlier.

The calendar had been predictably dominated by the presidential election, but even there, policing had yet to become a major focus of debate. For racial justice activists, the election was an opportunity to pressure candidates to adopt positions on policing and criminal justice reform, as well as to speak out on other issues of racial disparity. It remained to be seen how successful they would be.

"People know that the police are still killing people. What we've got to figure out now is what a victory looks like," Kayla Reed, the Ferguson protester still working for the Organization for Black Struggle in St. Louis, told me in early 2016. "There isn't going to be a single bill passed that will suddenly encompass all of the ways the system marginalizes black and brown people. We have to redo the whole damn thing."

Many of the young activists who had been driven into the street by the police killings of 2014 and 2015 had begun to move away from daily protesting and organizing work. Kayla Reed and Johnetta Elzie had both reenrolled in college classes. After his run for mayor, DeRay Mckesson had rejoined the Baltimore City Schools as an administrator. Shaun King, now a *New York Daily News* columnist, Kwame Rose, and Martese Johnson had all assumed roles as surrogates for the Bernie Sanders presidential campaign, rallying voters on his behalf.

Many of them and others in the movement felt they needed to catch their breath. Robust conversations circulated about the viralization of the deaths of individuals and the fetishizing of black death. Perhaps, some argued, not every video needed to be shared and played on a constant loop. "It's traumatic to see a hashtag of someone killed by the police every day; it messes with your psyche," Reed said. "And [the protest movement] is bigger than just the police." How could such a boisterous and seemingly omnipresent protest movement just fade from the streets? Where had the movement for black life gone?

As I finished a round of fact-checking, a tweet from DeRay Mckesson with the hashtag #AltonSterling caught my eye. It took me seconds to find the video, shot with a cell phone camera, of Sterling's final moments on July 5, 2016—two officers are yelling at him, they Tase him, they tackle him, and then the bullets are fired into his chest.

The *Post* has an overnight reporting desk, a team of night-owl reporters who handle late-breaking news, so I flagged the shooting for my colleagues to make sure they had seen it. And then I went home to wait.

I paced my living room, and later my bedroom, refreshing Twitter. I follow a few thousand people, and with each refresh of my phone a new group of them were voicing pain, anger, and outrage as they, too, watched the video.

We each cope with these deaths differently. I escape by reporting: making calls, digging into the police department that was involved, and tracking down the friends and family of the slain to better understand how the moment of their death fits within the context of the rest of their life. Doing this keeps my mind busy. Often we all have an urge to "do something." For me, reporting is that something.

The videos that surface at night are typically the hardest. The night of Sterling's death, I tried to do a little preliminary reporting, but I couldn't. It was too late to call anyone.

I set an early alarm, knowing that my job the next day would be to find witnesses, law enforcement officials, and context. And then I lay restless. How do you sleep when you know that soon you'll need to tell the story of the death of yet another black man? I was taken back to the countless days when the fierce urgency surrounding the latest black person killed by the police had dictated my sleep, work, and life. It felt like the night the video of Walter Scott was released, the afternoon the officer who killed Sam DuBose was charged, and the night the KKK was rumored to be at Mizzou after President Wolfe's resignation.

When my phone went off, I'd been asleep only minutes. I jolted out of bed. Before I could catch my breath, a frantic day of reporting and writing was already behind me. I stayed in the newsroom until late that night, finalizing our coverage of Sterling's death and the national outrage it had awoken.

Sometime around 11 p.m., a friend from college sent me a link to a live Facebook video feed from a woman in Minnesota. An officer had just shot her boyfriend, she screamed. As the camera panned, you could see a dying Philando Castile struggling to seize his final breaths. Over the woman's shoulder stood the officer who had shot him, his gun still trained on the dying man.

For the two years since Ferguson, it had been more or less my job to bear witness to pain and trauma. Once you're known as a reporter who covers policing and justice, your email accounts and voice mail boxes become depositories of death: pleading messages from mothers and widows of those who have been killed by officers who beg you to tell their story. Envelopes from inmates stuffed with legal filings and police reports arrived at work addressed to me. As hard as it is to be in receipt of so much rightful pain and sorrow, video of shootings, Tasings, arrests, and beatings is different. There is no way to filter it. The only way to decide what to cover is to watch them all.

To date, the hardest video for me to watch had been the extended version of Tamir Rice's death, in which his sister frantically raced to his body, only to be tackled by officers. But even that video hadn't brought me to tears. The video feed of Diamond Reynolds, Castile's girlfriend, was different.

"Fuck! I told him not to reach for it, I told him to get his hand out!" the officer screams at Reynolds.

"You told him to get his ID, sir, his driver's license," she insists in response. "Oh my God, please don't tell me he's dead. Please don't tell me my boyfriend just went like that."

Responding officers eventually removed Reynolds and her four-year-old daughter from the car where Castile was dying. In the video, as they take her into custody, Reynolds, who up until this point has been unbelievably composed, begins to lose herself to what has just happened. She cries, and then she prays. She pleads with

Jesus, a broken woman begging for divine intervention. As Reynolds then begins to scream, her four-year-old daughter interjects, "It's okay, I'm right here with you."

I sprang up from my desk and ran to the newsroom bathroom to throw up. Then I began reporting. Soon I was on the phone with Castile's sister, who was gathered with her family in a Minnesota hospital. She sobbed as she told me the only thing they knew: "He's gone."

The shootings of Sterling and Castile together prompted a reawakening. Among the cities that hosted major protests was Dallas, where the police had gone to great pains to support the protesters, cordoning off areas for demonstrators and posing for photos next to signs calling for reforms and justice. Unknown to the crowd, a single gunman would soon prey on this gathering, specifically attacking white police officers in what he later told police negotiators was a targeted retribution for the police killings of black men.

A week later, another lone wolf attacked officers in Baton Rouge, killing three. The deaths and injury of the officers in these two cities again shook the nation, underscoring with renewed urgency the depth of the anger and distrust toward police still coursing through America.

The attacks on police officers enraged the law enforcement community, who for years had worried about such targeted attacks. In a country with millions of easily accessible guns and an increasing national distrust of institutions — specifically the police — it wasn't hard to imagine the ease with which someone determined to harm officers could carry out such an attack. "With the number of police shootings that have occurred that seem to be totally unjustified, somewhere in this country, someone was going to do such a thing," John Creuzot, a former prosecutor and judge in Dallas, told me after the shooting.

Civil rights groups, and the young activists behind the protests that had propelled the movement, quickly condemned the shootings. But opponents of the protest movement blamed the rhetoric of the Movement for Black Lives for the murders of the officers in Dallas and Baton Rouge—a tactic not unlike the one employed by those who blamed Martin Luther King, Jr., and other civil rights leaders for the riots of the 1960s.

After the Dallas attack, President Obama convened a thirty-three-person conference at the White House, a conversation that ran for four and a half hours, which the president told attendees was among the longest single-subject conferences of his presidency. The attendees were a mix—young activists like DeRay Mckesson, civil rights stalwarts like Al Sharpton, police chiefs and heads of several major police unions, and government officials including Attorney General Loretta Lynch. "The president lived up to his reputation as a former law professor," NAACP president Cornell William Brooks told me after the meeting. "He spent quite a bit of time listening, probing, and guiding the discussion, occasionally deploying the Socratic method to get some of the day's best responses."

Among the first exchanges was one between St. Paul mayor Chris Coleman, who sharply defended his officers' actions in response to massive protests that had broken out after the death of Philando Castile, and Mica Grimm, a local Black Lives Matter activist, who had been leading the demonstrations. Coleman called some of the protesters "disgraceful," while Grimm shot back that it was their democratic duty to take to the streets—and the democratic obligation of the police to protect them. "I responded by telling him that the protests aren't going to stop until we see actual change," Grimm told me later. "And that begins with seeing an officer held accountable for killing somebody."

I'd first met Grimm months earlier, when I traveled to Minneapolis to cover the demonstrations in Minneapolis after the police shooting of Jamar Clark, an unarmed black man. As I followed a parade of marchers, Grimm was seated in the back of a pickup truck near the front, shouting protest chants into a bullhorn. But she spoke more softly in the White House. This was her first trip to Washington, DC, much less to the White House. As she sparred with the mayor and the police chief of her city, she received an unexpected expression of support. One of the other police chiefs in the room slid her a handwritten note, written on a sheet from a White House notepad. "Don't be deterred from speaking truth to power," read the note, written by Dean Esserman, the chief of the New Haven Police Department.

When it was his turn to speak, DeRay Mckesson drilled into Obama with a long list of complaints. He told the president that the language he used to describe the protesters had "come a long way," but he implored Obama to stop sprinkling into his speeches and addresses to black audiences urgings to vote. As Mckesson explained it, many in the community interpreted Obama's exhortations as condescending and reductionist. Mckesson asked the president to tell the FBI to stop having its agents drop in at the homes of prominent activists — in the weeks before the Republican and Democratic conventions, Johnetta Elzie, Bree Newsome, Mckesson himself, and at least half a dozen other prominent activists were visited by federal agents, which they believed to be an attempt to intimidate them. And, Mckesson noted, the president had been quick to visit Dallas after the officers were killed there, but even two years later had yet to set foot in Ferguson. "Well, I'm glad you have a long list for me," the president quipped in response.

As he facilitated the conversation, Obama often glanced to his left, at Brittany Packnett, a thirty-one-year-old Ferguson protester and Campaign Zero cofounder who speaks with unwavering confidence and poise. This was at least the third time Packnett had met with Obama, who after one meeting had been so struck by her command of the room that he pulled her aside to encourage her to one day run for office. Her father, Ronald Packnett, had been a prominent black minister and activist in St. Louis before dying in 1996 at the age of forty-five. Her mother, Gwendolyn Packnett, remains a well-known educator, community leader, and philanthropist. "My dad was an activist, and mom has always been in community leadership,"

Packnett recalls. "So, truth be told, my first protest was probably while I was still in a stroller."

Packnett recalls a childhood of relative privilege. Her parents, who had both grown up in households with meager means, had worked to ensure that their children could have the things they hadn't. They lived in a nice section of St. Louis, drove good cars, and went to esteemed private schools. But Packnett recalls being raised with a "double consciousness," having access to money and privilege but also feeling deep pride in her identity as a black woman, and as a black Christian. She read *The Autobiography of Malcolm X* and sat patiently next to her parents at evening Bible studies. "Our social responsibility was the most important thing," Packnett told me about her upbringing. "And I was raised in a liberation theology. We worshipped a table-flipping revolutionary Jesus with brown skin and Afro hair."

One evening when she was eight years old, her father and younger brother came bursting through the front door, her brother in tears. They had been out for a drive and had gotten pulled over. As the officer had approached the vehicle, he had asked Mr. Packnett to step out of the car, and then had thrown him onto the hood and put him in handcuffs. The officer didn't believe that this black man could possibly own the Mercedes he was driving.

The entire family was outraged, and Packnett's brother was traumatized. Her father, who was among the most politically connected black men in St. Louis, called the police chief and demanded that the officer apologize personally, in front of his son.

As she grew older, Packnett became an outspoken minority in her predominantly white private schools, sprinkling her class assignments with asides about equity and racial justice and helping to organize a regular seminar on diversity and inclusion. That drew backlash in the hallways of her majority-white high school. She recalls that one particular student, a young white man from a prominent local family who was a year ahead of her, began following

Packnett around in the hallways, mocking her. "Is my whiteness oppressing you today?" he would ask as she moved from class to class. She would ignore him. Then, one day, she didn't. She turned around, just outside the women's locker room, and told him to stop speaking to her that way. In return, he spit in her face.

Packnett said her track coach, one of her mentors in high school, insisted she tell the principal, who forced the boy to apologize. Immediately, the memory of her late father's interaction with the officer who pulled him over flashed back into her mind. That officer, like this boy, had been made to apologize. But had either actually been held accountable? Or did the system send the message that abuse of a black body can be negated and papered over by an "I'm sorry" no matter how reluctantly uttered?

"It's this idea that all a person had to do was say 'I'm sorry,' and then they never had to be held accountable for their actions," Packnett said. "Thinking about those two incidents is, for me, a constant reminder that this system was never built for us in the first place."

In the years since, Packnett had occupied a seat at some of the same tables at which her parents had sat, her activism undeterred by that incident. In college, at Washington University in St. Louis, she organized demonstrations and rallies on behalf of the campus food service workers, ultimately helping them win their first across-the-board wage increase in years. By the time Michael Brown was killed, she was working as executive director for Teach for America—St. Louis, spending many days in meetings with donors, leaders of non-profits, and community leaders. She saw herself as an inside-the-room advocate for radical change. "I had let a certain amount of comfort and privilege take hold of my social justice work," she said. "I wasn't sacrificing my body very much anymore in physical protest."

That changed in August 2014, when she showed up outside the Ferguson Police Department a few days after Michael Brown was killed. With demonstrations swelling beneath the summer sun, some city leaders invited Packnett inside the police station for a private meeting with the chief. It was the type of convening that often occurs in the days after a shooting—the powers that be assemble a group of black leaders, insist they are doing everything they can, and request that these leaders help cool the crowds. This time, Packnett said no. She wouldn't attend the meeting. She was staying outside.

"Sitting in a room with a corrupt police chief inside a building while traumatized black people protested outside was not the right step," Packnett recalled. "It was time to stop sitting in the ivory tower and hypothesizing and actually get back to doing what I knew in my spirit and in my upbringing was necessary to change these policing systems." By the end of the week, she was a protest regular.

But soon enough, the movement would call on her to sit at the table again. She applied for and was accepted to a spot on the Ferguson Commission, the task force convened by Missouri governor Jay Nixon after the unrest in 2014. Next, impressed after meeting her at his first sit-down with the young activists who had been awakened in Ferguson, President Obama invited Packnett to join his President's Task Force on 21st Century Policing.

"Everyone has a role," Packnett said after the post-Dallas White House meeting. "There are some people who need to be the revolutionary, and there are some people who need to be at the table in the White House. And I knew it was my job to translate the pain I had seen and experienced in the streets and bring it into these halls of power."

Packnett explains the protest movement as a series of escalating waves. Its conception came from the deaths of Oscar Grant, Trayvon Martin, and Jordan Davis, which mobilized black Americans in a demand for justice. Its grand birth, first in Ferguson and then throughout the nation in the fall of 2014, was prompted by the deaths of Eric Garner, John Crawford, and Michael Brown, the cases that showed those same black Americans that justice for those killed by the police was not forthcoming. As the list of names grew—each week, each day providing another—so did the urgency of the uprising that would become a movement. The year 2015 brought a third wave of anger and pain: Walter Scott, Freddie Gray, Sandra Bland, Sam DuBose—another round of death in which the now-pained calls for police accountability became insistent demands. The year 2016, which began sleepily, quickly saw the beginning of what most likely will become a fourth wave. As President Obama prepares to leave the White House, it remains to be seen whether the movement birthed by the broken promise of his presidency will live on through the season of his successor.

"The protests will continue," Packnett said confidently when I called her from Cleveland on the first night of the Republican National Convention in July. "Regardless of who is elected, we're going to work to continue this level of engagement with the next administration; there's just too much at stake." While the targeted killings of the officers in Dallas and Baton Rouge prompted some commentators and other members of the media to declare the Movement for Black Lives dead, the activists and organizers who have been the foot soldiers have not gone quietly into the night.

A few days later came the nonfatal shooting in North Miami of behavioral therapist Charles Kinsey, who was lying on the ground with his hands in the air, begging not to be shot, as he tried to soothe his autistic patient, when an officer fired his gun three times. Kinsey's hands were up, he yelled "Don't shoot," and the officer fired anyway. "I was thinking as long as I have my hands up . . . they're not going to shoot me," Kinsey told local television station WSVN from his hospital bed. "Wow, was I wrong."

In the days after the deaths of Alton Sterling and Philando Castile, thousands of people used an online tool provided by Campaign Zero to petition their local elected officials to demand police reform. Just before July 18, as the political media gathered in Cleveland for the GOP convention, thousands of demonstrators took to the streets in more than thirty cities across the nation in a weekend of activism they titled Freedom Now.

"We have no choice but to keep going," Packnett told me. "If one of the central demands of the movement is to stop killing us, and they're still killing us, then we don't get to stop, either."

July 2016, Cleveland

Acknowledgments

To the families and friends of those who in death have become national figures, Rorschach tests in a divided nation's debate of race and justice: thank you for sharing your pain, your mourning, and your humanity with the nation, and for extending patience and love to reporters like me who have shown up at your door at life's worst moments.

In the acknowledgments of his first book, journalist Chris Hayes described Vanessa Mobley as his "intellectual copilot." I heard from Chris almost as soon as I signed with Vanessa, letting me know how lucky I was to have landed the best editor in the game. By then, I already knew.

Her brilliance lies in her ability to reveal to me the things I knew but could never have said, to access the understanding I possess but never could have otherwise voiced. Her diligence and intellect forced me to heights that I could not have fathomed when we began. It has been an honor to copilot this project with her.

This book never would have made it into Vanessa's arms had it not been guided there by an amazing team. Thank you to Mollie Glick, for forcing me to sit down and write the original proposal for this book, even when I didn't think I could or wanted to. Anthony Mattero, my literary agent and friend, has pushed me and this project forward. Thank you to my agent, Traci Wilkes Smith, and the entire team at CSE, for believing and building in me.

The heartbeat of this project are the young people whose stories occupy its pages. For two years they have answered my calls, responded to my inquiries, indulged my theories, and helped me understand the depth of this moment. Without their stories, their work, and their candor and willingness to share both with me, there would be no book. To Johnetta Elzie, Alexis Templeton, Kayla Reed, DeRay Mckesson, Brittany Packnett, Clifton Kinnie, Bree Newsome, Kwame Rose, Shaun King, Jonathan Butler, Payton Head, Martese Johnson: telling your stories has been an honor.

And the many whose names and stories may not grace these pages, but whose work has nonetheless driven this movement and whose words and actions have crafted and challenged my understanding of what activism can be: people like Rachelle Smith, Dante Barry, Samuel Sinyangwe, Mervyn Marcano, Michael Skolnik, the folks at the Advancement Project, and the too-often-unsung Chelsea Fuller, my sister, confidante, and North Star.

Contextualizing the events of the last two years would have been impossible without conversations with people far smarter than I am: Chris King, Khalil Muhammad, Phil Goff, Ryan Julison, Chuck Wexler, Neal Peirce for sharing with me notes from his study of St. Louis, and many others.

I've been blessed with parents who have loved me, and have spent close to three decades sacrificing of themselves to provide for me and my younger brothers. My mother, Sheila, will always be the love of my life, the person I spend the most time trying to make proud. My father, Mark, has forever been my role model of what it means to be a journalist, an advocate for diversity, a Christian, and a man. Above my desk hangs an email he sent me in 2013, during what was for me a moment of frustration: "A journalist's commitment is to the truth.... We have no control over how people choose to handle the truth!"

I could not imagine having a more supportive family, both immediate and extended. You all are the rock on which I stand, and have provided the grounding of love, faith, and perseverance in which I'm planted.

I could never properly articulate what the love and support of my friends has meant to me during these last two years. This list is far from complete: Clinton Yates, Freeman Thompson, Travis Waldron, Sam McCullough, Aaron Edwards, John Ketchum, Gerrick Kennedy, Eric Burse, Dexter Mullins, Sarah Hoye, Corey Dade, Swati Sharma, Ashley Lutz, John Gruber, Kirsten Gassman, Adrian Walker, Joe Ragazzo, Amanda Lucci, Tom Suddes, Colin Jackson, Teddy Cahill, Mike Young, Chris Call, Cory Haik, Martine Powers, Julian Benbow, Sarah Cavender, Bartees Cox, Juan Diasgranados, and the 2012 *LA Times* Metpro class.

Danielle: thank you for being my partner in taking over the world. Never stop being you.

Every reporter is a team project, compiled and constructed by the editors, colleagues, and competition he or she encounters along the way.

I owe my love for journalism to Natalie Sekicky—my first boss, editor, and debate sparring partner. I'll always thank Marcia Jaffe for teaching a loudmouthed high school boy that, sometimes, it is okay to shut up and listen.

Much of this book leans on reporting and writing I've done while at the *Washington Post*. I'll be forever indebted to editors there who believed in and bet on me: Kevin Merida, Tracy Grant, Steven Ginsberg, Terence Samuel, Marcia Davis, Vanessa Williams, Lori Montgomery, David Fallis, Scott Wilson, Cameron Barr, and Marty Baron.

Kimberly Kindy and Kimbriell Kelly are the two older sisters I never knew I wanted but without whom I would be lost. Julie Tate, Jen Jenkins, and Steven Rich: so much of my journalism these last two years would have been impossible without you.

To the journalists whose work makes me better, and whom I am privileged to consider friends: Brittany Noble-Jones, Matt Pearce, Yamiche Alcindor, Nikole Hannah-Jones, Errin Whack (and your husband, and Ginger), Joel Anderson, Adam Serwer, Jamelle Bouie, Darren Sands, Jelani Cobb, Greg Howard, Trymaine Lee, Jamilah Lamieux, Jamil Smith, Vann Newkirk, Clint Smith, Rembert Browne, Ryan Reilly.

This book is dedicated to three men, gone too soon, who helped mold me into who I am today. I'll spend the rest of my life trying to love and be loved by as many people as you were, and are.

Notes

Preface

12. *Blessed Assurance:* Lyrics as they were sung that day, from my memory. Hymn by Franny Crosby, 1873.

13. *I wasn't escaping Ferguson:* A year later, St. Louis County charged Ryan Reilly and me with trespassing and interfering with a police officer in connection with our 2013 arrests. After months of negotiation, the county dropped the charges, and in exchange we agreed not to file a civil lawsuit.

16. *several efforts by citizen journalists:* Prior to the projects by the *Washington Post* and *The Guardian,* the website KilledbyPolice.net was the definitive count of those killed by police officers. In addition, Fatal Encounters (FatalEncounters .org), an effort led by a Nevada journalist, sought to collect information on several years of police killings.

16. *federal investigators would later conclude:* Investigation of the Ferguson Police Department, United States Department of Justice, March 4, 2015.

16. *one unarmed black person…990 of them in total:* The *Washington Post* police shooting database, 2015.

Chapter One

22. *had entered Ferguson Market & Liquor:* Marc Fisher, Kimbriell Kelly, Kimberly Kindy, Amy Brittain, "In Three Minutes, Two Lives Collide and a Nation Divides over Ferguson Shooting," *Washington Post,* December 6, 2014.

25. *would later be cited:* Ferguson Police chief Tom Jackson, in subsequent interviews with me and others, would say he regrets allowing Michael Brown's body to sit out for so many hours after the shooting.

32. *the same can be said for the violence in Ferguson:* Adam Serwer, "Eighty Years of Fergusons," *Buzzfeed,* August 25, 2014, www.buzzfeed.com/ adamserwer/eighty-years-of-fergusons.

33. *Baldwin wrote in 1963:* James Baldwin, *The Fire Next Time* (New York: Dell Press, 1963).

42. *These "Peirce reports":* A collection of many of these reports are available in Neal Peirce's *Citistates: How Urban America Can Prosper in a Competitive World* (Santa Ana, CA: Seven Locks Press, 1994). Many of the more recent reports are also available at Citistates.com.

43. *"I recall two poignant moments":* Comments from Johnson and Purcell provided by Neal Peirce.

48. *"bums" who had "spread destruction":* McCulloch described Murray and Beasley as bums during a September 2001 press conference.

69. *"Burn this motherfucker down!":* The reaction of Lezley McSpadden and Louis Head to the announcement that Darren Wilson would not be indicted was captured by various bystander and media videos.

Chapter Two

71. *a St. Louis blogger:* This accusation was leveled by Jim Hoft, known as the "Gateway Pundit," in a tweet on October 11, 2014.

74. *"I kept my eyes on the suspect":* From the sworn statement given by Officer Loehmann to the grand jury, released by the Cuyahoga County prosecutor's office, December 1, 2015.

75. *"weepy" and "distracted":* Human resources memo sent by Independence Police Department deputy chief Jim Polak on November 29, 2012.

78. *break your body:* The definitive writings on the perceived threats to the black body have been written by Ta-Nehisi Coates, most expansively in *Between the World and Me* (New York: Spiegel and Grau, 2015).

82. *Zimmerman told the 911 operator:* full transcript and audio of emergency dispatch tapes published by the *Washington Post,* May 20, 2012.

82. *Trayvon was pronounced dead:* Frances Robles, "A Look at What Happened the Night Trayvon Martin Died," *Miami Herald,* April 2, 2012.

85. *in a column:* Pat Buchanan, "What If Zimmerman Walks Free?" *Creators,* May 22, 2012, www.creators.com/read/pat-buchanan/05/12/what-if-zimmerman-walks-free.

89. *an essay on the protest movement:* Patrisse Marie Cullors-Brignac, "We Didn't Start a Movement. We Started a Network." *Medium,* February 22, 2016, medium.com/@patrissemariecullorsbrignac/we-didn-t-start-a-movement-we-started-a-network-90f9b5717668.

90. *Atop the list:* Tanya Sichynsky, "These 10 Twitter Hashtags Changed the Way We Talk about Social Issues," *Washington Post,* March 21, 2016.

93. *"That's the inconvenience of freedom":* Quote from December 11, 2014, press availability with Mayor Frank Jackson.

95. *137 bullets:* Mark Berman, "Six Cleveland Police Officers Fired for Fatal '137 Shots' Car Chase in 2012," *Washington Post,* January 26, 2016.

108. *"Tamir's mother, Samaria Rice":* Press release "Tamir Rice's Family Mourns for Tamir After Non-Indictment of Officers" issued December 28, 2015.

Chapter Three

111. *eighteen thousand police agencies:* U.S. Department of Justice, Bureau of Justice Statistics, "National Sources of Law Enforcement Data," April 2016.

111. *no comprehensive accurate national data:* Details on the lack of mandatory reporting and previous efforts to chronicle the number of police shootings is explored in my September 8, 2014, *Washington Post* piece, "How Many Police Shootings a Year? No One Knows."

113. *"Thousands Dead, Few Prosecuted":* Kimberly Kindy and Kimbriell Kelly, "Thousands Dead, Few Prosecuted," *Washington Post,* April 11, 2015.

Chapter Four

139. *In a survey conducted by the Balimore Police:* Police Commissioner Anthony Batts, "Public Safety in the City of Baltimore: A Strategic Plan for Improvement," report of the Baltimore Police Department, October 30, 2013.

148. *"There is a touching earnestness":* Jay Caspian Kang, "Our Demand Is Simple: Stop Killing Us," *New York Times Magazine,* May 4, 2015.

Chapter Five

176. *Dunn declared:* According to jailhouse recordings released by the Florida state's attorney and included in the documentary *3½ Minutes, 10 Bullets.*

Chapter Six

191. *mental illness as a factor:* Probed by me, and colleagues Kimberly Kindy and Keith Alexander, "Distraught People, Deadly Results," *Washington Post,* June 30, 2015.

191. *twenty-four unarmed black people:* Explored by myself and colleagues Sandhya Somashekhar and Keith Alexander, "Black and Unarmed," *Washington Post,* August 8, 2015.

192. *Among the twenty-four black men:* See "Black and Unarmed," above.
193. *6 out of the 248 cases: Washington Post* fatal police shooting database, 2015.

Afterword

221. *on pace to take more lives:* Analysis by me and Kimberly Kindy, "Fatal Shootings by Police Are Up in the First Six months of 2016, *Post* Analysis Finds," *Washington Post,* July 7, 2016.

Index